Selling Out America's Democracy

Selling Out America's Democracy

How Lobbyists, Special Interests,
and Campaign Financing Undermine
the Will of the People

Alan L. Moss

PRAEGER

Westport, Connecticut
London

Library of Congress Cataloging-in-Publication Data

Moss, Alan L.
  Selling out America's democracy : how lobbyists, special interests, and campaign financing undermine the will of the people / Alan L. Moss.
    p. cm.
  Includes bibliographical references and index.
  ISBN 978-0-313-34551-7 (alk. paper)
  1. Lobbying—United States—History—21st century. 2. Pressure groups—United States—History—21st century. 3. Campaign funds—United States—History—21st century. 4. United States—Politics and government—2001- I. Title.
  JK2498.M67 2008
  320.973—dc22   2008007901

British Library Cataloguing in Publication Data is available.

Library of Congress Catalog Card Number: 2008007901
ISBN: 978-0-313-34551-7

First published in 2008

Praeger Publishers, 88 Post Road West, Westport, CT 06881
An imprint of Greenwood Publishing Group, Inc.
www.praeger.com

Printed in the United States of America

∞™

The paper used in this book complies with the Permanent Paper Standard issued by the National Information Standards Organization (Z39.48–1984).

10 9 8 7 6 5 4 3 2 1

This book is dedicated to the memory of my father,
Irven Marty Moss

CONTENTS

PREFACE

If you are lucky, there comes a time when you see through the fog of confusing rhetoric and inexplicable events and understand a situation for what it is. If that epiphany involves the country you love, you are doubly blessed.

In 2002, after thirty-five years in Washington, D.C., I retired from the Federal Service and moved to the Jersey Shore. I left behind my years as American Political Science Association Congressional Fellow in the United States Senate, Chief Economist of the U.S. Department of Labor's Wage and Hour Division, and Adjunct Instructor at the University of Virginia's Northern Virginia Campus. I thought that my passionate interest in American politics, nurtured by PhD studies and day-to-day dealings in Washington, would begin to take a back seat to less stressful subjects.

Before long, my days of leisure became interspersed with occasional work as an economic consultant and the fulfillment of a lifelong dream to write fiction. While I found both these callings challenging and satisfying, the drumbeat of bad news from Washington and around the world denied me the peace one would hope for in retirement.

Why do we continue to lose young men and women in foreign misadventures? Why do we continue to defile our environment with carbon emissions? Why do we continue to deny workers a sufficient minimum wage? Why do we continue to see millions of Americans with no health insurance? Why do we continue to experience inner-city gun violence and record numbers of our citizens in prison? And why do we continue to underutilize the stem cell research that promises cures for many of our most devastating diseases? These were the questions that confronted me.

Removed from the seat of government and no longer beholden to support the policies of whatever administration happened to be in power, events became clearer and easier to analyze. Unable to resist, I pledged to seek answers and find solutions. Thus, for the past year, I have devoted myself to studying our misfortunes and determining how our system can be fixed.

As my new work progressed, one theme became evident. The ills that plague our nation are the result of the unchecked power of special interests and lobbyists, and their interaction with our method of campaign financing. The book you are about to read is the presentation of this general conclusion, how it was reached, and how we might modify our system of government to take account of our recent experience.

The problems we are suffering are not the result of random events. They are the predictable consequences of the absence of countervailing power to offset the impact of factions and their massive resources. Once you understand the way in which our democracy has been damaged and how we can reverse the harm that has been done, you will be empowered to become a political force for positive change with your vote and, if you wish, with activist contributions.

My research and the composition of this volume could not have been completed without the extensive help of many people. First, I would like to acknowledge the enthusiastic support and expert assistance provided by my two Praeger editors, Hilary Claggett and Robert Hutchinson.

Second, I wish to thank the Washington insiders who agreed to be interviewed. Each made unique and significant contributions to the understanding of how America's democracy functions in today's political environment.

Third, many experts were kind enough to provide data and explanations that assisted in presenting the wide range of issues included in this work. Special thanks are offered to David A. Love, writer for the Progressive Media Project; Ethan Nadelmann, Executive Director of the Drug Policy Alliance; and Ed Kirtz and Sarah Williams, Drug Policy Alliance staff members.

Excellent cooperation was also provided by staff members of the U.S. Department of Labor, Bureau of Labor Statistics; U.S. Department of Justice, Federal Bureau of Investigation and Federal Bureau of Prisons, Office of Justice Programs; U.S. Department of Commerce, Bureau of Economic Analysis, National Economic Accounts, and

Bureau of the Census, Census of State and Federal Correctional Facilities; and U.S. Department of the Treasury, Internal Revenue Service.

Finally, but most importantly, I thank my wife, Penny, for her unwavering encouragement and patience during this intense but satisfying project.

THE CHALLENGE

How have we gone so far astray?

The nation remains locked in ill-advised foreign interventions that take the lives of our young men and women and spend obscene amounts of U.S. resources. We continue to burn fossil fuels at record rates, stoking the furnace of global warming that promises environmental disasters for generations to come. Dependence on foreign oil drains consumer budgets, while efforts to develop alternative sources of energy languish. The minimum wage fails to cover the cost of living as more and more Americans fall below the poverty line. Inner cities resemble shooting galleries as actions to banish firearms and illegal drugs flounder. Millions lack health insurance, and the federal government ties the hands of stem cell researchers who likely hold the keys to curing humanity's most devastating afflictions.

Selling Out America's Democracy identifies how the forces of special interests, moneyed lobbyists, and our system of campaign financing work together to weaken political leadership, distort U.S. policy, and betray the legitimate interests of the American people. The volume utilizes a unique perspective, original research, and numerous telling interviews to support its thesis that self-serving forces flush with cash have corrupted the process of determining national priorities.

If we are going to turn things around, we must understand how our democracy was designed to work, what forces and procedures have twisted our government out of kilter, why policies intended to promote the greater good have been altered to benefit the few, and what steps must be taken to restore our democracy to its intended purpose.

We have been blessed with a heritage that offers the United States a unique opportunity for freedom and self-government. It would be nothing less than a tragedy if, after more than 230 years, we allow our dominion to fall under the control of those who care not for the American people but for personal or corporate wealth.

Begin your journey to untangle America's dilemma and once again set our nation's compass for the course our Founding Fathers intended. By mastering the information presented on the following pages, you will empower yourself to join those who are working to revive the purpose and spirit of our democracy.

PART 1

DEMOCRATIC AND POLITICAL ORIGIN

How do we evaluate the state of our democracy? "Of the many different ways of calling the common tradition to witness as to the right and the wrong of a current issue, none has been so favored among Americans as the simple and direct appeal to a standard presumably raised by the Founding Fathers."[1]

In Chapter 1 we explore the principles upon which the Founders established the American democracy. As we investigate the actions and impact of special interests and their lobbyists, we will discover the extent to which our democracy has strayed from the guidance of those with the original vision. We will return to the time, dreams, and ideals of the Founders to refresh our understanding of the democracy they created.

In Chapter 2 we examine the history and techniques used by special interests and their lobbyists. The playbook of today's lobbyists is opened so we may see how they serve special interest clients and utilize campaign financing to influence the positions of our elected officials.

CHAPTER 1

THE IDEAL OF AMERICA'S DEMOCRACY

The Foundation upon Which America's Democracy Is Based

INTRODUCTION

The Founding Fathers were possessed with a revolutionary vision. They would customize and apply the radical thought of political philosophers to create a democracy, a government ruled by the people. Unlike any before, the American republic would provide enlightened respect for common citizens and would require dedication, honesty, and virtue in its elected representatives. The scope of this democracy would be unprecedented, governing the lives of millions over a vast territory.

As this new American democracy planted seeds to serve the will of the people, its harvest was to promote the greater good of the nation. If they were with us today, the Founders would be delighted with and probably startled by many of our national accomplishments: free and open elections, presidential succession by law, an equitable judicial system, a vibrant press, a superior military, a man on the moon, world-class universities, a sophisticated industrial infrastructure, and vast economic wealth.

However, even from the earliest days, serving the public good was a difficult mission. For example, resolution of the fundamental issues of slavery and equal rights under the law required the Emancipation Proclamation, a civil war, constitutional amendments, *Brown v. Board of Education* (1954), and the Civil Rights Act of 1964 before African Americans and women won the formal protections promised by our Declaration of Independence.

Despite these great strides taken in the interest of the public good, the will of the American people is often denied by an unholy alliance of special interests, moneyed lobbyists, and the system of campaign financing. In the absence of strong political leadership, some promise funding to candidates to help them capture elected office; in return, some in positions of trust enact policies that favor their benefactors but may be contrary to the best interests of the nation.

Before we explore these unfortunate developments, we embark on a brief review of America's beginnings. Through these observations, we can understand the rationale for our democracy and how it was designed to work. By retracing the steps of our Founding Fathers, we can more fully appreciate the value of what is threatened by the siege of special interests.

PHILOSOPHICAL ORIGINS

The Founding Fathers were educated, well-read men schooled in the classics. Their concept of democracy was derived from building blocks laid by insightful philosophers such as Thomas Hobbes, John Locke, and the Baron de Montesquieu.

Whereas Plato and Aristotle contended that it was natural for man to form states and governments, Thomas Hobbes (1588–1679), the noted British political philosopher, believed the formation of governing states to be a product of rational decision-making. In his masterpiece, *Leviathan*, Hobbes explained that, without a governing force, men pursue their own self-interest, which invariably leads to social conflict.[2] To avoid such disputes and be free to focus on personal and family needs, men execute social contracts. They concede some of their freedom to a government that keeps order and provides protection. Hobbes believed that such a contract might only be practical if men were to submit to the supremacy of an indivisible sovereign power, preferably a monarchy with absolute authority.

In his *Second Treatise of Government*, John Locke (1632–1704), the Oxford academic, stated that the function of a legitimate civil government is to preserve the rights of its citizens to life, liberty, health, and property; to prosecute and punish those who violate the rights of others; and to promote the public good, even if such deeds impair the rights of some.[3] The origin of political rights is derived from the individual's ability to invest his labor, creating ownership in private property. The primary responsibility of government, therefore, according to this British philosopher, is to protect the citizen's investment.

Establishing a political community requires universal consent, and selecting the community's ruler requires a majority. This opens the door to the replacement of political leadership while the system of government is maintained. According to Locke, however, when a government fails to advance the interests of its citizens and violates their rights, the government no longer deserves obedience, and rebellion becomes legitimate. Locke opposed authoritarianism, advising individuals to use reason to search for the truth and avoid automatic acceptance of the judgment of those in power.

Although Locke believed in the rule of law, he recognized that situations would arise that were not covered by statutes. In these instances, the governing executive has the prerogative to act in the interest of and for the preservation of the public good. When the course established by the executive is questioned, the deciding criterion must be whether the action was taken for the good or detriment of the people. When those in power are mistaken or are unduly influenced by flattery or private ends, laws need to be established to revoke that prerogative and replace it with statute.

The French political philosopher Baron de Montesquieu (1689–1755) feared that corruption would defeat the good intentions of democratic government.[4] To avoid this danger, he recommended the separation of powers. With different bodies exercising legislative, executive, and judicial power, and each tied to the rule of law, despotism might be eluded.

This check of one power against the others is necessary because experience has shown that power corrupts. Montesquieu visualized two houses of the legislature, with both needed to establish law, including the power to tax. In his vision, the executive body would have the ability to veto legislative action, and an independent judiciary body would administer the law in a consistent manner.

In Montesquieu's view, democracy requires political virtue, "the love of the laws and of our country."[5] It requires that private interest be subservient to public interest. For democracy to function according to the public good, citizens must be educated as to their interests and the interests of their country. Democracy falters when its citizens promote their own private agendas at the expense of the needs of their neighbors.[6]

DEVELOPING AMERICA'S ECONOMIC AND POLITICAL BASE

With burgeoning political thought, including the conceptual development of the democratic form of government, brave souls from the old world traveled to America. The first permanent settlement in North America, established in the colony of Virginia in 1607, was Jamestown, an economic venture undertaken by just over one hundred business-men.[7] After several false starts, the Virginia colonists turned to growing and exporting tobacco, demonstrating the viability of their enterprise. Jamestown was the home of America's first representative assembly, which met in 1619 to provide "just laws for the happy guiding and gov-erning of the people."[8]

In November of 1620, the *Mayflower* landed on Cape Cod, and the Puritans, escaping religious persecution, initiated settlement of the New England colonies.[9] While the Chesapeake Colony in Virginia was mostly populated by men with economic motives, the New England Puritans of the Massachusetts Bay Colony included many women and children, families seeking to build lasting communities.

Over the next 150 years, a steady flow of colonists grew the economy of the New World and practiced many of the canons of democracy. The most common economic characteristic of colonial life was the family farm, which was able to meet most of the material needs of its occupants. The prominent political characteristic was the colonial legis-lature, which collected taxes and established a body of laws. Tobacco became the major cash crop of the South, leading to importation of African slaves to Maryland, Virginia, the Carolinas, and Georgia.

Self-government was an intrinsic aspect of colonial life. Legislators were either elected directly by the voters or appointed by elected houses. Governors were elected in some colonies, while in others the governors were selected by the King of England. In the latter, the colo-nists used the taxing power of their legislatures to influence executive policies. With small farms the norm, one-half to three-quarters of white adult men met property requirements and were eligible to vote.[10]

THE PATH TO INDEPENDENCE

The Founding Fathers saw the parallel between the dream of reli-gious freedom that attracted many to America and their right to self-government. They believed that their association with the Crown was voluntary and could be terminated if continued subjugation was no longer in their interest. Until the end of the Seven Years' (French and Indian) War, the loose British administration of the colonies posed little concern.

In fact, the colonists took pride in their business and community achievements and considered themselves to be politically and economi-cally far ahead of the masses they left behind in Europe. The testing years before the American Revolution built an American character that relied on the principles of political liberty, mistrust of government power, order in the community, the right to private property as a reward of labor, and the practice of tolerance for divergent religions and ideas.

The passive attitude of the British toward colonial administration changed dramatically when the Seven Years' War left the monarchy with a huge debt. The Crown was determined to tighten its control of the American colonies and tax them to increase revenues. The tense circumstances brought about by new British legislation, such as the Quartering Act and the Stamp Act, caused patriot Sam Adams to recommend that a Committee of Correspondence be formed in Boston. Before long, each colony had such a committee, developing and coordinating policy positions through written correspondence that went outside a colony, that is, to other colonies and to foreign governments. This committee network helped unify the colonies and laid the groundwork for eventual nationhood.

FOUNDING OUR DEMOCRACY

On September 5, 1774, the First Continental Congress met in Carpenters' Hall in Philadelphia.[11] The Congress issued a petition to the King of England with the intention of repairing the broken relations between the colonies and Great Britain. They requested the repeal of unjust legislation while they formed Committees of Safety to enforce a trade boycott.

Although most of the delegates believed they were fighting for reconciliation with the British, by the end of 1775 the King of England had called for the suppression of rebellion and sedition in the colonies and hired 18,000 Hessians to join his troops in America.[12] These actions and the publication of Thomas Paine's *Common Sense* ("These are the times that try men's souls") convinced a majority of delegates that independence was the only viable solution to the difficulties with British rule. Paine wrote:

> I am not induced by motives of pride, party, or resentment to espouse the doctrine of separation and independence; I am clearly, positively, and conscientiously persuaded that it is the true interest of this continent to be so; that everything short of *that* is mere patchwork, that it can afford no lasting felicity,—that it is leaving the sword to our children, and shrinking back at a time, when, a little more, a little farther, would have rendered this continent the glory of the earth.[13]

In the summer of 1776, with the war against the British more than a year old, the Continental Congress debated how it would declare independence from the Crown. A committee of five was appointed to draft this statement: John Adams of Massachusetts, Roger Sherman of Connecticut, Benjamin Franklin of Pennsylvania, Robert R. Livingston of New York, and Thomas Jefferson of Virginia.

It was Jefferson's knowledge of relevant political philosophy, his dramatic prose, and his strong beliefs in empowering the will of the people, reducing the authority of government, and respecting the value of freedom, autonomy, and the sufficiency of the individual that melded relevant political thought into the Declaration of Independence:

> We hold these truths to be self-evident, that all men are created equal, that they are endowed by their Creator with certain unalienable rights, that among them are life, liberty, and the pursuit of happiness. That to secure these rights, governments are instituted among men, deriving their just powers from the consent of the governed, that whenever any form of government becomes destructive of these ends, it is the right of the people to alter or abolish it and to institute new government, laying its foundation on such principles and organizing its powers in such form, as to them shall seem most likely to effect their safety and happiness.[14]

SECURING INDEPENDENCE

With independence declared, there was no turning back. The sacrifices made to establish our democracy would be enormous. Over the course of the Revolutionary War, 25,000 American revolutionaries lost their lives and as many as another 25,000 were seriously wounded or disabled.[15] The infant nation spent $37 million at the federal level, and the states spent another $114 million.[16]

In 1777, the Second Continental Congress adopted the Articles of Confederation. The purpose of this document was to provide an enhanced sense of unity and the framework required to direct the Revolutionary War. This first American constitution established the Confederation as the United States of America. It formed a Congress of the Confederation, whose members would be appointed by state legislatures, each state having one vote.

The Articles of Confederation restricted the conduct of foreign relations, the declaration of war, and the determination of weights, measures, and coins to the central government. The states would fund the central government, nine states were required to admit a new state into the confederacy, and amendments had to be approved by Congress and ratified by all of the state legislatures.

As commander-in-chief, President George Washington had a difficult challenge, dealing with an inexperienced militia and a limited number of regulars in his army. His incredible courage on the battlefield, superior knowledge of the terrain, and guerilla tactics, and supplies, ships, and men provided by the French, eventually allowed the Americans to prevail.

Facing unfriendly nations in Europe and the loss of support at home for the war, in 1782 the British House of Commons voted to end the conflict in America. The Treaty of Paris was signed on September 3, 1783, and ratified by the U.S. Congress on January 14, 1784.[17]

When victory was secured, the revolutionaries tackled the formidable task of defining their democracy and determining how it would serve the will of the people.

DEFINING THE AMERICAN DEMOCRACY

As the colonists returned to peacetime, they directed their attention to the Articles of Confederation. At the time that the Articles were adopted, the struggles with the British monarchy had created prejudice against a strong central government; now that stance was preventing effective administration of the nation.

The new U.S. Congress depended on the states for funding, but it was not able to levy taxes. At the same time, there was no procedure to require states to comply with requests for troops or money. The requirement that all states ratify amendments greatly limited the possibility for revision, and the one state/one vote provision was perceived as unfair by the larger states. With a weak financial standing, an inability to carve out an effective foreign policy, and a failure to attract strong public support and leadership, action was required.

On May 25, 1787, a Constitutional Convention was convened to deal with these issues and to establish a construct for effective governance of the infant nation's 3 million inhabitants.[18] Fifty-five men gathered at Philadelphia's Pennsylvania State House. General Washington was elected President of the Convention; Thomas Jefferson was in France as U.S. Ambassador; and Patrick Henry refused to attend, fearing that the establishment of a strong central government would lead to erosion of personal liberties.

"Until the year 1787, the entire history of mankind had never witnessed a single case of a successful and enduring representative republic over a large area."[19] This was the challenge faced by men like James Madison, age thirty-six; Gouverneur Morris, age thirty-five; and Alexander Hamilton, age thirty-two.

Entering deliberations, the majority of delegates agreed upon several key ideas:

1. The form of government would be a republic, a strong central government with executive and legislative bodies that would be selected directly or indirectly by the citizens.
2. A system of checks and balances would partition power centers to ensure that no one branch of government could dominate the population. This second canon recognized the concern about possible corruption and abuse of power, and it was intended to assuage states' fears of the central government.
3. For the system to work there would be a need for compromise. Checks and balances would require an ethics of responsibility under which the participants would recognize that, more often than not, a position or goal would have to be modified to obtain the support of the majority. For example, Madison signed the Constitution even though he opposed equal representation in the Senate.
4. In accordance with the Virginia Plan, developed by Madison and Virginia Governor Peyton Randolph, there would be three branches of a powerful central government: executive, legislative, and judicial. Under this structure, federal law would have command over state priorities.

Once the broad outline was agreed upon, the debate moved to more specific issues. Compromises were reached concerning state representation in the House of Representatives and the Senate, export taxes, slavery, and the process by which the President would be elected.

CONSTITUTIONAL ENCORES

Once completed, this constitution was sent to the states to be ratified. To promote approval of the groundbreaking body of laws, Alexander Hamilton, James Madison, and John Jay wrote eighty-five articles that were published in New York City newspapers.[20] A collection of all these essays, called *The Federalist*, was published in 1788. *Federalist No. 10* and *Federalist No. 57* are particularly relevant to the central theme of this work.

In *Federalist No. 10*, James Madison, inspired by the Scottish philosopher David Hume, dealt with the issue of factions, what today we would characterize as special interest groups.

"By a faction, I understand a number of citizens, whether amounting to a majority or a minority of the whole, (who) are united and actuated by some common impulse of passion, or of interest, adversed to the rights of other citizens, or to the permanent and aggregate interests of the community."[21]

Madison spoke of a population divided into parties, inflamed with mutual animosity, and much more disposed to vex and oppress each other than to cooperate for their common good. The most common source of their differences is the unequal distribution of wealth, as the landed, manufacturing, mercantile, moneyed, and lesser interests compete for their well-being. Thus, it is the principle task of government/legislation to regulate these various and interfering interests. To that end, no man is allowed to be his own judge because his interest would certainly bias his judgment, and, not improbably, corrupt his integrity.

On the other hand, Madison admitted that enlightened statesmen may not always be present to adjust clashing interests and render them all subservient to the public good. Because the causes of faction cannot be removed, Madison focused his attention on dealing with their effects.

Madison believed that if the views of a faction were represented by a minority, the majority rule provisions of the Constitution would ensure that such factions would be unsuccessful. Conversely, if a special interest were in the majority and held a view that would oppress, their views would be countered and their schemes would be foiled through routine functioning of the republic and its three branches of government. Elected representatives, through their wisdom, would discern the true best interests of the country and act out of patriotism and a love of justice.

However, Madison conceded that there may be instances in which representatives who appear to be just can betray the interests of the people through intrigue, corruption, or other means. In a large republic such as the United States, Madison believed that it would be more difficult for unworthy candidates to succeed because many free voters would be more likely to support men of merit and established characters.

In *Federalist No. 57*, the author (either Alexander Hamilton or James Madison) responds to a charge that those elected to the House of Representatives would be from the upper classes and would sacrifice the masses for the aggrandizement of the few. The essay contends that the aim of the Constitution is to provide for the election of administrators who possess the most wisdom to discern and the most virtue to pursue the common good of the society.

Once in office, the Constitution provides effective precautions to keep elected officials virtuous while they continue to hold their public trust. These provisions include

- term limitations;
- no qualifications for elected office involving wealth, birth, religion, or profession;
- the natural desire to win the honor, favor, esteem, confidence, and influence of the public;
- frequent elections and eventual return of elected officials to non-elective status (dependence on the people); and
- the realization that legislation introduced will, if passed, apply to themselves as well as their constituents.

The most serious objection voiced by the anti-Federalists concerned fear that the strong central government being created would be a threat to the rights of individuals. On February 6, 1788, the Federalists agreed to recommend constitutional amendments that would guarantee personal liberties. Five months later, New Hampshire became the ninth state to ratify the Constitution, which then became law.

Leaning on the writings of John Locke as well as George Mason's Virginia Declaration of Rights, James Madison proposed the first ten amendments to the Constitution on June 8, 1789, which guaranteed these fundamental rights:

- Freedom of religion, speech, the press, assembly, and petition for a redress of grievances
- The right to bear arms
- Freedom from soldiers quartered in private homes
- Freedom from unreasonable searches and seizures
- Due process of law
- The right to a speedy and public trial by an impartial jury
- Trial by jury in suits at common law
- No excessive bail or fines, or cruel and unusual punishments
- Enumeration of the Constitution would never deny or disparage other rights retained by the people
- Powers not delegated to the United States by the Constitution, or prohibited by it for the states, are reserved for the states, respectively, or for the people

On October 2, 1789, with Congressional approval, President Washington sent the amendments to the states. By December 15, 1791, the required three-fourths of the states had ratified the ten amendments, our Bill of Rights.[22] With that action, the founding era of the republic came to a close and the American democracy was defined.

SUMMARY AND CONCLUSION

When British fiscal and political demands intruded on the colonists' independent lives, the strong-willed colonists pushed back. Their taste of freedom and the benefits it afforded could not be denied. The more the British sought to repress their subjects, the more their subjects protested any infringement on their liberties. With separation from British rule the only perceived remedy, the colonists declared their independence. This is the tradition that is today threatened by the dominance of special interests.

With autonomy won, fifty-five of the most dedicated and educated Americans sought to design a republic that would promote and protect the moral truths of the Declaration of Independence. They drew upon their own experiences and the concepts developed by political philosophers to prepare the U.S. Constitution. Through a separation of powers, checks and balances, an independent judiciary, and a Bill of Rights, the Constitution that they fashioned recognized and guarded against the dangers inherent to a powerful central government. And yet the resulting government structure maintained the ability and vigor to protect the public, pursue noble deeds, and advance the greater good.

The Founding Fathers understood the dangers of special interests. In *Federalist No. 10* and *Federalist No. 57*, the nation was warned of the manner in which factions might undermine our democracy by seeking ends adverse to the common good. Furthermore, protections to guard against the influence of special interests were specified.

In Chapter 2, we will investigate the power and techniques used by today's special interests. This will be achieved in the context of an investigation of the history of special interests' influence on our nation.

CHAPTER 2

THE HISTORY OF POLITICAL INFLUENCE IN THE UNITED STATES

Tracing the Growing Influence of Those with Narrow Interests

INTRODUCTION

For years, political scandals have rocked Washington and driven the public's perception of elected officials lower and lower. Some of the more notorious disgraces include the 1922 Teapot Dome payoff for leased oil fields, Jack Abramoff's 2006 sentence for conspiracy to bribe members of Congress, and the recent discovery of $90,000 in "cold cash" in Louisiana Congressman William Jefferson's freezer as part of an alleged payoff to assist a tech company named iGate.[1] Over the years, the names and circumstances change, but one common conclusion may be drawn: Such efforts to win the influence of elected officials appear unmistakably illegal.

While today's special interest lobbying generally stays within the law, such legal activities can corrupt our elected officials with cash—this is the travesty of twenty-first-century Washington, D.C. Lobbyists and our representatives together have reduced the use of payoffs to an accepted practice that skirts the law and reinforces the perception that U.S. policy is not driven by doing what's right for the people. Instead, politicians manipulate laws and regulations to maximize their chances of raising campaign contributions, winning elections, and staying in office.

Our pursuit of maximum freedom and minimum government interference does not require us to leave the door open to the will of factions. Special interest control of government policy to the detriment of the nation is not an example of *laissez-faire* democracy; it is the opposite—it is blatant government regulation in the name of the rich and powerful.

There is nothing inherently troubling about special interests. Factions have greatly enhanced our democracy, winning the vote for women, protecting the civil rights of African Americans, and bringing an end to the war in Vietnam. However, special interests are a destructive force when they reach their goals at the expense of the common good or when they successfully distort the facts surrounding important issues. The Founders declared that the citizens of a democracy, to be an effective electorate, must know what's best for them and their nation, and that elected officials must strive to advance the public's interests.

For many, the complexity of our society and the grind of everyday life, which includes costly health care and inadequate wages—partly a result of the domination of powerful interests—provide a built-in advantage for narrow, moneyed factions. These groups, with the bottom line in mind, finance lobbying campaigns to turn specific issues to their advantage. At the same time, the average citizen may have no more than a passing interest in issues at play and would be at a loss to obtain and analyze all the relevant facts, let alone launch some kind of opposition.

This imbalance opens the door to government by the powerful, for the powerful. Equity in government now depends on countervailing public interest groups such as Common Cause and the Union of Concerned Scientists, organizations founded to protect and promote the greater good. Unless public interest groups are able to counter the impact of narrow interests, our environment, income, and health care will continue to be vulnerable to those who value profit over virtue.

MODUS OPERANDI OF TODAY'S LOBBYISTS

The modern version of Washington's lobbying industry was established in the 1970s as the federal government extended its influence into many facets of American society. Since that time, lobbyists have won significant battles for corporate clients, shaping our laws and the resulting fabric of our nation. Infrequent increases in the minimum wage, limitations to stem cell research, rising costs of health care, the absence of meaningful efforts to curb global warming, and unchecked inner-city crime are monuments to the effectiveness of America's lobbyists.

How do they do it? How do Washington lobbyists forward the agendas of their clients? For the most part, lobbyists serve their customers through five major activities:

1. Help large entities (corporations/unions) contend with legislative and regulatory issues. For example, the coal industry may anticipate problems meeting proposed emission standards or dealing with the negative impact of global warming. In response, their lobbyists draft bills to modify emission standards in their favor; these bills are provided to sympathetic Members of Congress for formal introduction.[2] At the same time, lobbyists for the coal industry work to obtain funding for the development of innovative equipment to reduce the emissions of greenhouse gases from their client's product.

2. Obtain government money to achieve a specific objective. Thousands of annual budget "earmarks" set aside dollars to build projects such as hospitals or research facilities that benefit selected constituents. Earmarks are included in appropriations bills but are rarely scrutinized by Members of Congress. Lobbyists develop ideas for projects that could be funded by earmarks and work to gain required Congressional support. Members of Congress who benefit from such earmarks provide lobbyists and their clients with favored treatment.

3. Manage an organization's campaign contributions to maximize their positive impact. Lobbyists direct the activities of corporate and union Political Action Committees (PACs) and organize fundraisers in support of friendly candidates. In addition to contributing to Congressional and presidential campaigns, lobbyists bundle the contributions of large numbers of client employees and others to provide significant sums for political campaigns.

4. Market goods and services to the federal government. For example, a business supply firm may seek to sell office supplies to federal agencies, so the firm's lobbyist might advocate more open contract procedures to provide the client with a better opportunity to compete.

5. Solve problems dealing with the government. A corporation may experience difficulty meeting quality-control requirements established in a government contract. The corporation's lobbyist might obtain additional information on contract conditions and propose alternative interpretations to soften the specifications.

Lobbying firms employ salesmen to recruit potential clients. Once the client is landed, the firm builds Congressional alliances for the client's benefit. This is often achieved by hiring former Congressional staffers who have easy access to their previous employers, are familiar with relevant statutes, and are able to readily develop legislation to assist their clients.

Over the eight-year period from 1998 to 2006, the nation's top lobbying firms spent $17.5 billion to promote their clients' interests. During that period, annual lobbying expenditures rose by more than 79 percent from $1.47 billion to $2.63 billion.[3] Some of these firms are dedicated exclusively to lobbying; others are law firms that also provide lobbying services.

Some lobbying firms support their clients by performing duties associated with public relations, Congressional consulting, polling, and grass roots lobbying. For example, public relations operations organize protests by contractors threatened by a planned reduction in Congressional appropriations. Complementary efforts include work to build the vocal support of friendly think-tank analysts, retired officials, newspaper editorial boards, authors of opinion articles, and entertainment personalities.

Congressional consulting includes building and updating databases that indicate the tendencies of individual Members of Congress with regard to hot-button issues. Analyzing such data allows consultants to predict the viability of alternative positions that require Congressional approval. If there is a need to take the pulse of the public to help sway Congressional sentiment, the lobbyist's polling capabilities are called into play.

Grass roots lobbyists organize local support for client initiatives. For example, the lobbyist provides opportunities for constituents to communicate their dissatisfaction with their Congress Member's position on a given issue. Communications take the form of e-mails, written materials, or visits with Members of Congress and/or their staff.

Direct access to legislators and executives is considered to be the most valuable service provided by lobbyists. A client's best chance of success with an initiative is to meet face to face with a Senator, Representative, or federal agency executive and make his or her case in person.

Lobbyists ingratiate themselves and their clients with Members of Congress through campaign contributions (especially with Members on appropriations committees and with leaders of the two main political parties) and by seeing that subcontracts are located in a given Congress Member's district, awarding honoraria to Congress Members to have them appear at posh locations, donating money to establish a university chair in the Congress Member's name, giving the Congress Member credit for lobbyist-inspired accomplishments, and sponsoring lavish entertainment at national political conventions and elsewhere to provide opportunities for a pleasant exchange of ideas between Members of Congress and other individuals of influence.

Some of these activities have been outlawed or restricted by the Honest Leadership and Open Government Act of 2007, signed into law by President Bush on September 14, 2007. Unfortunately, lobbyists often find clever ways around the types of requirements included in such legislation.

THE POWER AND EVOLUTION OF CAMPAIGN FINANCING

Winning and staying in office take money—lots of money. In 2006, successful candidates for the House of Representatives paid an average of $1.3 million to finance their campaigns, and successful candidates for the U.S. Senate paid $9.6 million.[4] Even after adjusting for inflation, these sums reflect an average increase of more than 300 percent over the past 30 years.

In 2004, the election campaigns of George W. Bush and John Kerry raised $457.0 million and $389.8 million, respectively.[5] These funds paid for the costs of primary campaigns, the general election, legal and accounting costs, and nominating conventions. The level of presidential campaign funding also reflects an increase of 300 percent since 1976, the first year in which matching federal funds were available and the first year in which primary elections played the most significant role in the selection of party candidates. For the year 2007, the 2008 presidential candidates raised $582.5 million and spent $481.2 million.[6] Thus, before the primary elections were completed, total expenditures exceeded spending for seven of the last eight presidential contests, including both primary and general elections. The Center for Responsive Politics has predicted that, for the first time, campaign financing for a U.S. election will exceed $1 billion. In spite of the many Internet contributions from individual donors, more than one-third of the money raised in 2007 was from ten industries: lawyers/law firms; those listing their occupation as "retired"; securities and investments; real estate; miscellaneous business; business services; miscellaneous finance; health professionals; education; and TV-movies-music.[7]

Campaign contributions are used to employ political consultants; pay for the advice of pollsters; purchase radio, television, and Internet advertising; and generate computer-driven mail. The significance of raising adequate campaign funds and the services obtained with these funds is clearly evident. In recent years, more than 90 percent of successful House candidates and two-thirds of successful Senate candidates outspent their opponents. In short, money is an important factor in winning elections.[8]

How have political candidates raised campaign funds? For most of the 1800s, the "spoils system" held sway as candidates promised federal jobs in return for financial support. Party loyalists who received government employment gave back portions of their government salaries to support activities of the political parties with which they were associated. These dollars became the primary financial base of political parties.

With the Pendleton Civil Service Act of 1883, eligibility for federal employment became largely conditional on competitive examinations.[9] This eliminated many federal jobs as a source of campaign funding; as a result, big corporate interests, representing banks, oil, steel, and railroads, filled the gap.

After President Theodore Roosevelt's 1904 campaign was criticized for accepting large contributions from big business, Congress passed the Tillman Act, which prohibited corporate contributions and gifts to federal candidates.[10] Then, in 1910, the Federal Corrupt Practices Act set campaign spending limits and established the first public disclosure requirements for federal campaigns.[11] However, despite these regulatory advances, the lack of an enforcement mechanism or effective penalties minimized their impact.

With the New Deal came the 1935 Works Progress Administration and federally funded jobs for millions of unemployed Americans. Because these positions were not covered by the Civil Service restrictions on political activity, there was fear that the spoils system would again rear its ugly head. To avoid that possibility, the Hatch Act of 1939 limited the political practices of these workers and prohibited the solicitation of political contributions from all federal employees.[12]

Recognizing the growing influence of union political contributions, the Taft-Hartley Act of 1947 made direct union contributions to political parties illegal. The Act also prohibited corporations and unions from purchasing ads and services on behalf of political campaigns, thereby circumventing the purpose of contribution limits.[13]

To avoid restrictions on union contributions, PACs were organized. These committees were supported by union members who made voluntary payments to PAC budgets. Unions used the PAC vehicle to fund numerous federal candidates, voter registration drives, and other party activities. Corporations began to use the PAC funding mechanism in the early 1960s.

With the growing popularity of television in the 1950s and 1960s, personality trumped party in election politics. General Dwight David Eisenhower—everyone's kind old grandfather—and John Fitzgerald Kennedy—the young, vibrant, handsome icon—proved that a winning presence on television could carry a candidate through to election victories. Although political parties were still a major source of funding, individual candidates became the focus of raising political contributions.

At the same time that the responsibility for raising money shifted to the candidates, the cost of campaigns skyrocketed, mainly as a result of the added expense of television advertising. For example, between 1956 and 1968, media bills for presidential elections rose by nearly 500 percent.[14]

Out-of-date spending limits, disclosure requirements that failed to capture substantial contributions, and concern about the ever increasing costs of election campaigns led Congress to fashion new legislation. In 1971, the Federal Election Campaign Act (FECA) attempted to curtail rising campaign costs by limiting the money that a candidate could provide to his or her own campaign and spend on television advertising.[15] The new law also increased the reporting burden for those who contributed funds above predetermined amounts to political parties and campaigns.

With no enforcement mechanism in place, however, the rise in campaign costs failed to slow, and the Watergate scandal magnified the dangers of unfettered political contributions. Congress went back to the drawing board and passed the 1974 FECA Amendments.[16] These additions to the law strengthened reporting requirements, further limited political contributions, substituted overall spending boundaries for media limitations, restricted party spending on behalf of candidates, and established the Federal Election Commission (FEC), an executive agency charged with enforcing federal campaign finance laws.

An innovative feature of the 1974 FECA Amendments was a program of federal funding for presidential elections. Using dollars set aside by a voluntary contribution selection that is available on individual federal income tax forms, the program continues to offer matching subsidies for primary elections, grants to help pay for presidential nominating conventions, and a single grant to cover the costs of the general election. Eligibility requires that candidates agree not to raise any private funds for their general election campaigns and to limit their own contributions.

Unfortunately, the dollars promised by FECA campaign financing have failed to keep pace with the huge funding capabilities of today's political machines. As a result, most leading presidential candidates have declined to participate.

In 1976 the Supreme Court threw a wrench into the workings of the FECA campaign-spending requirements. In the landmark *Buckley v. Valeo* decision, the Court found that spending on political campaigns was tantamount to free speech, guaranteed by the First Amendment.[17] Therefore, the court concluded that the government could not restrict political spending, although it could regulate contributions as a means to avoid corruption. As a consequence of these findings, FECA was again amended, this time to eliminate the cap on the amount a candidate could provide to his or her own campaign. However, the cap was maintained for those who accepted public financing.

Despite the long history of attempts to temper the influence of campaign contributions, the 1980s once again saw the floodgates open to unregulated campaign financing. This was a consequence of a 1970s FEC decision to allow the political parties, at the federal and state levels, to use unlimited amounts of corporate, union, and individual contributions on non-federal, party-building activities and for administrative costs.

Beginning in 1988, this "soft" money became a major source of support for presidential campaigns. Candidates and the political parties requested soft-money gifts from lobbyists and special interests with stakes in federal policy. With little objection from the FEC, these funds were used for voter registration and get-out-the-vote campaigns, as well as candidate-specific issue ads that promoted candidates but did not ask voters to cast their ballot for a certain individual. This technicality avoided the Supreme Court's restriction on the use of soft-money contributions.

The abuses that derived from the lure of soft-money contributions were predictable. In 1996, the presidential election featured contributions to party committees by foreign nationals (banned by FECA), access for soft-money donors through coffee klatches with influential White House staffers and officials, sleepovers in the Lincoln bedroom, corporate and union funding of candidate-specific issue ads, and the establishment of non-federal PACs by federal candidates.

To combat such practices, Congress passed and the President reluctantly signed the Bipartisan Campaign Reform Act of 2002 (BCRA), also known as McCain–Feingold.[18] This law required national party committees to use only "hard money" raised in accordance with federal contribution limits to sponsor political operations. At the same time, the statute widened the definition of prohibited advertising on behalf of corporations and unions.

However, a five-to-four ruling of the Supreme Court struck down the advertising provision of McCain–Feingold on June 25, 2007, reasoning that the restrictions were unconstitutional.[19] Critics of that decision claim that it represented a big win for special interests and big money. In addition to this setback, there is an indication that soft money may continue to be sheltered through the status of special tax-exempt groups, including those labeled as advocacy entities and social welfare organizations. Thus, the 2008 presidential election promises a financial arms race between cash-laden special interests.

SUMMARY AND CONCLUSIONS

We have seen the powerful arsenal of tools used by lobbyists to influence the content and course of U.S. political and policy agendas. The funding that lobbyists provide to those who seek elected office is the heart of the special interest groups' ability to steer the nation. Unfortunately, efforts to restrict and regulate campaign financing have fallen short.

Where has the legislative journey to limit the influence of special interests through campaign financing restrictions taken us? First, it has resulted in a hodge-podge of shifting and confusing federal contribution and spending regulations that make compliance difficult, even for well-intentioned candidates.[20] Second, given the history of political campaigns in our country, one must conclude that, regardless of the controls put in place, candidates, parties, and special interests and their lobbyists will continue to find ways to circumvent the rules. When new barriers are erected, innovative means are found to get around them.

This leaves the door open to the solicitation of contributions by candidates and parties with the understanding that campaign contributions will be recognized with Congressional favors. Donating special interests take advantage of legislation written to meet their needs. As noted earlier, such bills are often written by lobbyists themselves. Special interest advantages gained include federal subsidies, entitlements, tax cuts or tax breaks, and other policies and fiscal remuneration that serve special interests but not the public good.

The lure of campaign financing and the election victory that it enables is the lobbyist's carrot that may tempt any political figure to compromise his or her convictions and dishonor our democracy. Therefore, it is not surprising that Members of Congress, Presidents, and their senior staffs typically spend significant portions of their time in office raising money. Such efforts take the form of telephone calls to lobbyists and union and corporate executives; holiday fundraisers; and breakfast, lunch, and dinner events to capture donations, just to name a few. In fact, the amount of time that Congress spends in session has been significantly reduced by the perceived need to raise campaign funds—and because those who make political contributions are among the wealthiest in the nation, is it any wonder that federal priorities have shifted away from serving the poor and middle classes?

In Part 2, we will present interviews of knowledgeable parties intimately involved in the U.S. system of government to learn their perspectives on special interests, lobbyists, and campaign financing.

PERSPECTIVES OF POLITICAL PLAYERS

To effect change, we must understand the mindset and motivations of those who drive our political system. What do Washington insiders think about special interests, lobbyists, and campaign financing? If we can effectively answer this question, we can begin to see how mechanisms of change may be designed and integrated into our political life to return America's democracy to the people.

Six interviews were conducted to obtain information on the political perspectives of those who work to make the wheels of government turn. Information was provided by the staff of a citizen advocacy organization, a thoughtful conservative, a seasoned Washington progressive, a candid Washington lobbyist, a European diplomat (to provide an international perspective), and a media expert. To maximize the frankness of responses, those interviewed were assured that sources would not be identified. In some cases, transcripts were edited to maintain a consistent style and to clarify interview information.

CHAPTER 3

VIEWS OF CITIZEN ADVOCACY STAFF

Special Interests, Lobbyists, and Campaign Financing

Q: What's your view of the importance of public financing for Congressional and presidential elections?

A: We think it's important to have a public financing system for the President as well as for Congress. We have been working for several years starting around 2000 to update the current presidential system to higher amounts and earlier disbursements of funding that would coordinate with the timing of campaigns these days. The Republican-controlled Congress of the recent past opposed public financing for presidential elections. So, we realized that there was no chance to fix things for 2008; 2012 would be the soonest that we could use an updated system.

Q: I've read that in the recent past 95 percent of all House candidates who won their elections outspent their opposition, and two-thirds of all Senate candidates who won outspent their competition. So, that leads me to believe that public financing would really have to guarantee parity. Candidates know these statistics as well, and they wouldn't accept it without the assurance that enough funding would be provided to run competitive campaigns.

A: A lot of people on the outside like public financing because they think that you'll have many new Representatives in office and the crooks will be gone. But, based upon what we know from public financing of State legislator elections in Maine and Arizona, the actual numbers of incumbents don't seem to change that much. Even if you provide public money and balance that out against those with private financing, the incumbent still has better name recognition and contacts. It does allow for greater diversity of candidates. My personal belief is that even if you have the same people in office, if you have public funding, their decision-making process would at least appear to be more genuine. It's still important for that reason.

Q: What is your overall take on where we are on the influence of lobbyists and the dollars they provide in the name of special interests?

A: I think our take would be that their influence is big and is getting bigger because the amount of money that you need to run a competitive campaign for the Presidency or Congress is going up a lot faster than the contribution limits in force. The way people do it now is modeled after the "Bush Rangers." The politician relies on the lobbyist who might know fifty people who could each write a $2,000 check. Not only the big money-givers, but the people who can gather people who write checks to help the candidate keep pace with the rapid increases in the cost of campaigns.

Q: What are the forces that are driving costs upward?

A: I know that a lot of the cost increase is due to media buys ... TV. I think that's primarily it. Talk to any voter and they say "I've seen enough of this guy." But if the opponent can raise $3 million and spend it on TV, the other candidate feels he has to do the same thing. It's a vicious cycle.

Q: What about the primaries? When I was a kid there weren't many primaries. The presidential candidates were mainly selected at the conventions. You'd get twenty-four-hour-a-day TV coverage trying to track the back-room deals being made to help determine who the presidential and vice presidential nominees would be. Once the conventions were over, you just had a few months until the election. Now, we're starting so much sooner because in recent elections the candidates have been determined by the primaries. Look at the presidential race today. The serious candidates started months ago, because they thought that the February 2008 primaries would likely select the candidates. So, wouldn't you agree that the extended time and expenses involved in the primaries have been an important factor in adding to campaign costs?

A: Yes, you need a big organization and millions of dollars. That's part of why we realized that if we want to make public funding a viable option for presidential elections there needs to be a lot more money a lot sooner.

Q: So what are the plans to get public financing implemented?

A: Our strategy is to divide and conquer. There is a coalition of groups that's working on the presidential system. It's not a full public financing system because there is a matching program. Some groups think you have to do full public financing. However, none of the proposals require full public financing because there are First Amendment problems with that. There are those who don't want to invest too much time on this because they don't think it will solve the problem. We think that full public financing would be best, but we support improving the current presidential system.

We also have a coalition of six groups working on Congressional funding. One of the key strategies is that we've reached out to bring in other groups to endorse our proposal. For example, we have received the endorsements of the American Federation of Labor and Congress of Industrial Organizations (AFL-CIO) and the Service Employees International Union (SEIU). We also have the backing of major environmental and civil rights groups, as well as the National Counsel of Churches. Although we're off to a good start, we need to build a lot more power. We meet every week and talk about strategy for the Hill. Some Senators have cooperated with us and we have people on the ground in thirty-four states working for this. We're essentially doing what most groups proposed, an inside-outside strategy.

Q: Will the candidates for 2008 endorse this proposal?

A: The top three candidates on the Democratic side have all endorsed public financing at one time or another. Obama is co-signing the bill that introduces our proposal in the Senate. Edwards has said that he supports it, and Hillary says she supports it. So, our goal is to get them to prioritize public financing and to pass it. We have groups in Iowa and New Hampshire who will pop the question to candidates appearing there. We're also going to have sit-down meetings with any candidate who would be willing to talk about the system. The surprising thing to me is that a lot of candidates and people in general just don't fully understand how it works. They think it's mandatory, required, or really easy and that any fringe group could obtain public financing.

Q: So you have to educate people as to what the system really is?

A: Yes. It's not welfare for politicians. That's a talking point against it. We hear that it's hard to combat that one line—it resonates.

Q: People also think that the public is against public financing of federal elections.

A: I hear that, too. People use the percent who check the box on their income tax to use a dollar in support of public financing but that's not a fair measure. We've polled the public and found that 70 percent like the idea.

Q: Some tell me that rather than systemic problems like campaign financing, the nation has suffered from the unusually dogmatic views of the current Administration. They agree that there are systemic problems that need to be handled, but over the last several years they feel that we have been subjected to a very conservative Administration that is tied too closely to the business community. So, a lot of the systemic problems are magnified because you have a lot of those kinds of personalities running the show. They contend that if you had a traditional Democratic or moderate Republican Administration in office, you'd have some difficulties with special interests and lobbyists but nothing like what we've experienced recently. Looking at issues like global warming, you'd have more reasonable decisions made.

A: I think that's a very convenient argument. I won't argue that the Bush Administration, with their ties to big money, has been pretty obvious. We see the stamp of corporate America on a lot of their policies. I don't disagree with that. But I think almost any person in office says, "I have to deal with raising money and I don't like it, but I take it with a grain of salt and I make my own decisions." They'll all say that, but the level of access has a very significant effect ... it's all about access. Who has the ear of the decision-maker? No doubt the groups with money have the access. The guys who donate the money get to sit down and have a forty-five-minute meeting with a Senator as opposed to a fifteen-minute meeting with a staffer. Each individual says they're not influenced, but if you look at their decisions they track pretty closely. Their argument falls flat.

Q: Assuming that the campaign financing problem will be solved, would we still need to deal with the problem of lobbyist practices, or is it the money that allows the lobbyist to win undue influence?

A: If you're asking would we still need to monitor lobbyists, then yes.

Q: Would we still need this kind of control over things like bundling and the revolving door of Congressional staffers who end up working for lobbyists?

A: My initial gut reaction would be yes, although I think it would be a lot different. We've never had a problem with people hiring lobbyists to represent their interests. But watch-dogging to make sure there is no corruption would be a good thing. Unless the Supreme Court case (*Buckley v. Valeo*) that forces public financing to be voluntary is over-turned at some point, we'll still have some private financing, so we will need a parallel set of rules. If we could overturn that decision, which says spending money on campaigns is comparable to free speech, then we could pass required campaign financing and that would solve most of the problems. We're not trying to get money out of politics. But it's the big money and the influence it buys that is the problem. The revolving door issue is still one we need to address. It shortens the Congressional careers of talented staff and it provides an unfair advantage to some lobbyists.

There are seven states that have some version of public campaign financing that applies to state offices. Most seem to be successful. Maine and Arizona are the two that have comprehensive programs for their legislatures. Maine has a website that includes a study of their successes.

Q: Many of the restrictions included in bills to limit the influence of lobbyists simply shine a light on questionable practices, but they don't outlaw them. For example, bundling can continue, but the lobbyist has to report the amount of money that has been provided and who provided it. If you're the guy that bundled, is that enough to restrict that practice? Do you care that you had to report that information?

A: The alternative is not to have anyone report.

Q: But if I represent an oil company and I get twenty $2,000 checks and I turn them over to a political campaign and report what I've done, do I really care that I had to provide that information? I still have the belief that the funding I've provided will likely buy me some influence sometime down the road.

A: The thinking behind it is merit. The public should know who is raising money and where the money is coming from. Over the course of the last few decades that kind of report has been required. You can go to the website www.opensecrets.org and see who has been providing money to each political candidate. That's good because the public should know. I think it's a good thing, but will not have a drastic impact. It will inform voters so they can make an informed decision as to whom candidates are likely to represent.

Q: Take global warming. Lobbyists for the oil, gas, and coal companies have really determined U.S. policy. This information is readily available; but has it really made a difference? The guy who wrote the Bush policy supposedly is a former Exxon/Mobil employee. Everybody knows it—where is the outrage? Why isn't the American public more upset and proactive?

A: I guess I have a few reactions to that. One is that I feel like it shouldn't take outrage from the entire population to influence a commonsense decision. Thinking about the global warming example; it's taken years to educate the public. They want us to do the right things, but Congress and the Bush Administration have done nothing. Voters make decisions about electing their Representatives to the House, the Senate, and the White House. There are a whole set of issues that come into play and most people aren't single issue–minded. There are groups—Exxon/Mobil, Chevron—they are interested in a single issue and they can raise tons of money and channel it into the campaigns of important decision-makers.

So, I think, even if voters are really concerned about global warming, they are also concerned about other things. They cast a vote for a candidate that has positions on many issues. It seems to me that the contention that people concerned about global warming should throw out the politicians who have done nothing is too simple an argument. It's a tough parallel. Powerful special interest groups are focused on that one issue while the public has a whole array of issues with which they are concerned. Even if they don't approve of the global warming position of an elected official, maybe there are other positions of that candidate that they do approve of.

Q: If you go back and look at the Founding Fathers and how they believed that our democracy would work, they made an assumption that elected officials would usually do what's best for the country. Maybe not all the time, but on the big issues, and if they don't, people would protest or eventually vote them out. There would be some noise. It just seems to me that we've lost something here. There's an acceptance of policies that we know are wrong-headed and probably aimed at satisfying a special interest that has provided campaign funding.

I remember marching against the Vietnam War. The country was outraged. People were getting drafted and killed for what proved to be an unnecessary and unwise conflict. Today, we have a parallel situation and clear violations of trust, and yet the nation accepts what's going on. Polls show that people don't like what's going on but they seem to accept it. Maybe it doesn't matter that politicians are taking contributions; it just seems so blatant. I know people have a lot to worry about. They have their jobs, family, health insurance, and college tuition for the kids. But what kind of America will the kids inherit if issues such as global warming fall by the wayside?

A: I generally agree. It seems like people just throw up their hands instead of going out into the streets and protesting. The whole mantra that one person can make a difference has given way to a belief that the powers that be won't be moved so easily. People get frustrated and opt out.

I think another thing is how important raising lots of money is— being a candidate. There are two parties and both of them have to go out and raise a lot of money. There aren't many places where you can raise that kind of money. When they get to that point, they start formulating their platforms and figuring out how to represent their constituents. But this is affected by the money question. Do you please your constituents and anger potential sources of funds, or do you strike some kind of balance?

This ends up limiting what constituents are able to get. That may result in the public not being so excited by elections—there may not be a difference between the candidates because they have to sell themselves out to the wealthy. This creates a huge crisis of trust. I think that a system that removes the influence of big money might restore people's trust. It might get them engaged if they believe more in the system.

Q: Do you think that the problem you just described is a factor in low turnout for our elections? No one is representing what I want, so the hell with the election.

A: I think that's got to be part of it. I don't want to say that we'll ever get 100 percent turnout. But certainly we should be doing much better. The media, of course, is another relevant issue.

Q: Are there any plans to try to restrict the amount of time in which campaigns can take place?

A: I don't think you can because it's a First Amendment issue. The public financing system includes guidelines, dates on when you get the money, at what point you must qualify, etc. So that's built into it. But you can't restrict candidates in terms of when they will begin their campaigning. By the way, our Congressional financing plan also includes media vouchers and discounted TV time for those who participate in public financing.

Q: If the new lobbying restrictions that have been introduced on the Hill are enacted into law, do you think that lobbyists will find a way to get around them?

A: It's a finger in the dike. Don't get me wrong. I think the restrictions are a good idea. The revolving door provisions that require Congressional staff to wait for a year or two before they accept employment are a good idea. But, based upon past performance, I think the lobbyists will find a way to get around most of the new restrictions.

Q: How about issues like stem cell research? It's religion rather than money that seems to be blocking action. Do you think it's an interesting case study?

A: Yes. It's a different kind of motivation but just as powerful as the profit motive.

Q: If you were writing this book, is there something else that you'd cover?

A: Given your outline, I think the relevant topics are well covered. However, I think you should also stress the impact of the media.

Q: The media are supposedly the truth tellers. We rely on them to tell the truth, and yet the lobbyists are very skilled at putting out their version of the facts. If the press just accepts arguments made by those with a stake in the conclusion, and no other group goes up against it, then the public doesn't really know the facts. Again, if you go back to the beginning of our democracy, there is an assumption that people will know what's best for them and for the nation. How can they make informed decisions if they don't know the facts?

A: For the project that I'm working on, we're also looking at the profits that broadcasters make out of political campaigns. Who makes the money when more and more people are buying TV ads ... it's the broadcasters. How do they turn around and talk about the issues in an unbiased manner, even when some of their biggest advertisers may be damaged by the truth?

Q: So they may be compromised by money as well?

A: I'm sure they'd tell you that they keep their business separate from their reporting. But you know if someone is calling the shots at the top, in the end everything is a money issue. But I'd be careful to discuss media in your book because of its complexity.

CHAPTER 4

VIEWS OF A MEDIA EXPERT

Media and America's Political Process

Q: What role do the media play in electing political candidates to public office?

A: The huge amount of money spent on candidate ads for political campaigns is unprecedented. At the same time, now we have tremendous amounts of money spent on issue ads. Most times you don't really know who is financing the issue ads. They come in with names that are generic—this group or that—so you don't know who is behind the ads.

The reason television is used so much is the power of TV. As many years as I've been in it, the power of TV can't be denied. You really can sell ice to Eskimos. What the political people have discovered about TV is its incredible power. I've always thought retailers have underestimated what TV can accomplish. On the other hand, politicians now understand it.

The politicians have found that TV works, and the reason TV works as compared to newspapers, magazines, and other print media is that with print media you must make a conscious effort to understand the information being provided. With TV you can avoid the conscious effort required by print media. So what happens is you sit down and you listen and maybe you watch the TV ads, and even though you may contend that you aren't paying attention, most of the time those ads have an impact.

The reason it has become so important in the political process is because politicians have realized that their product is no different from paper towels, cleaners, or dog food. They are selling a product, and the public can be sold. Evidence of this is the Swift Boat episode and how effective it was—I don't think they spent more than $2 million with those messages and yet they changed the outcome of the election.

The other thing that politicians have discovered is that the media will latch onto anything. Just give them a reason to be there, and they'll show up. TV has become a very important part of the process because of its power. This year [2008] it is estimated that they [political candidates] will spend $400 million in political ads. You have to have media, and if you don't you can't win. The other guy will pound it and pound it, and if you can't retaliate, you're dead in the water.

By the time an election reaches crunch time, let's say four weeks before a primary, the politicians will reach a point where they'll purchase an incredible number of rating points a week. They'll buy time on every newscast you have during the day. They come in and inundate the public with airtime. In all my years, I've never seen anything like it. They can't sit back because if they do the opposing candidate takes the advantage. They're buying so much media that you can't avoid their message. The public is the public. They're not that well informed, and they can be sold.

I think an unfortunate thing that has happened in this country is that the public has such a good time with these elections. I really believe that 80 percent of the undecided voters aren't really undecided. They say they are because it makes them feel important. For example, with the Bush–Kerry election, with one week left, there were huge numbers of undecided voters. What the hell were they waiting for?

So what happens is that the public has bought into the political-media drama. They like to be part of things going on in the media. It's like everyone in Los Angeles thinks they're in show business, and everyone in Washington thinks they're in politics. Of course one of the benefits for the media is that if there are a lot of undecided voters, the politicians have to spend more money to court those potential votes.

The other factor that has become a big issue is the entrance of soft money into the campaign process. The McCain-Feingold Act was to have a major impact in controlling those dollars. But when the Supreme Court overturned the restriction on using candidate names with issue ads, that again opened the floodgates for soft money into the political process.

Q: To what extent do political ads contribute to media profitability?

A: It's huge. I can't put a percentage on it, but it's huge. There's really no way to figure it out because it varies so much depending upon the political circumstances. In 2004, in Philadelphia, you couldn't avoid political advertising. One hundred miles north in New York, there was nothing because Kerry had it won and there was no reason to spend on media. Of course, one year you might have a governor's race and the next year you don't. That could make a big difference. Regardless, political ads are the only segment of the TV industry that is increasing in value.

Q: Some campaign finance reform proposals would have the federal government instruct the media to provide free or cut-rate TV time to political candidates. How would the networks respond to that type of suggestion?

A: We've seen those proposals more than once and they receive a terrible reception. Anyway, I don't know if those proposals would have the desired outcome. You can't stop campaigns with greater financial resources from buying more media exposure than the opposition, even if a certain number of hours is provided free of charge. What I would do is shorten the period of time in which campaigns can be conducted. However, the problem is that such a proposal would likely be found to violate the First Amendment.

Can you imagine that they're talking of spending $3 billion for the 2008 campaigns? The only way to restrict such spending is to cut the amount of time in which campaigns can be conducted. It's all about raising money, getting on TV, and getting yourself sold. We all know that Bush isn't the brightest, but his handlers used TV to push all the right buttons, and they got him elected, twice. The second time, his camp had a very willing partner in the Democrats, who failed to respond adequately to Republican charges.

Q: Is there a relationship between the reporting/editorial sides of media and the business side? If yes, how does it work?

A: I have never seen cooperation between the two sides. If anything, I've seen conflict between them. These two sides are kept very separate. Every once in a while you have a situation where the news department goes after an employer who happens to be a large advertiser for the station. It doesn't make the business side happy, but that's just the way it is.

Q: What responsibility do the media have to report truthful information? Is this a high priority, or is the highest priority to attract advertisers and make acceptable ratings?

A: The highest priority of a TV station is to keep your license, attract advertisers, and make good ratings. TV stations are in business solely to make money. They are supposed to represent the public interest, which they do to a degree.

Q: Let's say you sell a certain amount of time to one of these issue groups. They broadcast a five-minute message that you know is dead wrong. It's very convincing, but you know they're 180 degrees wrong. Is that just the way it goes, or do you have an obligation to do something about it?

A: The truth is that nobody is paying very much attention to the validity of the content of most political ads. It's really a self-regulating industry. The stations are required to take political business. If someone gets on the air with a candidate ad that says that my opponent sleeps with boy scouts, you can't question, you must show it. They may come after the individual making the charge but they won't come after the TV station. On the other hand, if you run a commercial that tells the public to use *toothpaste A* because if you use *toothpaste B* your teeth will fall out, then the sponsor as well as the station running the ad may be charged with libel.

However, what's happening now with regard to issue ads is that some stations are asking for backup information. They are looking for substantiation of the comments made. But there's a lot of stuff that gets by, and rarely are the messages examined closely. If you know that a message is wrong, you should really get it off the air. But the truth is the stations aren't equipped with the expertise or the time to examine the truthfulness of the huge array of messages that they are asked to broadcast.

Q: So, conceptually, do you think that the media adequately serves America's democracy?

A: I think it does, but I think it's unfortunate that there aren't more restrictions on the volume of political advertising. It's serving, but it's also serving for its own good. Political money, whether it is candidate or issue money, it's all paid in advance. There is no credit. So they *really* like political money. The industry puts few roadblocks in front of these people because the rest of the business isn't all that good.

Q: Do you have any other ideas to improve things? For example, what if a consumer group with no financial stake in the outcome of an issue bought TV time to explain how certain ads have been deceptive and then provided accurate and relevant information concerning the issues addressed? Might that have a positive impact?

A: I guess I'm somewhat cynical about the viewer. Most people are satisfied with the surface. They don't want detailed information; they don't have the time or patience. Just tell them what they have to know and which way to vote.

CHAPTER 5

VIEWS OF A THOUGHTFUL WASHINGTON CONSERVATIVE

Special Interests, Lobbyists, and Campaign Financing

Q: I'd like to start off with some rather general questions. How do you think the Founding Fathers would judge our progress in realizing their dream of America's democracy?

A: I think it would be a mixture of positives and negatives. In terms of the positives, we've retained a lot of reforms of representative government. The Founders established an indirect democracy of representative government where the people rule but not directly. In some cases we've probably done better than the Founders were able to do under their political circumstances to achieve a wider base of consent of the governed. In terms of requirements for voting for members of the U.S. Senate, for example, the Founders left it up to the state legislatures. We've determined a better way of going about it with direct election of senators.

On the negative side, the delegation of legislative power to an expert bureaucracy is a real deviation from the Founder's model. The bureaucracy has been turned into a policy-making branch of the government. Experts are making policy instead of carrying out the *will of the people*. The level of emissions that can come out of your car, the fuel efficiency of an airplane, these are all established by bureaucratic agencies who are only accountable in an indirect way. For the most part they are unaccountable because of civil service regulations. So, in general there has been good and bad. The Founding Fathers would have a problem with legislative acts flowing from an executive agency.

Q: The Founders visualized an ethics of responsibility under which our political leaders were expected to make compromises in order to make progress on important issues. Some say that this ability to compromise is something that we've lost in recent years. What is your view?

A: Recent historical research has shown that party battles in earlier days were almost as fierce, but not fiercer than what we have today. The Founders did understand the importance of compromise. They understood that the only way to achieve a principle is by adapting what you do in a particular circumstance so that you might achieve the principle in the long run. For example, the Constitution included a compromise in regards to the question of slavery. If that compromise had not been reached, we would not have established a framework in which slavery was eventually abolished.

They all understood that the compromise was necessary to achieve attainment of the principle. If they hadn't compromised on this, we might have two countries, one free, and one slave. The Founders believed in compromise on issues that they felt were high and noble. It's not shameful to compromise as long as you're not compromising the principle. You are in effect compromising the route you will take to get to the principle.

The crucial distinction is that today we think of compromise as giving up on principle, but the Founders believed that compromise is not about giving up on principle but adapting to what you have to do in a given circumstance to achieve the principle in the long run. The Founders disagreed on a wide array of certain practical policies, but they all agreed on the fundamental principles. For example, they all agreed on the principles in the Declaration of Independence.

Today, there is no consensus on whether the Declaration's principles are legitimate. So, when you have a broader range of disagreement, compromise becomes much more difficult.

Q: What kinds of disagreements do you have in mind when it comes to the Declaration, for example?

A: Conservatives would say that the central principle of the American democracy is equality. The natural equality of all human beings leads to the principle of government by consent because there are no natural rulers. In fact, we have natural rights by virtue of our humanity. The Declaration calls for limited government to protect the individual so that you can have the opportunity to acquire property. It doesn't give you a claim to property, or a claim to positive government benefits.

I think there is a new idea of equality wholly divorced from the Declaration that operates in modern liberals. Hence, the idea that equality means equality of outcome, not accepting the inequality which necessarily results from your equality of rights. If rights are applied equally you're going to have inequality of outcomes. So, the idea of equality has at least been modified to the extent that it means something very different as determined by modern liberals.

Q: There are recurring themes in our nation's founding involving the ability of voters to identify men of merit and sound character and the assumption that, in general, our political leaders will have the wisdom and virtue to promote the common good and to pursue noble deeds. Do you think we're on track with that or have we slipped in the last twenty-five years or so?

A: We're not doing a very good job in terms of identifying representatives who possess wisdom and virtue to promote the common good. I think that the Founders understood that the only way to reconcile the two central ideas in the Declaration of Independence, mainly, consent of the governed and the protection of rights, is to have an enlightened citizenry. This is one area where the country would benefit if we all read the *Federalist Papers*. Obviously, those two requirements may not always work out. For example, you could have a majority that tramples on the rights of a minority; consent might yield a policy that fails to protect natural rights. To guard against such outcomes, you have to make sure that the voters are virtuous enough and wise enough to select the right kind of representatives.

So, in the *Federalist Papers* and in Washington's farewell address it's constantly stated that in a democracy religion and morality are indispensable supports. If you're going to have government based on the consent of the governed, you must have those two assets so the people can rule themselves. The idea of a republican government requires civic virtue. In other forms of government, for example, monarchy, where the people don't rule themselves, you could have people without virtue because they're not the ones making policy. Democracy and republican government only work when you have the right qualities in human nature cultivated in the citizens.

In Number 57 of the *Federalist Papers*, Madison (or possibly Hamilton) says that in all political constitutions in human history men must have the wisdom and the virtue to pursue the common good of citizens. So, the first goal of the citizen is to identify the right people for leadership and to elect them. And then you have to figure out how to keep them properly oriented once they're in office, because power tends to corrupt. I think the Constitution's features, such as specified terms of office, help to take care of the second requirement, keeping them oriented once they get in. But you have to rely on the people to get the right officials elected in the first place—that's where we've failed, and I think that rests in a large measure on our educational institutions. We need to get back to studying our political principles in high school and college and train young men and women to be politically motivated and to understand that their interests lay in following politics and selecting the right people for office.

Q: There is an assumption in our Constitution that people will be capable of determining what policies will benefit them and what policies will benefit the nation overall. I think today doing that is very difficult for the average person because there are strong arguments on both sides of an issue. Take global warming, for example. For many, many years, it was dismissed as baloney and the average citizen believed that. To a large extent, our representatives also failed to believe that it was a threat and established a policy that didn't take serious steps to combat it. Isn't it difficult for the average person to try to understand such complex issues?

A: Yes, in general, some of these issues are complicated, and it's difficult to find people with the background and attention span to understand them from beginning to end and to make a proper decision. Difficulty also results from the opposite side of the coin; that is, we don't have political leaders who are willing to communicate these difficult questions to the people in a way that puts the choices to them so that they can make informed decisions. Since the rise of bureaucracy as a policy-making branch of government, what we try to do is let science and factual knowledge make the decisions for us. We try and take the decisions out of the hands of the people. There should be no surprise then that after a long time of seeing the decisions taken out of their hands, the people aren't interested in making the decisions when it comes time. So, we're not planning about global warming, we're having someone at the EPA [Environmental Protection Agency] plan it for us.

Q: So, where do you see special interests in all of this? If you take an issue like global warming: The oil, coal, electric companies put together a lobbying group that provided disinformation in order to convince the public and the government to refrain from significant action to curb carbon emissions. As a result of that campaign, the Byrd–Hagel Resolution passed in the Senate and that dissuaded the nation from joining the Kyoto Protocol. How does the average person make an informed judgment if you've got major public relations firms working the wrong side of the street?

A: I think the best thing that helps to counter the influence of special interests is action taken by corporations and individuals on their own. It's interesting to see how private companies have voluntarily taken action to reduce global warming. The idea is to create a culture through which corporations and individuals will make the right decisions. Now, a lot of marketing commercials are based upon who is the greenest. This is a much healthier way of getting corporations under control rather than having the government require certain steps.

The big problem with special interests is what is described in the literature as diffused interests versus concentrated interests. If a particular committee of Congress is about to make a decision, they're not going to be lobbied by citizens who have a very small stake in the outcome. They're going to be lobbied by those who have a very concentrated interest in the outcome and have the time and money to lobby. The diffused interest reflects the malaise—the malaise of the people we were talking about a little while ago.

Our self-government has fallen away—America has let government do too many things, rather than having its citizens more involved in government decision-making. I think the phenomenon of diffused interest is really part of that. In many ways it results from a central invasion of power. You're one of 300 million, so you feel you cannot make much of a difference. You get more attention from your state legislature than from the federal government in Washington, DC. Therefore, centralization has given rise to the growing impact of special interests.

Q: As an average person, say you have two kids in school and you and your wife are working full-time. Is it realistic to spend time researching a complex issue like global warming and lobbying your representatives? I mean, I can see where a corporation, where the bottom line is affected by the result, would feel it a necessity to learn about the issue and lobby one way or the other. Plus, the corporation would have the resources to do that. But in the end, the average person only has the power of the vote. You know, finding a candidate who represents their views and will benefit the country is another difficult set of decisions. I think your theory sounds good, but I'm not sure of the extent to which it would work in a practical sense.

A: You do find that people, in spite of their busy schedules, take an interest in these issues, and I think if they didn't there would be no incentive for corporations such as Starbucks to make it a point to tell you how green they are. The magazines abound with environmental issues, and corporations are responding to the popular movement for more environmentally friendly good-news to the public. I think, although not to use this example too much, people have other means of changing society and culture. Mainly, how they spend their money. People will change the way they spend and the way they behave. I think people's strong opinions on an issue can have important consequences.

Q: I've seen some surveys on global warming, and there is a clear majority for action to be taken, certainly a lot more than has been taken. The government policy is basically what it's been all along. I agree that some corporations are taking action on their own, but it seems there are a number of issues where the popular sentiment is one way, and government policy is the other. I think that might discourage citizens more than anything else; that the public's sense on these issues is not reflected by the positions of their own representatives.

A: My first response is that that's not necessarily a bad thing. There are plenty of scenarios in which it might be good for representatives not to follow the will of the people. The representatives who have been elected may have greater foresight than the citizens that they represent. The wonderful thing about our system is that representatives can resist popular opinion, but not for too long because everyone shows up for reelection at some point. At the end of the day, elected representatives will have to respond to public opinion. So, the institutions aren't designed to respond immediately to public opinion. In fact, the people's representatives can interpret the sentiments of the people and modify their recommendations with their own judgments and perceptions.

The Senate was designed to be this cold, deliberative body that could interpret and correct the people when their opinions were erroneous. So, this gives you rule by the sense of the majority, rather than the actual majority on a day-by-day basis. Policy doesn't follow immediately from public opinion. It could be that global warming is not going to be affected by stricter control on emissions in America. It might be that developing countries need to be given new technology, and that would have a more beneficial result. It might be that the economic costs that the United States would have to incur (relative to the benefit) would be too great. If you tell the people that the world is getting warmer and ask if we should do something about it, they will say "yes." But the representatives must form a more sophisticated policy that will serve the long-run interests of the people. In the end, people have ultimate control, because they can remove those elected officials from office.

Q: Where do you see campaign financing in all this? We're trying to find leaders who will tackle the noble deeds and take action that's for the common good, and we're talking about $3 billion that are going to be spent in the 2008 presidential elections. The guys running for House and Senate seats, 95 percent of those who win their House seats have outspent their opponents, and two-thirds of those who won Senate seats have outspent their opponents. So, these guys spend much of their time raising money from special interests so they can buy TV time and get elected. How does that reconcile with the clean functioning of America's democracy?

A: There is certainly cause for alarm in those figures. On the other hand, it's possible that the money discrepancy in terms of spending is not the cause of the victory but an effect of other variables, such as the ideas that the candidate projects to the electorate. Presumably, if you raise the most money, it's because you connect with the most people. For example, Hillary Clinton and Barack Obama aren't raising the most money because they're the wealthiest; it's because their ideas are connecting with the constituents. It's because their ideas are more attractive to the American people. It's ironic that for the 2008 election so far, the Republicans are being outspent significantly by the other party.
    As far as I'm concerned, the more important problem is the perpetual campaign that the candidates must run and the continual pandering to the people. That's a problem that's been created by the modern media. There's a market for these kinds of things.

Q: I interviewed a media expert, and he said that politicians have discovered even more than retailers that you can use the power of TV to sell almost anything. The furniture stores don't understand how much TV can impact their sales, but politicians understand it. And that's why they're lined up to get special interest dollars, so they can buy more and more TV ads.

A: There's always going to be the influence of money in politics, and it's going to come from the special interests. I think the most important thing in the 2008 election is how Barack Obama is raising millions of dollars from unorganized young voters. They seem to be giving him a lot of money, not because they have an immediate interest, but because they find his ideas inspiring. The money is an effect of whether you're an attractive candidate.

Q: So what do you think of public financing, getting rid of the need for perpetual fundraising? Just let folks campaign up front, raise many small donations to show that they have a real following, and then, after that, provide the funding necessary from the government?

A: Any proposal would have to overcome several objections. First, campaign financing regulations may restrict what you can say, and this would be a violation of the First Amendment. The second objection would be the sort of danger inherent in a state-run election. There are many examples around the world where people who want to stay in office can manipulate the voting machinery and get unfair advantage to stay in power.

Q: Several citizen advocacy groups are promoting a proposal for federal funding of congresional elections. The federal government would provide dollars to all the candidates once they reached a certain level of support. It's similar to the current presidential system except the dollars provided would be increased as election costs rise.

A: If they had proposals that would work their way around my objections that would be fine. It might be possible to structure a proposal so it wouldn't violate the fundamental principles I've described.

Q: Of course, such proposals would have to be voluntary. As you know, in *Buckley v. Valeo* the Supreme Court found that spending money on an election is comparable to free speech, which can't be restricted. However, one benefit that public financing might bring is a broadening of the candidates running for office. There are people who would like to run but don't want to go out and raise all that money. If they knew that once they hit that certain prerequisite of support that the government would provide the rest of the required dollars, they might change their minds and get into elective politics.

A: I suppose it would. Of course, most candidates tend to be pretty ambitious and enjoy working to get into office. Some people think that's one of the problems with one recently declared Republican candidate for president. He gives the appearance that he wants to be president, but he doesn't want to do the difficult work. One of the essential characteristics of good candidates is that they want to get out ahead of the people and sell their ideas. They want to persuade the public and shape public opinion by communicating with the people. So, I think all the difficult tasks required to win an election is a necessary screening device to make sure the right candidates stay in the race. If the state provides you with the money, you might get candidates who aren't suitable for office, but since they get public money, they can stay in the race.

Q: Many years ago I was a Congressional Fellow in the U.S. Senate, and I saw really bright professionals spending half of their day on the phone trying to raise money for an upcoming campaign. I can't image that the Founding Fathers would have visualized this—that talent, investing all that time, trying to raise money so you can buy TV time. It just doesn't seem like a wise expenditure of time and talent.

A: I agree that is a problem. You don't want to be spending your time pandering to people as opposed to meeting people. It's an unfortunate situation that we have today, but I'm not sure what the alternatives are. It seems like that time should be spent communicating with the people, not just asking for money. I would agree that perpetual pandering is a problem.

Q: I interviewed a lobbyist and he claimed that his best strategy is to get someone elected who already agrees with his client's position. It's much tougher if you get an independent-minded candidate in office and then have to convince him of your position. However, he believes that access is extremely important in terms of policy formation. What these lobbyists do is get their client in on a one-on-one session with a Senator or Congressman so they can make their points in person. It's that opportunity that the lobbyists are compensated for, demonstrating that they can provide access to the policy maker.

A: I think that works most effectively when you have what we talked about earlier—diffused interests versus concentrated interests. I think it's sort of inevitable that you're going to have factions or special interests try to persuade Congressmen to vote for a particular issue, like approving new coal-fired power plants. Maybe the best way to counter that is to work with the diffused interests on the other side. For example, the reason the Congressman provides access is so he can get campaign finance money with which he'll be able to buy TV time and obtain votes. But if those on the other side of the issue can deliver a greater number of votes, then that nullifies the impact of the special interests. If you have a mobilized constituency that's going to vote against the special interests on a particular issue, the Congressman is not going to look for money from the special interests because he understands that the majority of the votes are represented by the other side. If you can effectively mobilize the diffused interests, you can counteract special interest money and influence. Some organizations, such as the Heritage Foundation and the American Enterprise Institute, do a good job of explaining complex issues and rallying citizens to support their thinking.

So, the scale can bounce back in favor of the people, and therefore they have a much greater say than they had before when they were just a diffused interest. There are always going to be special interests. It's just a matter of human nature. But like the Founding Fathers, we should not try to change human nature but to work with it. We take ambition for granted, so we need ambition to counteract it. I think the ambition of the lobbyist is always going to be there, so we need to organize a motivated and mobilized citizenry that will not just accept special interest legislation. This would require Congress to take into account the common good before it reaches a decision.

Q: It seems offensive to me that a U.S. Senator is going to provide access for a lobbyist's client because he knows that he's going to get a certain amount of money down the road. It just doesn't seem right that he should be able to do that. If the lobbyist client has important, relevant ideas then he should be able to get that meeting on his own, on the basis that he's a constituent or that the problem that he's raised or the issues he has in mind merit a meeting. It seems to me that the dollars involved subvert the answer to whether or not the meeting is legitimate.

A: I think sometimes the distinction between legitimate interests on the part of the lobbyist versus the lobbyist getting the meeting only because of the money is a distinction that works out more neatly in theory than in practice. I'm not saying that it's not a valid distinction, but we tend to see corruption where there might not be corruption. For example, if I'm a Congressman representing a district that includes a large manufacturing facility, a faction might lobby me to vote in a particular way. That may appear to be corruption. On the other hand, the Congressman may vote that way because he's trying to protect the many jobs in his district that are in that manufacturing plant. That vote might be to restrict environmental requirements that would cause the plant to move overseas, for example.

Q: I agree with that completely. The only problem I have is that I don't think the Senator should be paid in order to sit down with the special interest. Even if it's just the appearance of impropriety, why should you have the appearance?

A: It's interesting you should use that phrase—appearance of impropriety. This is similar to the phrase that the Supreme Court used in its case of *Buckley v. Valeo*. As you know, the Court said that corruption, or the appearance of improper influence, is sufficient to justify these laws that seem to go against free speech by sustaining limits on individual campaign contributions, disclosure and reporting requirements, and the public campaign financing scheme in place. It's not just the reality of improper influence, but the appearance of improper influence. I suppose I understand that argument, but the appearance of corruption is not necessarily corruption. Hillary Clinton came out and said it—that taking lobbyist money is not necessarily a bad thing.

Q: Of course, she's taken a lot of their money.

A: Right, but I think she's making a legitimate point. Many times lobbyists have a legitimate role in representing special interests. The fact that they use special interest money to influence policy is not necessarily a sign of corruption.

Q: Is there anything that I haven't covered that you think would be worth including in the book?

A: I think one of the things that we've lost in modern nomenclature is the meaning of the word "democracy." Technically, it means rule by the people. In several of the *Federalist Papers* it is pointed out that there is a difference between a pure democracy, where the people all get together and decide on something, and a representative democracy or republican model, which is what we have, along with separation of powers and an independent judiciary. The republican model requires that all offices are accountable to the people who elect them. I think the idea of a republican form of government is something that we've lost.

I don't think anyone really expects that we ought to use each person to make a decision on every issue before the government. This is sort of a practical consideration that administrators carry out decisions that have been made. I think that's a distinction that probably will have to be reintroduced, and we should recapture the meaning of the republican form of government. One of the problems I think is if you talk about republic versus democracy, people get confused and think that the Republicans want a republic and Democrats want a democracy.

Q: What about our election process? We've talked a little about the dollars, but can you think of any ideas that might improve the way we're going about electing our officials other than campaign financing? When I was a kid growing up, the candidates were selected out of the conventions, and then you had a few months for the presidential campaign. Now, you have the candidates selected by primaries that take months and take a huge amount of dollars. So now you have this very long timeframe and candidates who sell themselves by looking good on TV.

A: If Lincoln were running today, in the age of TV, because of his appearance there's no way he'd be elected. I think the Progressive Era in the early 1900s was when the primaries were first used. During that period you also had the movement of democracy shifting to the bureaucracy, civil servant regulations. So, on the one hand they promised direct democracy, and on the other hand they took the power out of the hands of the legislature and gave it to the merit or civil servant appointees—sort of promising democracy but really giving you government by the experts.

One of the things that the primaries do is create this really long campaign, which has positive and negative effects. The negative effect is of course the money required to stay in there and the election fatigue experienced by the voters.

One of the other problems with it is that there is really no control anymore. There used to be a party platform, and you could read it and you would know what the candidate stood for, and you could make a semi-informed choice. Now, a Republican candidate could be Ron Paul, or it could be Rudy Giuliani, each with very different policy positions. So, parties don't stand for a clear definition of policies like they used to. This makes it more difficult for people to select a candidate in an informed way.

But there are also positives with this process. When you have such a long campaign it's almost impossible for you to dupe the people. At some point, the real personality of the candidate is bound to come out. So, it's a good protection for the people because there is a long record that they can observe for each of the candidates. There are advantages and disadvantages, but no one is going to be a flash in the pan over the many months of the campaign.

CHAPTER 6

VIEWS OF A SEASONED WASHINGTON PROGRESSIVE

Special Interests, Lobbyists, and Campaign Financing

Q: Based on your experience, how do you feel about the topic of special interests, their lobbyists, and campaign financing?

A: From the beginning of our history, Americans have always been concerned about what they perceive as the excessive power of special interests. Although the degree of public dissatisfaction ebbs and flows, I suspect that cynicism about special interests will be with us for a long time—to some extent, for good reason.

Q: What do you feel personally about the influence of lobbyists on Capitol Hill?

A: People with common interests who are organized, well-funded, and focused on specific issues clearly have an advantage over those who are not. If Congress is considering legislation that would affect your industry directly, you're probably going to care about it and work to influence the outcome. That's not necessarily a bad thing, as it is appropriate that Congress understand the industry's perspective and how the legislation might be implemented in the real world. The problem is that if there's a broader public interest on the other side, that interest may not be represented as effectively. This creates a systematic bias that is a real problem, even if it, to some extent, may be unavoidable.

While special interests do have disproportionate power, however, the influence of lobbyists, per se, is often overstated. Lobbyist influence is largely a function of their clients. So, for example, if the House of Representatives passes a bill that tilts housing policy in favor of realtors, that is more likely to reflect the power of the many realtors in Members' districts rather than the unique skills or influence of their lobbyists.

In any case, while I don't mean to minimize the disproportionate power of special interests, I'm actually more concerned about the fact that our political system in recent years has been dominated by radical conservatives, largely on behalf of those with enormous economic power. While lobbyists disproportionately represent those with economic power, that's not always true, and many lobbyists do serve the public interest. For example, when lobbyists from organized labor, senior groups, and other public interest groups lobbied in opposition to President Bush's plan to privatize Social Security, I thought that was a good thing. Of course, generally speaking, those aren't the types of lobbyists who have had most of the power lately.

My impression is that many lobbyists sell themselves to clients and claim to have more influence than they really have. And reporters also love to write stories about lobbyists influencing the process. This builds on the public's long-standing distrust of special interests and, for many, has created the impression that Congress now bows to their will like little marionettes. That's a caricature. In fact, I'm skeptical of claims that lobbyists, per se, have substantially more power today than they had ten or twenty years ago. However, I do think that the very wealthy have been much more influential over the past several years because they have had such a champion in the White House and because the Republican majorities in the Congress were so consumed with serving their interests. That, to me, is the fundamental problem.

Q: Did you read the "Citizen K Street" series in the *Washington Post* about the evolving techniques used by today's lobbyists? The articles provided a vivid picture of how lobbyists use the experience of former Hill staffers and others for the benefit of their clients. It seemed like a very complex and powerful process. For example, it appears that the oil, gas, and coal companies have been able to dictate the nation's policy when it comes to global warming. Isn't that an example of how lobbyists have steered U.S. policy to the detriment of the nation?

A: There is no doubt that Republicans have refused to deal with global warming largely because of opposition from industry. Lobbyists clearly are an important part of that process, though I suspect that the Republicans would have been similarly responsive to industry even if Members of Congress were dealing, not with registered lobbyists, but with corporate CEOs and other executives within industry. Put another way, the enhanced power of large corporations and the wealthy probably has more to do with the current nature of the Republican Party—its radically conservative ideology and its support for big businesses—rather than with a proliferation of lobbyists or other intermediaries.

Q: But isn't it true that campaign financing helped put Bush in the White House? And isn't that indicative of a systemic problem?

A: Yes. Clearly, money plays too great a role in politics, and those with lots of money have disproportionate power. It's a real problem, and always has been, as far as I can tell. Having said that, money is not the only reason why special interests have disproportionate power. In any democracy, vocal, intense minorities have a built-in advantage over majorities who may have conflicting interests but who are not as passionate, engaged, and organized.

Q: That's not a bad thing, necessarily, is it?

A: To some extent, it's appropriate for decision-makers to consider intensity of opinion. On the other hand, if narrow interests can determine the outcome of a policy issue to the detriment of the majority, then it can be a problem—especially if a minority of already powerful people repeatedly prevails in policy disputes.

Q: Doesn't it come back to one of the principle tenets of a democracy, promoting the "greater good"? Isn't it assumed that a democracy's leaders, when it comes to decision-making, will generally seek to serve the greater good? Doesn't the campaign financing situation today negate much of that? You can see Congressmen making decisions based on campaign funds they can raise, rather than making decisions that would benefit the country the most.

A: Of course, Washington is supposed to make policy on behalf of the common good. And I think most elected officials do care about doing the right thing. But, often, reasonable people disagree about what that means, and there's no obvious right answer.

The current campaign finance system does give more power to special interests than would a publicly funded system. Having said that,

I'm not convinced that the relative advantage provided by the campaign finance system has increased all that much over the past decade. I suspect that the reason why multimillionaires and special interests have had so much influence recently has less to do with any changes in the campaign finance system, and more to do with the fact that an ultraconservative group of ideologues has been in power.

Q: If you look at the number of earmarks included in legislation each year, it has grown tremendously. Isn't that a reflection of the greater skill that lobbyists practice today? Also, haven't the increased campaign funding requirements of recent years put more pressure on politicians to play ball with lobbyists so they can raise the necessary dollars?

A: I'm sure that lobbyists, like other professions, get more sophisticated over time. And no doubt candidate requirements to finance their campaigns make many elected representatives responsive to those lobbyists who help them raise funds. But lobbyists have been influential for a long time, and while their influence may well have increased as campaigns have become more expensive, it's not clear to me that the difference is that dramatic. The explosion of earmarks probably is more a reflection of the dominance of the Republican Party and the way they govern. People like Newt Gingrich and Tom DeLay were unusually focused on the accumulation of power, and they were very aggressive in using earmarks and many other means to increase their power. Democrats care about power, too, of course. But it's a matter of degree and balance. And, as I see it, the Republicans have just pushed things way too far.

Q: Why didn't President Clinton make an effort to campaign for the Kyoto Protocol to allow the U.S. to take meaningful steps to try and prevent global warming? The Democrats had the White House then and yet there was little effort to take a stand for the environment.

A: My impression is that the Republican Senate was never going to approve that treaty no matter how hard Clinton tried. Republicans were too tied to industry, and at that time the public was not engaged. In addition, I suspect that at least some Democrats were concerned that the treaty failed to ensure that many other countries, like China and India, would share the burden of addressing the problem.

Q: Isn't that kind of a kid's excuse? Because China and India aren't being required to cut greenhouse gas emissions we will continue to pollute the atmosphere. Why not go ahead and set an example and then turn to China and India and request that they restrict their pollution? If they don't take meaningful steps we could always exact a price on them through trade restrictions or other similar means.

A: I personally agree that the United States should lead the way in addressing this issue, and do what we can to get the rest of the world involved. The problem is too urgent to just sit and do nothing while waiting for other countries. At the same time, I understand the view of those who argue that it's unfair to ask Americans to bear a greatly disproportionate share of the burden, whether in terms of higher prices or fewer jobs, if countries like China and India are refusing to make meaningful changes. You can agree or disagree about whether this perceived inequity should have led to a rejection of the treaty. But, to be fair, the fact that Members of Congress were concerned about this type of equity issue does not, by itself, prove that they were motivated more by lobbyists than by concerns over the public interest.

Q: Well, couldn't we have enacted trade restrictions against China and India to convince them to take the proper steps?

A: Sure. I suspect there would have been real costs to doing so, especially when you consider how dependent we've become on borrowed money from countries like China because of the record deficits we've been running. But we could have imposed sanctions, and perhaps that should have been considered more seriously. Honestly, I don't know enough about it to have an informed opinion. But my impression is that, right or wrong, there was a feeling among many in the Senate that Kyoto failed to adequately ensure that the costs associated with addressing global warming would have been shared broadly and equitably. In other words, the outcome was not exclusively the result of special interest lobbying, though no doubt the views of industry were critical, especially for most Republicans.

Q: So overall, your feeling is that problems we are experiencing with special interests, lobbyists, and campaign financing are mainly a function of having the Republicans in power?

A: To me, the fundamental problem is not that lobbyists have more power than in the past. It's that the government has been run largely on behalf of multimillionaires and powerful industries at the expense of the middle class and those in real need. The Republicans operate differently. They have a different vision of the proper role of special interests. They're not embarrassed by it. They think that yielding to the demands of wealthy special interests is a good thing.

Special interests have gained not because of a structural change in the system or a dramatic increase in the power of lobbyists, but because Washington has been under the control of highly ideological conservatives like George Bush and his supporters in Congress. Democratic majorities will help, and already have led to improvements, like a major increase in student assistance, an increase in the minimum wage, and ethics reform, to name just a few things. To really make progress, though, we'll need a Democrat in the White House and many more progressives in the Senate.

While too few people understand this, being in the majority in the Senate is very different than being in control. You need sixty votes to break a filibuster, and that is very difficult to achieve when you're dealing with controversial legislation that imposes burdens on powerful industries. So adding just a few more Democrats won't be enough to change things all that dramatically.

Q: But don't the Democrats have their own special interests, such as labor unions and Hollywood producers?

A: It's certainly true that Democrats have their own constituencies, such as labor. Just like Republicans, Democratic politicians have to get elected if they want to stay in the game, and they're not going to ignore the views and interests of those who put them in office. Politicians, like everyone else, continually have to strike a balance between altruism and self-interest. Even Mother Teresa had to survive in order to do good work.

It's also worth remembering that sometimes, believe it or not, the special interests are right. Sometimes, politicians propose legislation that sounds good to the public but that would lead to unacceptably large hidden costs or other serious unintended consequences. In such cases, it's a good thing that there are lobbyists to point out the problems and to prevent them from happening. And that's true whether the special interest is an industry group or a labor union.

To be clear, though, all this doesn't mean there's no difference between the parties. There is, and it's significant. When you get right down to it, Democrats are Democrats largely because they care about serving ordinary people. To a large extent, that's what defines us as a party. We support the middle class and working Americans not only because they are our constituency, but because we believe it's the right thing to do. So I think it's wrong to suggest that both parties are equally beholden to the same kind of special interests.

Q: Is campaign financing a serious problem for a party trying to develop policies that best serve their constituents and the nation? And if your answer is yes, do you believe that public financing of Congressional and presidential elections would go a long way toward solving that problem? This would remove the financial hold that many lobbyists have on political candidates. Lobbyists would no longer be able to trade campaign financing for favors that benefit their clients.

A: I think establishing a system for presidential public financing was a good thing. For a long time most candidates participated in the program, but now the amounts provided are insufficient and most major candidates have opted out.

Q: But if those problems were taken care of, wouldn't that be beneficial? Also, it would allow people to run who don't have the kind of financial contacts that would give them the big bucks needed today.

A: Personally, I like the idea of financing campaigns with clean money that is completely separated from special interests. But public financing for Congressional campaigns has not been politically viable largely because much of the public won't support it; too many consider it to be welfare for politicians and don't like the idea of their tax money financing campaigns of those with whom they disagree.

Q: I've seen a survey that disproves that belief. It found that 70 percent of the population favors public financing of federal campaigns.

A: That seems inconsistent with other public opinion research, but I don't know. A lot depends on how you ask the question. In any case, my recollection is that the votes in Congress on public financing for Congressional elections generally have not been close. My impression is that the Republicans almost universally oppose it because their constituency has more money; the Democrats are split on the issue. I think the majority of liberal Democrats support public financing, but many moderates and conservatives do not. While I know a lot of cynics assume that their opposition is based primarily on their own ability to raise funds, my impression is that much of their concern is based on the opposition of their constituents. Many of these Members probably would love to get out of the game of raising money, if they could.

Q: In recent years, 95 percent of all House candidates who won their elections outspent their opposition, and 67 percent of all Senate candidates who won their elections outspent their opposition. I would think that if you're going to do public financing you'd better guarantee parity.

A: I agree that money plays an important role in the outcome of campaigns. At the same time, those statistics may reflect the advantages of incumbency more than the impact of campaign spending. Incumbents tend to get more contributions than challengers, and spend more. But even without this spending advantage, they would enjoy many other advantages of incumbency. Also, many Members of Congress, especially in the House, are elected by homogeneous constituencies and would have safe seats regardless of the type of campaign financing system.

Having said that, a publicly financed system, if properly constructed and implemented, would reduce the power of incumbency. Of course, there are many questions about such a system. How do you distribute the money? Who gets it? How much do they get? How do you avoid giving excessive money to the established parties? And what if some candidates opt out of public financing and spend huge amounts of their own resources?

Q: I've seen a proposal for federal campaign financing of Congressional elections. It seems to answer most of those questions. You qualify for federal funding by starting out on your own and raising a number of small contributions to show that you have a base of support. Then you receive a grant that reflects an estimate of what a viable campaign should cost for the area/population covered. If the opposition is privately funded and spends well over the grant initially provided to the publicly funded candidate, an additional grant is issued to the federally funded candidate. Would such a plan be operable?

A: Personally, I like the idea, even if it's not a cure-all. At a minimum, it should help address the concerns of those who cynically believe that all Congressional decision-making is driven by campaign financing. That's not true, but it can be hard to convince people of that when a politician's votes happen to coincide with the interests of his or her contributors.

Q: Some have set up 527 tax-exempt groups and utilize millions of dollars to get their message across. What's your view of that?

A: I have mixed feelings about 527s. I don't have a problem with Americans expressing political views, and some 527s have advocated effectively for the public interest and made a real, positive difference. At the same time, I am concerned when a narrow minority of very wealthy people is able to enjoy such a disproportionate degree of influence solely because of their wealth.

Q: The philosophers who developed the concept of democracy believed that the ethics of elected leaders would have to allow them to compromise on important issues. Have we lost some of that today?

A: Over the past few years, I think that Washington has been controlled by people who are more ideological and less willing to compromise than in the past. Most importantly, George Bush and Dick Cheney. But many Congressional Republicans, from Newt Gingrich to Tom DeLay, also have been extremist ideologues who have been philosophically opposed to compromise with those from the other party.

Q: So if the Democrats were in the White House that would change things? Would they be more willing to compromise?

A: I do think that all the leading Democratic presidential candidates would be more willing to compromise than President Bush.

I know there's a tendency for many commentators to complain that Washington isn't working and to blame the system rather than particular leaders or the party in power. That's easy to do. Americans usually are willing to believe the worst about Washington. Blaming the system allows one to avoid creating the impression of bias in favor of one party or the other. But sometimes, the problem isn't with the system, but with the specific people who happen to be in power at the time, their ideology, and their approach to governing.

As I see it, the biggest problem is not that there's something structurally wrong with our political system that has given special interests substantially more power than they've had in the past. The fundamental problem is that our country has been governed by a bunch of radical conservatives in the White House and Congress who have adopted a very ideological and partisan approach to governing, made a lot of very bad choices, and refused to change their approach even in the face of obvious failure.

Q: That's an interesting observation. It's a matter of ideology, not special interest?

A: I'm not disputing that special interests have too much power—clearly, they do, as they probably always have. We should try to make structural changes, like reducing reliance on special interests for campaign financing, which could help. In fact, the Congress has now enacted some lobbying reforms that have made a modest difference in the way Washington operates. But structural change can go only so far if you've got the wrong people in the White House and the Congress.

Q: The idea of the book is to see the way the Founding Fathers envisioned our democracy working and to see what is and what could be. Are you saying that we can solve the problems of influence and financing simply by electing Democrats?

A: Again, I'm not arguing against campaign financing or any other reforms. But I think things would be very different if we had a Democratic president and sixty progressive Senators. If the President and the Congress were working more consistently on behalf of ordinary Americans, there probably would be less public concern about the power of special interests.

Q: The political philosophers who inspired our democracy spoke of elected officials promoting noble deeds that would benefit the population. Some would say that over the past thirty years it's difficult to recall more than a few of these. The U.S. worker is on the job longer hours than workers in any other nation. Wages adjusted for inflation haven't kept pace with increases in medical costs, college tuition, and other expenditures important to many Americans. What substantive efforts have been completed by the federal government for the benefit of the average person?

Carter came in concerned with zero-based budgeting; Reagan mainly wanted to cut domestic programs; the first President Bush had no domestic initiative of note from his term; President Clinton attempted universal health care but abandoned the idea when the First Lady ran into roadblocks; and our current President can point to "No Child Left Behind" and the prescription drug plan, but it is generally agreed that the first is underfunded and the latter is a boondoggle for the drug companies.

A: You're right that the past thirty years have not been marked by much progressive legislation—though, of course, we had an explosion of such legislation in the 1960s, when we enacted everything from civil rights to Medicare and Medicaid. To a large extent, the government became more conservative because the country did. In the intervening years, Americans have been unhappy with Washington and with the failure to adequately address problems like health care. But, generally speaking, I'm not sure there's been a broad consensus in favor of specific policy changes.

Meanwhile, many Republicans believe that if you hand out enough tax breaks to people at the top and then leave problems to the market, everything will be fine. Democrats have a fundamentally different view. We want to strengthen the middle class and help those who need it the most. And while we understand the need to be smart and practical about it, we're not willing to just sit on our hands and assume that the market, left alone, will magically solve all of our country's problems. But until we have someone in the White House who shares our view— and, just as importantly, until we have sixty votes to cut off Republican filibusters in the Senate—it will be very difficult to make progress at the federal level.

Q: I wonder if part of the problem is a general disdain of government.

A: I agree. Americans' distrust of government in many ways is self-defeating and self-reinforcing. Congress often finds it impossible to enact change because Americans don't trust the government to do the job right, and thus it is easy for opponents to persuade the public that pending legislation is bad. When the legislation gets stalled, public cynicism only grows.

Generally speaking, conservatives and those they represent benefit from cynicism about government, and they feed that perception at every opportunity. There are plenty of news reports about waste in government and few reports about government's achievements. That's not to say that government doesn't have real problems—inefficient bureaucracies drive all of us crazy, especially those people in need who rely on government the most.

I don't mean to imply that conservatives and Republicans don't believe what they're saying about government—they do. Most leading Republicans really have a visceral hostility to government. They're not just playing to their campaign contributors. George Bush is an ideo-logue who would love to abolish everything from Social Security to Medicare to student aid, if he could. And many Republicans now in Congress feel the same way.

Consider this: If today we did not have Medicare and Democrats proposed to create this large, new, federal program to provide health care to seniors, do you think there's any chance that Republicans would support it? Of course not. They'd be screaming bloody murder about the dangers of socialized medicine, just as they are doing today about a small increase for the children's health insurance program.

Q: So, if you were me, and were writing this book?

A: I'd recommend that you take a close look at the Republican opposition to raising the minimum wage and their absolute obsession with eliminating the inheritance tax. They've misled a lot of people into believing that inheritance tax repeal is designed to help small businesses, a goal most Democrats share. But Republicans really are focused on handing out massive tax breaks to just a handful of politically connected and extremely rich families. In the end, of course, it would be the middle class who would be forced to make up the difference.

Q: Do you think lobbyists should be able to donate money to political candidates either through their campaign committees or leadership PACs?

A: Personally, I think it would be better to have a clean-money system in which campaign funds come without strings from anyone.

Q: But you can't limit it to public financing because the Supreme Court has found that spending money on a campaign is the same as free speech, guaranteed by the First Amendment.

A: It's true that the Supreme Court, in *Buckley v. Valeo*, made it much more difficult to enact reforms designed to reduce the power of special interests. But it hasn't closed the door on public financing. Nor has it prevented the public from doing the one thing that would make the greatest difference: electing the right people.

CHAPTER 7

VIEWS OF A CANDID
WASHINGTON LOBBYIST

Special Interests, Lobbyists, and Campaign Financing

Q: Being a longtime Washington lobbyist, how do you visualize the combination of special interests, lobbyists, and campaign financing affecting U.S. policy?

A: Well, I don't know if I'm a typical lobbyist. Most lobbyists, I think, operate differently. My view is that when you are dealing with a Member of Congress, do no harm. In other words, I'm still very sensitive to the Congressional point of view. I talk to people on the basis of, this is my client, this is my problem, and here's what we would like; but I never ask a Member to do anything that would cause problems either campaign-wise or personal-wise. So I guess in that respect my first concern is that I'm not asking for something they cannot do. They'll tell me when a request is off-limits because I have a good personal relationship with Congress. I never, never push something, if they say this is an issue they're not comfortable with. I'll go somewhere else and see if there is someone else who might assist my client.

I think lobbyists feel like they serve a good purpose in that most Congressmen have so many things on their plate that they can't be all-knowing about every issue, every industry cause. Often, through lobbyists, they are exposed to a cross section, every side of an issue, so that a Member of Congress is not being tricked because he doesn't know the other side of an issue. Most of the time they will talk to people who represent different interests, and from those discussions the Congressman knows what's going on. Oftentimes the lobbyists are former staffers from the Hill, so these people have access to the Member, and the Member gets both sides or some version of both sides.

Sure, they present their clients in the best possible light. So, it's not a situation in my opinion where Members of Congress are unduly influenced by lobbyists. It's more like they're exposed to differing opinions, and it's not like they're each not without self-interest. Surely, the people who talk to them have an interest and present the issue in a way that would support their client. That's just one phase that comes to mind. It's not harmful to the process, in my opinion.

I have witnessed a number of other things I do not think are proper. For example, trips in which the Member is wined and dined. You've got big companies backing entertainment, and to some extent you have to believe that if one accepts these gifts that they have a tendency to lean towards that particular issue or client. So to me, that's one of the things that should be dealt with in the new ethics law. And that's one of the things that has unduly influenced legislation and direction.

Of course, this is true of staffers as well as Members. I sometimes think that you do better if you can sway the influential staffers because the staffers who work, for example, with the Ways & Means Committee, often these people have more to do with what actually happens than the Member. Because here again the Member has many, many things [on his plate] and wears many, many hats. He is always concerned with his constituents, his public image, voting, committee work, etc., so he winds up with little time to legislate, if you will, and depends a great deal on his office staff and relevant committee staff.

In fact, in my opinion, one of the biggest problems today is the fact that staff has more influence on what happens than Members do, I think, because a lot of times Members rely on staffers to know what's in a bill and rely on the staff to negotiate with other staff to see how a bill might be brought together in conference. If the staff chooses to tell the Member that they couldn't get this done or that done, you wind up with staff determining what goes into a bill and what doesn't. To me, having non-elected people determining the content of legislation is wrong. I just think it is totally wrong to have people who are not elected influencing the content of legislation, which will not make me very popular with staffers. I think that staffers believe this as well; some of the Members try to deny it, but it's there.

Q. What about campaign financing? Did you ever help a client provide campaign dollars to a particular Member of Congress?

A: How would you mean? For instance, if, say a railroad wanted to raise money for a particular candidate, I would help them to do that, and I would contribute myself. In fact, I have come close or usually maxed out for many Members of Congress each year. I think I'm allowed something up to $2,300 per contribution per campaign and up to $25,000 per year. Sometimes lobbyists "bundle" campaign contributions. They go out and collect money from a lot of people and package it to the Member. In a recent presidential election, lobbyists would get fifty people to raise $20,000 each for the candidate. And that got each of them membership in an exclusive club that gave them certain prestigious perks, like attendance at White House receptions. Another common method of raising money is where a particular industry sponsors a fundraiser, and the money goes to a person designated by the Member.

Q: Do you think that raising those funds and the cost of campaigns today contribute to Members not having enough time to devote to their work? They're putting a lot of effort out there raising dollars?

A: The problem is with the Constitution, setting up two-year terms for Members of the House of Representatives. I don't think our Forefathers ever anticipated that it would cost the time and money it does to run for office, campaign for Congress. And I think that does affect the ability of Members to do what they should do. And I don't see an answer to it because costs keep going up, and new restrictions on raising money or using their own money in campaigns have been struck down by the courts, so the problem continues. And it's a big problem; I mean, it takes up a great deal of time.

The phenomenon today is that there is pressure put by the leadership of the parties themselves in Congress to require the Chairmen or the ranking Members of committees to go out and raise a lot of money for the general fund of the party. And this requires a tremendous amount of time. And it puts a great deal of pressure on the Member of Congress to raise money for the so-called general fund or for a political action committee (PAC) to help all the party's candidates.

Q: So do you think public financing might be an answer to that?

A: Well, I've not given it a great deal of thought. The problem would continue to be that as long as the law could not prohibit a person from using their own money or using other private donations, it would be hard to ensure that those who accept public financing could compete. Take a person who has plenty of money, who chose to participate in a presidential election. That would give him a tremendous advantage over the person who was getting public financing because they wouldn't be bound by the same rules and regulations.

Q: What if public financing provided dollars equal to the amount raised by the privately funded opposition? Then you would pretty much have parity, wouldn't you?

A: Well, that's true, but how do you set up the law that determines how the money is allocated? If a candidate spends $50 million of his own money on his campaign, then the public would have to provide his competition with another $50 million? I don't know. It would be difficult to come up with a law that covers all the bases.

Q: So if you helped to raise money for an elected official, and he knows that your client helped him get elected, doesn't that influence him or at least make it appear that he is going to lean your way?

A: If you're asking if it gives an appearance, it certainly does, because an appearance is perception, and a perception is whatever a person believes. And if the public believes that it gives an advantage, there is an appearance because it is something beyond the control of the Member or lobbyist or anybody else. Does it? I think it depends on the individual Member. If there are two sides to an issue, and the lobbyist on one side makes a contribution and the other side doesn't, then the one making the contribution will get the audience and the other might not. And therefore, your contribution gives you an advantage in influencing the Member of Congress, but I still think you have to make a case.

I would say that most Members go the way they would go anyway, because of the very nature of the job. All that anyone can ask, if they give money, and if they're in their right mind, would be an audience. In that regard you do have an advantage. A Member can't see or talk to everybody that requests a meeting. They're going to talk to their constituents first, and then they're going to talk to people who support them. So from the standpoint of getting an audience, certainly I would guess that a Member would give time first to one who has supported him. It's just human nature.

Now whether they would go with the proposed position is a whole lot less than people would think, because you get money from so many sources; you might be getting money from people on both sides of an issue. They're pulled in a lot of different directions. Generally, they will base their decisions on a lot of things, not just who gave them the most amount of money. Now, I believe that's the truth.

If I were a consumer advocacy group, I would certainly argue that the ones who give them the most money are the ones who'll get the most consideration, that they'll go their way. I know most Members have dozens of former staffers, and those former staffers are spread out over the lobbying industry and they deal with the Members on a regular basis. Every time a Member goes to make a decision, he has former staffers on this side and on the other side. So, which way is he going? He's going the way he thinks.

Q: If you took your lobbyist hat off and you're just thinking strictly as a U.S. citizen, why should a Congressman, an elected official, be able to take anything from anybody? I understand the industry viewpoint that they want to get an audience with the Congressman and make their case, but as an individual citizen in terms of how our democracy should work, shouldn't the Member really be putting the nation's interest ahead of anything else? Wouldn't you want it set up in a way that these fellows basically act on the facts and make decisions that would be best for the country, instead of shading things one way or the other? Why should they be able to take anything?

A: If we were operating in the world of Voltaire, and everything was the best of all possible worlds, perhaps. But I think that would be even worse than what we have now because Members would lose contact with folks who rely on them. Now, you know the public in this country. Even though it's their government, their business, they don't have time to study the issues. And they do not as a rule keep in touch with their Member. So if you were to remove the ability of industry, labor, and other organizations to have the opportunity to contact Members, you would have much worse laws than you do now.

Q: But I'm not talking about not meeting with special interests, I'm talking about not accepting campaign financing and other gifts from special interests and their lobbyists.

A: I don't see it that way. If you have a perfect system, I would agree. I think that most Members would agree. If my campaign could be financed by the public, that would be great. If they didn't have to accept anything from anybody or ask anything from anybody, that would be great. If I can have what I need in my opinion to do the things I need to do to get elected, then fine.

I find very few Members who enjoy fundraising. It's the worst part of the job. When I was a Congressman, I would have loved not to have raised money. It would have been great not to have taken money or anything else from anybody. On the other hand, to say they can't take anything would to some extent thwart democracy, the ability to communicate. How many Members have the money to go meet somebody for lunch and pick up their own tab and do all these things?

Yet these contacts are good and necessary, in my opinion, to learn what the problem is. I don't know what the problem is in a particular industry. I don't know if we word a certain piece of legislation a certain way what it would do. See, I think that one of the biggest problems is that when laws are made language is used, and oftentimes the staff or the Member doesn't know the effect of what is written.

They don't know what it's going to do. So if you take away the communication, and communication comes in many forms whether it's over lunch or a dinner or meeting or whatever, you would in my opinion lessen the ability of the Member to know what he's talking about or what he was doing.

Now you say you don't have to give them anything to communicate. Most people look at their salaries and say that's a tremendous amount of money. But I know that it didn't go very far when I was in there, and I don't think that the salaries go very far for the Members today. Most of them could certainly do better in the private sector if they choose so they don't have any grounds to complain, but to answer your question, if you prohibit any kind of entertainment or meals or whatever I think that you decrease the ability of the Member to be well informed. As to campaign money, I say sure, if you've got a system that will make sure that everyone has the same opportunity to run a campaign and get their message to the public, take away contributions, absolutely.

Take for example this Congresswoman who called me out of the blue and says she's in the middle of a campaign and could use some help. Well, I sent her $1,000. I knew that she probably didn't think my way on most things but I just sent her $1,000 because she asked. Then she got another $1,000 out of me, and she just recently called me again and I haven't sent her another $1,000 because I'm just a working stiff. You can only send so much but the point is I think that whether you're liberal, Republican, or whatever, you're a Member and you think for yourself and whatever you come up with is fine with me.

Q: Wouldn't public campaign financing really make the lobbyist's job more interesting because you'd not be relying on the money? You'd be relying more on your arguments, fashioning an argument that will win on its merits.

A: Well, I don't know how much it would change things. I think that with some Members it possibly would. But by and large I think the Congressmen basically end up doing what they think they should be doing anyway, no matter how much money or anything else goes their way. In the extreme cases, where you have Members taking bribes, and things like that, that person is flawed anyway, but by and large there may be some influence without the Member even knowing it.

So sure, I would take a system whereby no money would need to be raised for a campaign, but I would not say that you couldn't buy someone lunch because I think that's against human nature, because if I want to talk to you, I feel that I should pay for lunch if our discussions are over lunch. I don't care if you're a Member of Congress or who you are. If you're asking someone to lunch, then you should pay. On the other hand, I think to take someone on a trip and pay their expenses and do these kinds of things should not be allowed.

Q: Some of the chapters in the book are going to present case studies, issues that appear to have been influenced by lobbyists. One of the cases concerns global warming and the campaign that was put on by oil, gas, and coal before the Kyoto Protocol to keep us out of it. And really, what they did years ago was factually all wrong. But their position was accepted by the U.S. government and is still in force today. So it seems to me that lobbyists, when they attack one issue, can have a large effect on the nation and even on the world in this case.

A: I can give you another one. A similar case was the tobacco industry and how they delayed anti-smoking legislation for years and years. Global warming, I don't know what the industry came up with. I personally have not exhausted the scientific evidence pro and con about global warming. So, I'm not sure if I'm convinced about global warming. I know that we're seeing melting of ice caps and so forth, but I'm not certain about the causes. I'm not sure that the government is taking into consideration that certain pollutants seem to cancel each other out.

But back to your original point, that certain industries can have an adverse effect on the policies of this country. I would agree with that concept. In my opinion we could have developed all kinds of alternative sources of energy over the past fifty to one hundred years. All kinds of inventions have been created which would reduce our dependency on the internal combustion engine, oil products, etc., and they have been thwarted by the industry. So I agree with you that they can have an improper effect and have had in many instances.

Q: Hasn't lobbying been one of the ways they have accomplished this?

A: Well, I would certainly agree with that. Lobbying which would include a lot of things that I don't even engage in. A big industry certainly can put all kinds of money in the right place at the right time to get friendly candidates elected who will act to build up their business. They have elected people who already believe what they want them to believe. I think that they have had a greater influence that way than when an independent person gets elected and the lobbyist attempts to shape his views.

You know, a person who's elected independently, he's going to think independently, and you're not going to buy him with a lunch, a trip, or a campaign contribution. That person is still likely to be an independent person. But if you get out there and work for somebody and get somebody elected who already agrees with you, then I think you have an ally more than if you try to shape the opinions of someone elected independently, independent thinkers who are not elected by a particular industry.

Q: That gets back to campaign financing.

A: That absolutely gets back to campaign financing, but it gets at it a different way. What I'm saying is that campaign financing can elect a like-thinking person to an industry, and that is of a great deal more help to me than buying a Member of Congress lunch or giving them $1,000 for their campaign. You're not going to get that Member to change his philosophy for you no matter what you do. What you've got to do, and what that industry did, was elect people that think the way they do.

Q: A couple of people that I've interviewed have indicated that lobbying problems under the current Administration have been more serious than in other Administrations because of the strict ideology of the conservatives in power.

Do you agree with that? Maybe some of the abuses we are seeing are not typical and are due to the very close ties between this Administration and corporate America. Have you noted a difference or is it pretty much the same as always?

A: I don't think there's any question that anyone who has been in this town knows that when the Republicans took over that Tom DeLay made it clear that only Republican lobbyists would be seen by the majority, Republican Members of Congress. In my opinion, this was improper. He tried to make up for the many years when the Democratic majority in Congress dealt with Democratically controlled lobbying firms and helped them to get things done. What he tried to do was to reverse that trend, and basically he said that only Republican lobbyists would be seen. I think that certainly had an influence because the Republicans are friendlier to business and large corporations. And that's been true up until this year, so in that regard I don't think there's any question about it.

Q: Are there other issues that we've yet to discuss that you think I should include in the book?

A: I think I would cover the incestuous relationship between federal agencies and Members of Congress. You've got people going back and forth, the IRS, for instance. If they want to get something passed, they can because they have people who are with the IRS but working on the Hill. It's like a family, and it's true of other departments as well. Not to the extent it is for the IRS, but I think as a result you have Members not even knowing what's in the bill that they passed. And there are provisions in there that the staff has put in that the Member is unaware of. That's one of my pet peeves.

I think the system creates too much reliance on the staff, the technicians, because the Members don't have time to do all the other things they need to do. And that doesn't have anything to do with lobbying. What we have is the bureaucracy running the country. In terms of lobbying, as I've said before, I think putting up money and helping people of like thinking to get elected is the bigger problem. Once they get in Congress you don't have to do much to get them to vote your way.

Our system is sick when it comes to raising money for campaigns. I think Members hate raising money. It's the worst part of the job. If we had a system of public funding for campaigns that would be fair to everybody, I would love to see it. And the question of lobbying, I think the bills they've introduced pretty well put a lot of restrictions on how money is raised. I know that it's changed a good number of things people can do now.

Q: What about grass-roots lobbying? I believe it's still permitted under the bills that have passed their respective Houses.

A: I don't think you would ever want to do away with the grass-roots lobbying. That's a part of representative government. If you can't even talk to your constituents, then I don't know.

Q: Aren't they talking about lobbyists organizing for a particular issue at the local level?

A: I think what they are talking about is going back and telling the employees of a given firm that there's something Congress is trying to do that's going to affect you in a negative way. Then the lobbyist organizes those workers to voice their concerns to their Congressmen. Would you want to do away with that?

Can I tell you something that you probably already know? When a Member gets all of these postcards or e-mails that all say the same thing, you treat that as one thing. You don't think that all of those people are individually thinking to contact you. I never gave much credence to those kinds of campaigns. We sent the same response to all of them. They had the influence of one group. And so I don't have any problem with them doing that. I don't think it's very effective.

As a general rule, if it was up to me, I would say to lobbyists that you can do anything but you have to report it.

Q: I guess to a large extent we're dependent on the press to explain these issues?

A: That's pretty bad, isn't it? Sometimes with the press there are very few people who will go into the depth necessary to really explain an issue. There are superficial writers that just try to get the sensational issues, and they don't understand what they're talking about. I've sat with reporters and tried to explain things, go into depth, and they aren't interested in that. They just turn off after the first two minutes. Of course, we have to have a free press, that's one of the things you can go to when you've got corruption everywhere else. It doesn't serve us very well anymore, in my opinion, except in the extreme instances.

Q: Do you think a problem with the press is that they are also compromised by money because the way they characterize certain issues may impact wealthy advertisers? Because they're making so much money from these campaign ads?

A: No. I don't think your reporters, your writers give a damn about the business part. You've got a separation there. The people who make the paper go and the people who are doing the writing are separate. I don't think that's a legitimate complaint.

CHAPTER 8

VIEWS OF A EUROPEAN DIPLOMAT

Special Interests, Lobbyists, and Campaign Financing

Q: Most people seem to believe that money is very influential in determining federal policy in the United States. This is because skilled lobbyists use campaign financing to establish policies that serve their clients, but often are not in the overall interest of the public or the nation. How are these issues handled in your country?

A: First, our system, as a political system, is different than the Americans'. We have a Parliamentary system. Our constitution was written to modify the State from the Monarchy and the government in power during World War II. Our constitution is very recent, and it's got a very strong division of powers. We have a bicameral Parliament, a separate judiciary, and an executive branch composed of a Council of Ministers, which is our cabinet. The cabinet is led by the President of the Council (Prime Minister), which is composed of selected Members of Parliament. The President of the republic is elected by the Parliament for a seven-year term. He's the Chairman of the Board of the Council of Ministers.

So, all this implies that the fight for money is not among single candidates—it's between the parties themselves, and coalitions of parties. The lobbying system as it is here in the United States is forbidden in most of the rest of the world. The U.S. system is a case study for students at our universities. One of the first things I studied at university was the U.S. system and how small interest groups were able to present their arguments to legislators. I believe its origins date back to when politicians used to wait for the President to make their arguments in the lobby of the Mayflower Hotel, hence the word "lobbyist." It may happen through other means in my country, but clearly, it's illegal.

Q: What kind of means?

A: Contributions of corporations and other organizations to political campaigns is frowned upon here. Morally, such contributions, if discovered, would be condemned by the public. Also, there are limits to the amounts of money that do come into play. So, many of these corporations do not do it openly, because they are afraid of the public scrutiny that would result. If you are a political candidate and it is learned that you are being financed by one of our large auto manufacturers, you would be hanging yourself. So, if you have a policy about CO_2 [carbon dioxide] emissions and global warming, and you receive money from a car manufacturer, the public will accuse you of not having their best interests at heart.

For the most part, our political parties are financed by the state. Parties can accept some private money, but they generally deny it. There have been many scandals that have sent more than a few politicians to jail. But the U.S. system would be criminal in most European countries. Lobbyists are not allowed on the Parliamentary grounds. Your *K Street* people take their little bags to the corridors and make their arguments. We wouldn't let them in the door. If someone from the pharmaceutical industry or auto industry wanted to see a legislator, he would never meet with him in his office for fear that the meeting might be discovered.

It doesn't mean that we don't have corruption. We have had some serious scandals. But our campaigns aren't very expensive because most of the funding comes from the government. Also, members of each party subscribe, give a contribution. It's like paying dues. So the bigger the base of the party (the number of votes received in the previous election), the more money they get from the government and from their own members. However, there is always a minimum guarantee from the government for each party.

Remember too that our elections are among the political parties more than presidential candidates. Once a new Parliament is formed, they will elect the President.

An important resource here is that each party has its own newspaper paid for by the government. And before elections, the parties are provided free TV time on the state-run channels. Like campaign grants, the amount of TV time provided is proportional to each party's support, and two months before the vote parties are restricted in terms of the campaign activities allowed so as not to overload the public.

The government also provides money to privately run TV stations to sponsor debates and similar events. Basically, the system is characterized by two-thirds state-provided money and one-third private money (party members and others). But very large donations are forbidden and those in the government are not allowed to donate money to political parties.

Q: Are there other institutions that get involved in political elections?

A: Unions, which are also partly financed by the government, are very active. It has been estimated that 40 percent of our workforce are union members. Since they have many more people enrolled than do the political parties, they have a lot of influence. They may speak directly to politicians, expressing the views of their members. The unions and union confederations coordinate their positions before expressing their demands to management or lobbying the government.

Q: Could a business or another group generate political TV ads of their own?

A: Ads must be done by the political parties who take advantage of discounted rates. There are parties that have a lot of money. Some Prime Ministers have had much personal wealth, and they have used it to help finance their parties. Of course, since personal wealth may be derived from corporate wealth, sometimes it's hard to tell exactly who is providing the funding. If Mike Bloomberg runs, he's not officially going to use *Bloomberg News* money—he'll use his own, which he received from *Bloomberg News*.

Q: There are some who would say that much of the U.S. problem regarding political integrity is really a problem of perception. What is proper and what is not proper? It sounds to me that your population doesn't tolerate practices that we don't like but think they are just par for the course.

A: That's correct, but put it in the framework of people in my country versus people in the States. We believe that American society is very raw. In Europe, we have a welfare state that takes care of our citizens. And many of the corporations in the United States that employ lobbyists and influence your policy, in our country, are publicly owned corporations.

So you have a different relationship with your government and your corporations.

We have organizations comparable to labor unions that represent all sectors of our population. For example, there are groups who represent the Catholic workers, corporate executives, shopkeepers, and lawyers, and each such organization interacts with the political parties to create consensus. So, in other words, they play the role that in the United States is played by lobbyists. In other terms, in the United States you have the system of special interest, and then you have Congress, then in the middle, the lobbyist. Your groups of interest pay money to lobbyists. In Europe, it's a bit different. For example, the energy field is run by the state, so there is no group lobbying the state about energy policy.

Unions for taxi and bus drivers, train conductors, organizations representing corporate executives dialogue with people in Parliament, but without lobbyists—there's no middleman. There is a legal and illegal flow of cash, but it's a different system.

We are starting to see some corporations give money to political parties publicly. But as I said before, it's not viewed very well by the population at large. We have universal health care, so there are no insurance lobbies or HMOs expressing interests contrary to much of the public. We have totally socialized medicine. We do have a private-sector pharmaceutical industry, and they probably finance certain political interests, but if the public were to know about it, it's not going to be very happy because the recipient party will tend to serve the industry rather than the public. In the United States there is no public condemnation.

Another difference is that we have always been a society of professional politicians; but in the United States, your government is different. Ours is made up of the same politicians who are in Parliament. Our cabinet members are also members of Parliament. When you go to the level below, you have civil servants, people like me who have worked for the government all their life. In the United States, your cabinets often are composed of technicians who serve at the pleasure of the President. For example, Secretary Rice was a professor; others may come from Halliburton or Goldman Sachs. They may be political but they are not necessarily familiar with the workings of Congress. Often, such people don't have the same appreciation for government and what it can accomplish.

The lobbying that is done in my country is carried out by consultants who work directly for the firm trying to impact policy. For example, the title of such people would be Director of Institutional Relations, not Lobbyist. The guy that is discussing regulations with the government—he would be the Vice President of Institutional

Relations for the company. The corporation would not employ a lobbying firm. I remember from my university years when I was studying the American system that I found it hilarious that lobbyists could offer Congressmen advantages from this corporation or that corporation—it doesn't mean that in Europe it doesn't exist, it's just illegal.

Q: The fact that it's condemned limits the extent to which it takes place?

A: Yes, but there is more hypocrisy in our system. As I said before, we have had major scandals in which many politicians were found guilty and jailed. But there is one truth told to me by a Prime Minister that I try to always remember—politics has a cost. We cannot just forget or prohibit everything. We cannot create the immaculate politician like the Holy Mary who gives birth and remains a virgin—we cannot imagine politicians giving birth and staying a virgin.

Basically, you have to give up some freedom in order to leave some space, because politics has a cost. There has to be an agreement on what you authorize and what you don't. We have an agreement by which the state finances elections, which is also criticized by many who say they don't want to spend their taxes on politicians. But if we abolish that, then we have to authorize people to get their money somewhere else, and then we have to tolerate all the problems that accompany that policy.

I think today the system in my country works because, morally, the public tends to accept state-run financing of the political parties, but does not accept private financing, which is exactly the opposite of the U.S. system. You would morally condemn a government that gave money to political parties, but you accept funding of politics by the private sector.

We also have a different mentality when it comes to the law. We have a common law system; you have a civil law system. You have been able to create a system of lobbying that fits in between the laws. In our system, to make your lobbying system legal, we would have to pass laws that authorize it. In our system, everything is illegal unless there is a law that permits you to do it. As you know, much of your system is derived from the concerns of your Founding Fathers and how they wanted to be free from government interference.

THE LEVERAGE OF WEALTH

Case Studies of Special Interest and Lobbyist Success

Thus far, we have dealt with the philosophical and historical construction of America's democracy, the means by which special interests and their lobbyists attempt to steer U.S. policy, and the perspectives of insiders engaged in the world of government and politics. Now it's time to get down to the facts. If special interests are a real problem, what specific policies have they created to the detriment of the nation? Have they focused on distinct issues that affect few Americans, or have their targets been more consequential?

Part 3 provides five case studies that show how key issues have been affected by special interests, their lobbyists, and the use of funding for political campaigns. We will document how Washington lobbyists, through the many tools described in Chapter 2, have shaped the world in which we live.

CHAPTER 9

GLOBAL WARMING: THE SPECTER OF CLIMATE CHANGE

How Special Interests and Lobbyists Prevent U.S. Efforts to Curb Global Warming

INTRODUCTION

When it comes to judging the significance of a policy issue, it's difficult to imagine a subject that carries more weight than one that threatens the air we breathe, the water we drink, and the land on which we live. We begin, therefore, with the issue of climate change, alternatively labeled greenhouse gases and global warming.

THE ALARM IS SOUNDED

You didn't have to wait for Al Gore and his movie to understand that global warming is a vital issue that requires government action.[1] The world's most respected scientists have urged society to take steps to reverse the causes of global warming for some time. They have claimed that signs of this threatening phenomenon are everywhere:[2]

- Eleven of the last twelve years rank among the hottest years since 1850, when adequate records first became available.
- Over the past fifty years, cold days, cold nights, and frost have become less frequent, while hot days, hot nights, and heat waves have become more frequent.

- The intensity of tropical cyclones in the North Atlantic has increased over the past thirty years.
- Storms with heavy precipitation have increased in frequency over most land areas.
- Boundary zones between desert and more fertile areas have become drier, adding stress to water resources.
- Since the 1970s, droughts have become longer and more intense, and have affected larger areas.
- Since 1900, the Northern Hemisphere has lost seven percent of the maximum area covered by seasonally frozen ground; mountain glaciers and snow cover have declined; since 1978, Arctic Sea summer ice has shrunk by more than 20 percent.
- Rising sea levels have been caused by ocean absorption of heat that has been added to the climate, melting glaciers, and losses from the Greenland and Antarctic ice sheets; the oceans have increased in acidity, coral reefs have been bleached, and wetlands have been lost.
- Enormous tracts of Siberian peatlands, with vast stores of carbon, are beginning to thaw and release carbon dioxide and methane into the atmosphere.
- The Larson B ice shelf in Antarctica has lost volume, as large chunks (some as large as the state of Rhode Island) have broken free and melted.
- Plants and animals are changing their habitation ranges, sometimes dramatically; for example, there has been increased growth of allergy-inducing pollen, and robins and mosquitoes are for the first time being found in the Arctic.

The scientists warn:

> We have a small window in which to avoid truly dangerous warming and provide future generations with a sustainable world. This will require immediate and long-term action to reduce our heat-trapping emissions through increased energy efficiency, expanding our use of renewable energy, and slowing deforestation (among other solutions).[3]

Without such action, the following consequences have been predicted:

- Within a couple decades, hundreds of millions of people won't have enough water, and tens of millions of others will be flooded out of their homes.

- Tropical diseases like malaria will spread.
- By 2050, due to their disappearing habitats, polar bears will only be found in zoos.
- By 2080, hundreds of millions of people could face starvation.
- The Mount Kilimanjaro glacier, which has survived the past 11,000 years, is at risk of disappearing by 2020.

Three-fourths of carbon emissions from human activities are from the combustion of fossil fuel; the remainder is mostly from deforestation. The United States is responsible for 24 percent of carbon emissions; China, 14 percent; Russia, 6 percent; and Japan and India, 5 percent.[4]

Given the U.S. level of carbon emissions, its relative wealth, and pioneering spirit during times of crisis, one would have expected the American government to take a world leadership role in establishing agreements to reduce global warming. Instead, the nation has shrunk from this opportunity.

Has U.S. inaction been based on a reasonable interpretation of the available information and a sincere concern for the nation and the world, or are other factors in play? These are the facts.

THE BEARERS OF BAD NEWS

Concern over rising global temperatures was expressed at the First World Climate Conference held in Geneva in February of 1979. Sponsored by the World Meteorological Organization, the attending scientists issued a statement urging governments "to foresee and to prevent potential man-made changes in climate that might be adverse to the well-being of humanity."[5]

The conference identified increased atmospheric concentrations of carbon dioxide, deforestation, and changes in land use as the primary causes of global warming. To provide more information about these problems, the Conference instituted the World Climate Programme to conduct scientific research into the causes and effects of climate change. Sponsoring agencies included the United Nations Environmental Programme and the International Council of Scientific Unions.

The 1987 Montreal Protocol on Substances that Deplete the Ozone Layer encouraged further action to study and curb global warming. Under that international agreement, the production and consumption of compounds that deplete ozone in the stratosphere—chlorofluorocarbons (CFCs), halons, carbon tetrachloride, and methyl chloroform—were to be phased out by 2000. The success of this agreement demonstrated how coordinated international action might be taken to reverse global warming.

A major step forward was taken in 1988 when the United Nations established the Intergovernmental Panel on Climate Change (IPCC). Its mandate was to coordinate climate research and evaluate the risk of climate change brought about by human activity. The organization was set up to conduct no research but to draw conclusions based on peer-reviewed and published scientific and technical literature.

The IPCC is directed by government scientists but also includes hundreds of academic scientists and researchers. It is organized into three working groups: Group I assesses the scientific aspects of the climate system and climate change; Group II weighs the vulnerability of socioeconomic and ecological systems and human health, consequences, and adaptation; Group III surveys options for restricting greenhouse gas emissions and other measures to temper climate change. A Task Force on National Greenhouse Gas Inventories conducts work on inventory-related methodologies and practices; for example, if you're going to cap the output of greenhouse gases, you have to be able to measure them.

A global network of authors, contributors, reviewers, and other experts produce reports issued by the IPCC. Before reports are finalized, two distinct reviews invite the comments of experts and government officials regarding accuracy, completeness, and overall balance. The IPCC currently comprises 450 lead authors, 850 contributing authors, and more than 2,500 expert reviewers from 130 countries.[6]

While some have criticized IPCC findings, for the most part scientists involved in climate research accept the IPCC's conclusions as accurately summarizing the state of knowledge. The work of the IPCC has been characterized as a unique example of science in the service of society.

THE GREENHOUSE EFFECT AND GLOBAL WARMING

Without the greenhouse effect the earth would be too cold for life to flourish. In fact, our average surface temperature of 59 degrees Fahrenheit would be zero.[7] While the sun's rays heat the earth's surface and atmosphere, a portion of that energy escapes back into space, but gases in the atmosphere—mainly carbon dioxide and methane—trap some of those rays and form an insulating layer that keeps the earth's temperatures moderate.

Global warming occurs when increases in heat-trapping gases raise the earth's temperature. As noted above, the principle source of these gases is the burning of fossil fuels. Carbon dioxide is released from gasoline that enables our automobiles, oil and natural gas that heats our homes, coal that fires power plants, and deforestation, mainly in the tropics, that clears land for development and provides wood products.

Carbon emissions are produced by four economic sectors: electricity generation creates 42 percent; transportation, 24 percent; industrial processes, 20 percent; and residential and commercial uses, 14 percent. Major industry sources of greenhouse gas emissions are manufacturers of cement, steel, textiles, fertilizer, and aluminum and coal mining. Increases in methane have been generated by rice cultivation and cattle raising. The energy source that is most disruptive to the climate is the coal-fired power plant because coal is almost pure carbon. Coal burning is also the main source of mercury deposits that pollute freshwater lakes and streams.

EARLY IPCC ASSESSMENT REPORTS
AND GLOBAL ACTION

Most of the world's leaders concerned with global warming and the environment have looked to the IPCC for guidance. Every five or six years, the IPCC issues an Assessment Report that provides the latest scientific evidence on the magnitude of human-induced climate change, its impact, and options for adaptation and mitigation.

The first IPCC Assessment Report was issued in 1990 and included the following major findings:[8]

- The natural greenhouse effect is being substantially enhanced by human activities that result in increased emission of carbon dioxide, methane, CFCs (used as propellants in aerosol cans), and nitrous oxide; this results in warming of the earth's surface, increased water vapor, and further global warming.

- The emission of carbon dioxide is responsible for more than half of the enhanced greenhouse effect.

- To stabilize greenhouse gases at 1990 levels, human emissions would have to be reduced immediately by more than 60 percent.

- Global mean surface air temperature has increased by 0.3 to 0.6 degrees Celsius over the past 100 years; assuming no action to curb greenhouse gases, current models predict further increases of 0.3 degrees Celsius per decade, which would be temperature hikes larger than those seen over the past 10,000 years.

- There are many uncertainties associated with the predictions made; for example, while the degree of warming observed is consistent with climate model predictions, it is also of the same magnitude as natural climate variability. Therefore, higher temperatures could be largely due to natural variability.

As a result of the 1990 IPCC Assessment Report and the 1992 IPCC Supplementary Report that confirmed the 1990 findings, a United Nations Conference on Environment and Development, known informally as the Earth Summit, was held in Rio de Janeiro, Brazil, in 1992. It resulted in the United Nations Framework Convention on Climate Change (FCCC), a treaty to reduce greenhouse gas emissions in a widespread effort to reduce global warming and prevent dangerous human interference with the climate system.

Initially, the FCCC set no mandatory requirements on greenhouse gas emissions and included no enforcement mechanism. However, it established ground rules for later agreements, called protocols, which would set required emission limits. It also established a greenhouse gas inventory to account for the level of national greenhouse gas emissions, which are to be submitted regularly by treaty signatories.

One of the more significant provisions recognized common but differentiated responsibilities, with greater responsibility in the near term assigned to developed/industrialized nations. Such countries are the source of most past and current greenhouse gas emissions.

The treaty places the signatory nations into three groups. The developed/industrialized countries, called Annex I Parties, include member nations of the Organization of Economic Cooperation and Development, which includes the United States and the European Union, plus countries with economies in transition (EIT), including the Russian Federation, the Baltic States, and several central and eastern European states. These nations were expected to stabilize their greenhouse gas emissions at 1990 levels by the year 2000.

Annex II Parties consist of the Annex I members of the Organization of Economic Cooperation and Development, but not the countries with economies in transition. Annex II Parties were encouraged to furnish financial resources and to share technology with developing countries; this would enable developing countries to undertake emissions reduction activities and help them adapt to the adverse effects of climate change.

Non–Annex I Parties are for the most part developing countries. Because economic development is vital for the world's poorer countries, no emission restrictions were placed on them; their output of greenhouse gases was expected to grow in coming years.

Certain groups of these states were recognized for their special vulnerabilities, such as low-lying coastal areas or zones particularly susceptible to drought. Others, such as countries that rely on fossil fuel production, were highlighted for their economic vulnerability to greenhouse gas reduction. Also, forty-eight of these nations were recognized as least developed countries and were given special consideration because of their limited capacity to respond to climate change and adapt to its adverse effects.

On September 8, 1992, President George H.W. Bush transmitted the FCCC Treaty to the U.S. Senate for ratification. The Foreign Relations Committee approved the Treaty and reported it out on October 1, 1992. The Senate consented to ratification on October 7, 1992. The President signed the instrument of ratification on October 13, 1992, and deposited it with the U.N. Secretary General. With more than fifty countries' ratifications in hand, the agreement entered into force on March 24, 1994.[9]

SPECIAL INTEREST AND LOBBYIST TACTICS

In 1989, U.S. industry began its global warming lobbying effort by forming the Global Climate Coalition. The group's mandate was to stifle measures that might be taken to ease the effects of global warming but in the process negatively affect the bottom lines of the nation's energy corporations.

The Global Climate Coalition was formed at the same time that the world's nations were laying the groundwork for substantive action to reverse global warming. This was a business lobby group supported by Exxon/Mobil, Ford Motor Company, Royal Dutch/Shell, Texaco, British Petroleum, General Motors, Chrysler, and many other employers and trade associations. The organization claimed to represent 6 million businesses in every sector of the economy, and it channeled business participation into the debate on global climate change and global warming; its primary targets were claims made by the IPCC.

The Global Climate Coalition waged an extremely effective public relations campaign to discredit the concept of global warming and to maximize perceptions of the negative impact of joining agreements that would require lower levels of carbon emissions and other greenhouse gases. Through its Global Climate Information Project, visions of unaffordable gasoline and deep economic recessions and unemployment were woven into the psyches of the American public and its representatives. This was achieved through glossy publications, lobbying at international climate negotiation meetings, and a video claiming that global warming will increase crop production and help feed the hungry.[10]

Such efforts were bolstered by corporate jawboning conducted by firms such as Exxon, which was said to have provided the second Bush Administration with advice on energy policy. According to papers obtained by the *Guardian* through a Freedom of Information Act request, America's most valuable corporation claimed that joining a treaty to cut carbon emissions "would be unjustifiably drastic and premature."[11]

THE 1995 IPCC ASSESSMENT
AND THE KYOTO PROTOCOL

For some, the uncertainty that was expressed in the 1990 report on the issue of human influence on the global climate opened the door to criticism and hesitancy to act. However, in 1995, the IPCC issued its second Assessment Report, and its primary finding was that "the balance of evidence suggests that there is a discernible human influence on the global climate."[12] Other 1995 assessment findings included the following:

- Greenhouse gas concentrations had continued to increase.
- The previous estimate of climate change over the past century (an increase of 0.3 to 0.6 degrees Celsius) was confirmed.
- Although uncertainties remained, improved statistical models indicated that global warming was expected to continue in the future.

When the FCCC was established, it was agreed that the signatories would meet annually in a Conference of the Parties to assess progress and work toward legally binding greenhouse gas reductions of the developed countries. The first two meetings worked toward the establishment of targets and mechanisms to allow emission reductions. The third such session, held in December 1997 in Kyoto, Japan, resulted in a landmark agreement, the Kyoto Protocol.[13]

The Kyoto Protocol is a legally binding agreement to reduce greenhouse gases worldwide. These gases include carbon dioxide, methane, nitrous oxide, hydrofluorocarbons, perfluorocarbons, and sulphur hexafluoride. Overall, the Protocol pledges a level of greenhouse gas emissions at least 5 percent below 1990 levels. This is to be achieved over the commitment period of 2008 to 2012. To meet their targets, Annex I Parties must put in place domestic policies and measures to cut emissions. Had the U.S. participated, its reduction target would have been 7 percent below its 1990 level of emissions. If a Party fails to meet its emissions goal, it must make up the difference in the second commitment period, plus a 30 percent penalty reduction.

Parties may offset their emissions by increasing the amount of greenhouse gases removed from the atmosphere by so-called carbon sinks. These include the planting of new forests, restoring forests that have been destroyed, following the best practices in crop and grazing land management, and revegetation. Credit may also be received for building projects that reduce the emissions of non–Annex I Parties.

Under the Kyoto Protocol, emission reduction quotas are set for Annex I countries; then these nations set corresponding quotas for resident businesses. Should a business go beyond the required level of reductions, it is rewarded with a proportionate number of carbon credits, representing the excess tons of carbon emissions reduced. These credits may be sold through market mechanisms that have been established for such trade; businesses that have not met their targets may purchase credits to offset their excess emissions.

Requirements of the Kyoto Protocol have been characterized as a "cap-and-trade" system. One carbon credit represents one ton of carbon dioxide emissions. The carbon credits create a market for reducing greenhouse emissions by giving a monetary value to the cost of polluting the air.

Initially, many of the eighty-four signatories of the Kyoto Protocol were hesitant to ratify the agreement until specific rules were delineated. Over the next several years, negotiations were conducted to finalize such provisions.

THE 2001 IPCC ASSESSMENT REPORT
AND THE MARRAKECH ACCORDS

The 2001 Assessment Report verified previous conclusions and presented a more authoritative picture of continued global warming. Its major findings were as follows:[14]

- Increasing signs of a warming globe were provided by surface temperatures that increased by about 0.6 degrees Celsius during the twentieth century, rising temperatures in the lowest eight kilometers of the earth's atmosphere during the past four decades, and declining quantities of snow cover and ice.
- There was new and stronger evidence that the warming experienced over the past fifty years had been due to human activities and not natural variability.

- Global average temperatures and sea levels were projected to rise throughout the twenty-first century.
- From 1990 to 2100, the average surface temperature was projected to increase by 1.4 to 5.8 degrees Celsius, and the sea level was estimated to rise by 0.1 to 0.9 meters; actual levels within the stated ranges were predicted to depend upon the extent of efforts taken to restrict greenhouse gas emissions.

With the third Assessment Report in hand, the Protocol rulebook was finalized at the seventh Conference of the Parties meeting in Marrakech, Morocco, held from October 29 to November 10, 2001.[15] The Kyoto Protocol entered into force on February 16, 2005. The European Economic Community and 168 additional countries have signed and ratified the Protocol.

From November 28 to December 9, 2005, a meeting of the Parties to the Kyoto Protocol was conducted in Montreal, Canada.[16] More than 10,000 delegates attended the session that approved an agreement (the Montreal Action Plan) to "extend the life of the Kyoto Protocol beyond its 2012 expiration date and negotiate deeper cuts in greenhouse gas emissions."

UNITED STATES DECLINES MEMBERSHIP
IN THE KYOTO PROTOCOL

Of the world's industrialized countries, only the United States and Australia refused to ratify the Kyoto Protocol and join the community of nations to curb greenhouse gas emissions. However, the recently elected Prime Minister of Australia has pledged that one of his highest priorities is to see that his nation becomes a party to the agreement. This would leave the United States as the only developed country to refrain from signing on to the Kyoto Protocol.

This victory for the U.S. energy lobbyists was achieved years ago through the concentrated efforts of the Global Climate Coalition. The group's crowning achievement was U.S. refusal to enter into the Kyoto Protocol. The instrument used was the Byrd–Hagel Resolution (S. Res. 98) passed in the U.S. Senate on July 25, 1997, five months before work on the Kyoto Protocol was completed.[17] The Resolution objected to the global warming proposals under negotiation because of the disparity of treatment between Annex I Parties and developing countries and because the level of required emission reductions could have resulted in serious harm to the U.S. economy, including significant job loss, trade disadvantages, increased energy and consumer costs, or any combination thereof.

The Resolution provided that the United States should not be a signatory to any protocol or other agreement that would either mandate reduced greenhouse gas emissions for the Annex I Parties unless it also does so for the developing countries, or that would result in serious harm to the economy of the United States.

If the Senate were called upon to ratify such an agreement, the Resolution states that the request must be accompanied by an explanation of new legislation and regulations that would be required to implement the agreement. Also, the request must include a detailed analysis of the financial costs and other impacts on the economy.

On November 12, 1998, Vice President Al Gore symbolically signed the Kyoto Protocol.[18] However, the Senate would not act upon the agreement until it was modified to specify emissions reductions for developing countries. With such action out of the question, President Clinton did not submit the Protocol to the Senate for ratification.

In 2001, the Bush Administration made clear its intention not to forward the Kyoto Protocol to the U.S. Senate for ratification. President Bush objected to the agreement on the basis that there was still a great deal of uncertainty about climate change projections, that the Protocol would damage the U.S. economy, and that the exemptions granted to the Peoples' Republic of China (the world's second largest emitter of carbon dioxide) and India represent serious flaws in the Protocol.

Some in the Administration viewed the Kyoto Protocol as a contrivance to slow U.S. growth and to transfer wealth from the world's industrial powers to developing nations. Others objected to the use of the year 1990 as a benchmark because that was the year before the Soviet Union break-up, when energy efficiency there was at its worst. Therefore, the selection of the year 1990 provided Russia and the European Union (which includes the former East Germany and eastern European countries) with inflated benchmarks against which reductions are to be measured. Still others objected to failure to use per capita emissions as the measurement criteria. This would have reduced the sense of inequality between developed and developing nations.

On December 7, 1997, a *Los Angeles Times* article estimated that the Global Climate Coalition spent $13 million on its 1997 campaign against the Kyoto Protocol.[19] According to a Common Cause study, $63 million in political contributions were made by members of the Coalition from 1989 to 1999.[20] At the same time, Coalition members, such as the National Coal Association and the American Petroleum Institute, launched coordinated publicity campaigns opposing proposed restrictions on fossil fuel emissions.

Despite its successes, the Coalition lost many of its members between 1997 and 2001 as a result of reports from the IPCC and other scientific organizations that confirmed the existence of human-induced global warming, its negative effects, and the impending global problems if emissions are not reduced. For example, DuPont and British Petroleum left the group in 1997, Royal Dutch/Shell left in 1998, Ford left in 1999, and Chrysler, General Motors, and Texaco left in 2000.[21] While the change in stance of such employers may well have resulted from legitimate concern for the environment, some have speculated that apprehension over possible litigation, as has been common against the tobacco and drug industries, may have played a role.

In March of 2000, the Coalition restructured its membership by only representing associations as opposed to individual employers. This was a strategy to encourage members to continue their support for Coalition positions while insulating individual firms from public boycotts and other steps taken against those who were still denying global warming and its likely effects.

The Global Climate Coalition ceased operations in early 2002. However, its legacy remains as a potent force in determining U.S. climate change policy. This includes the failure of the United States to join the Kyoto Protocol, a refusal to adopt mandatory emissions reductions, and the concept of reliance on development of new technologies to reduce greenhouse gas emissions.

Since the demise of the Global Climate Coalition, public efforts by employers such as Exxon/Mobil and associations such as the American Petroleum Institute have recognized global warming and the problems that it likely causes. However, their recommended remedial actions continue to avoid the idea of mandatory emissions reductions, emphasize projects to limit emissions through innovation, and pilot efforts to test and apply cleaner energy-producing processes and technology.

THE 2007 IPCC ASSESSMENT REPORT

On February 2, 2007, the fourth IPCC Assessment Report was issued. The report included the following key conclusions:[22]

- Warming of the earth's climate is unequivocal, "as is now evident from observations of increases in global average air and ocean temperatures, widespread melting of snow and ice, and rising global mean sea level."

- There is a more than 90 percent likelihood that most of the observed increase in global average temperatures since the middle of the twentieth century has been caused by human-generated greenhouse gas emissions.

- Global atmospheric concentrations of carbon dioxide, methane, and nitrous oxide have increased markedly as a result of human activities since 1750 and now far exceed "the natural range over the last 650,000 years."
- During the twenty-first century, global temperatures are likely to rise from 1.1 to 6.4 degrees Celsius. Impact of this phenomenon is likely to cause
  o a rise in sea levels of 18 to 59 centimeters;
  o increased frequency of warm spells, heat waves, and periods of heavy rainfall (90 percent certainty); and
  o an increase in the frequency of droughts, tropical cyclones, and extreme high tides (66 percent certainty).

- Both past and future human carbon dioxide emissions will continue to cause warming temperatures and sea level expansion for more than a millennium; however, the extent of these changes will depend on the extent of fossil fuel use during the next century.

U.S. GOVERNMENT—LIMITED ACTION

In 2002, the Bush Administration introduced a bill to establish the Clear Skies Act.[23] According to the Environmental Protection Agency, this new law would "dramatically reduce and cap emissions of sulfur dioxide, nitrogen oxides, and mercury from electric power generation to approximately 70 percent below 2000 levels."[24] According to the Administration, it was "proposed in response to a growing need for an emission reduction plan that would protect human health and the environment while providing regulatory certainty to industry."[25]

However, two attempts to pass the Clear Skies Act in the U.S. Congress, in 2003 and 2005, failed. This was attributed to analyses of the proposed legislation by environmental public interest organizations. They concluded that the bill, if enacted, would have resulted in significantly fewer reductions of air pollutants than are currently provided by the Clean Air Act. In addition, the bill would have created a loophole to exempt new and upgraded power plants from being required to comply with modern federal emissions limits.[26]

As part of the Clear Skies Act initiative, the U.S. announced a goal of an 18 percent reduction in carbon intensity by 2012.[27] Carbon intensity is a ratio of carbon emissions to economic activity. For example, one might compute carbon intensity by dividing gross domestic product (expressed in millions of dollars) by carbon dioxide emissions (expressed in thousands of metric tons).

However, environmentalists pointed out that the carbon intensity measure may fall despite an increase in carbon dioxide emissions.[28] For example, from 1990 to 2000, the carbon intensity of the U.S. economy declined by 17 percent, yet total carbon emissions increased by 14 percent.[29] Estimates found that by 2012 total carbon emissions would be 12 percent above the 2002 level and 30 percent above the level of 1990. By 2020, a 19 percent increase in carbon emissions would be expected from the total in 2000.

Therefore, while Bush policies were expected to slow the rate at which carbon emissions increase, their absolute quantity would continue to increase. According to the U.S. National Environmental Trust, carbon intensity is "a bookkeeping trick which allows the Administration to do nothing about global warming while unsafe levels of emissions continue to rise."[30] According to the American Enterprise Institute for Public Policy Research, which recommends a long-term, federally funded initiative to develop radically new technologies to reduce emissions, "America remains an international pariah for its refusal to participate in it [the Kyoto Protocol]. President Bush has been able to prevent ratification of the Protocol, but has not made the effort needed to convince people that there is a better way to approach the issue."[31]

The United States did join the Asia-Pacific Partnership on Clean Development and Climate.[32] This pact, introduced on July 28, 2005, also involves Australia, China, India, Japan, and South Korea and allows its signatories to set their own goals for reducing greenhouse gas emissions, with no enforcement mechanism.

At the initial meeting on January 12, 2006, the signatories agreed to a Work Plan to use government–industry task forces to develop sustainable solutions to shared challenges through bottom-up practical action. As a result, eight Task Forces are working on projects to promote cleaner production of fossil energy, renewable energy and distributable generation, power generation and transmission, steel, aluminum, cement, coal mining, and buildings and appliances.

While the Bush Administration has been opposed to mandatory emission reductions and has not set a cap-and-trade program in place, the federal government continues to spend billions of dollars in initiatives that benefit climate-change objectives.[33] For example, recent annual budgets provided close to $5.0 billion for global climate change. Another five-year, $4.6-billion commitment has been made in the form of tax credits for development of renewable energy sources. The tax credits are mainly for the production of wind energy, for biomass power, for energy produced from landfill gas, and for the purchase of residential solar heating systems and hybrid, electric, and fuel-cell cars.

The Climate Change Technology Program provides direction and organizes about $3 billion in federal spending for climate change–related technology research, development, demonstration, and deployment initiatives to reduce greenhouse gas emissions and power economic growth. The program is organized around six complementary strategic goals: Reduce emissions from energy end-use and infrastructure; reduce emissions from no- or low-emission technologies; capture, store, and sequester carbon dioxide emissions; reduce emissions from non–carbon dioxide greenhouse gases; enhance the measurement and monitoring of emissions; and strengthen scientific contributions to development of climate change–related technology.

President Bush has called for a 20 percent reduction in U.S. gasoline use over ten years. He also proposed greater use of alternative fuels such as ethanol, targeting a sevenfold increase in annual production by 2017; however, ethanol produced from corn is an energy-intensive process that adds its own pollution to the atmosphere. Therefore, he has proposed $1.6 billion for research for renewable energy, focusing on ethanol sources other than corn.

In terms of Congressional action, several bills have been introduced to establish cap-and-trade programs in the United States. The McCain–Lieberman Climate Stewardship Act would require mandatory, domestic, economy-wide emissions reductions. It also would set up an emission trading program, a climate research initiative, and an emission registry. The reductions required by this bill would be much stricter than the Bush "emissions intensity" goal but less stringent than what the Kyoto Protocol would have mandated.[34] Democrat Nancy Pelosi, Speaker of the House of Representatives, organized a Congressional subcommittee to examine global warming when the Democrats won the majority in the House of Representatives in 2006.[35] This may give new life to global warming legislation generated from the House of Representatives.

INDEPENDENT INITIATIVES

A number of corporations are working to develop the next generation of green-friendly technology as more definitive data about human-induced global warming and its impact on the earth's environment and population have been released to the public. According to Yale's Daniel

C. Esty and Andrew Winston, "billions of dollars of venture capital are flowing into alternative energy and pollution control technology."[36]

To some extent, investment in wind and solar power, hybrid automobile engines, lightweight vehicles, high-efficiency LED lighting, smart appliances, and green buildings is based on an assumption that the next U.S. President will lead the nation back into climate change negotiations and commit to the next stage of serious international greenhouse gas reductions. Under such a scenario, with carbon emissions bearing a price, these investments should pay significant dividends.

On January 19, 2007, the U.S. Climate Action Partnership urged lawmakers to pass mandatory curbs on greenhouse gas emissions, including those of power plants, transportation, and buildings.[37] The group includes more than twenty-four of the nation's major corporations and six environmental advocacy organizations. The partnership is advocating a cap-and-trade system constructed to reduce emissions by 10 to 30 percent over the next fifteen years. The partnership is guided by six principles:

• Account for the global dimensions of climate change.
• Create incentives for technology innovation.
• Be environmentally effective.
• Create economic opportunity and advantage.
• Be fair to sectors disproportionately impacted.
• Reward early action.

According to the Electric Power Research Institute, without significant action, global carbon dioxide emissions will more than double by 2050.[38] On March 30, 2007, sixty-five large pension funds and corporations wrote to President Bush, calling for a 60 to 90 percent reduction of greenhouse gas emissions from 1990 levels by 2050.[39] This group is promoting a market-based system that would give companies incentive to reduce the growth of harmful emissions. The investors, who manage $4 trillion, claim that in the long run the nation's inadequate steps to curtail emissions will hurt business much more than the adoption of a comprehensive plan to reduce global warming. A spokesperson for Merrill Lynch & Company said the investment bank sees big business in a potential global market for trading carbon emission credits. Their experts claim that a 60 percent reduction from 1990 levels will effectively stabilize the global warming phenomenon.

Wal-Mart, the nation's largest retailer, has set a goal to reduce store energy use and is pressuring its 60,000 suppliers to do the same.[40] The company aims to increase the fuel efficiency of its truck fleet by 25 percent over the next three years and double it within ten years. By 2020, these initiatives are expected to save $494 million annually. The firm is also planning to design a store that is 25 percent more energy-efficient than current stores.

With regard to its customers, Wal-Mart is determined to place compact fluorescent lamps (light bulbs) into 100 million homes. These bulbs use 75 percent less electricity, last ten times longer, produce 450 pounds fewer greenhouse gases, and save consumers $30 over the lifetime of each bulb. If the retailer meets its light bulb goal, Americans would save $3 billion in electricity costs and reduce electricity requirements of the equivalent of 450,000 homes.

In addition to U.S. corporations and environmental groups, state and local governments have taken their own initiatives to reduce greenhouse gas emissions. Almost 200 U.S. cities with a combined population of 50 million have committed to reducing greenhouse gas emissions to 7 percent below 1990 levels.[41]

California's 2006 Global Warming Solutions Act commits the State to reducing emissions to 2000 levels by 2010, 1990 levels by 2020, and 80 percent below 1990 levels by 2050.[42] These savings are to be achieved mainly through tighter automotive emissions standards, increased use of renewable energy in the production of electricity, a mandatory emissions reporting system, and market mechanisms to provide incentives to businesses to reduce emissions while safeguarding local communities. Because the state of California has the world's sixth largest economy, the impact of these steps should be significant worldwide.

However, on December 19, 2007, Federal Environmental Protection Agency Administrator Stephen L. Johnson denied California's petition to limit greenhouse gas emissions from cars and trucks, overruling the unanimous recommendation of the agency's legal and technical staffs. Environmentalists claim that the EPA action was in response to lobbying by Ford and Chrysler, whose representatives met with Vice President Cheney on the issue in November. It is anticipated that the state will successfully challenge the EPA directive in court.[43]

In a similar effort, the state of New Jersey has enacted its own pollution reduction legislation. Through the Global Warming Response Act, global warming pollution is to be reduced below 1990 levels by 2020 and 80 percent below 2006 levels by 2050.[44]

The Regional Greenhouse Gas Initiative is a seven-state agreement signed in 2005 that involves the state governments of Connecticut, Delaware, Maine, New Hampshire, New Jersey, New York, and Vermont.[45]

These states have pledged to reduce carbon dioxide emissions from power plants utilizing a cap-and-trade program with a market-based emissions trading system.

EUROPE TO GO BEYOND KYOTO

On March 9, 2007, the European Union approved an agreement that will require an overall reduction in greenhouse gas emissions of 20 percent below 1990 levels by the year 2020.[46] The Kyoto Protocol calls for a 5 percent reduction below 1990 levels to be achieved by 2012. The new pact's reduction would be bumped up to 30 percent if the United States and China sign binding climate change agreements. This 2007 pact requires that the European Union derive a fifth of its energy from renewable sources such as wind and solar power by 2020. Currently, renewable energy sources account for 7 percent of their energy mix. In addition, by 2020 10 percent of the cars and trucks in the European Union must be able to use biofuels made from plants.

European heads of state believe the agreement raises them to a leadership status in fighting global warming. They hope to use this pact to push the world's biggest polluters—the United States, China, and India—to tackle climate change in a more diligent manner and to correct some of the problems of previously implemented cap-and-trade schemes. Implementation of this agreement will be made more difficult because countries from the former Soviet bloc are far behind in the use of cleaner energy and economic development. As a result, the European Commission will set individual targets for each nation.

SUMMARY AND CONCLUSION

There is no question that global warming is a complex issue. Understanding its characteristics requires objective and accurate presentation and study of scientific information. To correctly gauge this issue when it first surfaced, a special effort would have been required to bring the public, Members of Congress, and the President on board. Instead, industry and their lobbyists moved quickly to launch a disinformation campaign that led the nation in the wrong direction. Even as U.S. states, cities, and corporations seek to reduce greenhouse gases on their own, the current Administration has failed to reverse its position and greenhouse gas emissions continue to grow. The damage resulting from U.S. inaction is inestimable, including continued pollution that will degrade the environment for hundreds of years, diminished national prestige in the world community, and a lost opportunity to call on Americans to sacrifice in the name of a noble cause.

CHAPTER 10

MINIMUM WAGE: INCOME DENIED

How Special Interests and Their Lobbyists Stymie Timely Updating of the Minimum Wage

INTRODUCTION

The *New York Times* recently ran a series, "Age of Riches," that described the past twenty-five years as the New Gilded Age.[1] The series explained how government action in combination with favorable market developments have given birth to incredible wealth for a very small number of Americans.

The federal government's contribution to the development of this high concentration of riches has been unprecedented deregulation of industries such as banking and investment firms, as well as acute reductions in tax rates. For example, today's marginal tax rates on income (35.0 percent) and on capital gains (15.0 percent) have been cut by 50.0 and 61.5 percent, respectively, since the late 1970s.[2] These advantages, provided to entrepreneurs and large companies, have been combined with lucrative opportunities offered by expanding global markets, innovative management, and huge stock options emanating from higher stock market prices.

Only twice before over the last century has 5 percent of the national income gone to families in the upper one one-hundredth of a percent of the income distribution—currently, the almost 15,000 families with incomes of $9.5 million or more a year, according to an analysis of tax returns by the economists Emmanuel Saez at the University of California, Berkeley, and Thomas Piketty at the Paris School of Economics.[3]

A lack of concern over income inequality is another common characteristic shared by the Gilded Age of industrial titans before World War I and today's Gilded Age of global innovators. While the very rich of both eras have given generously to their favorite causes, they continue to seek lowest-wage workers to provide the goods and services they market. At the same time, they oppose higher taxes and seek new tax breaks (the inheritance/death tax elimination, for example), thereby further reducing the chances for meaningful income redistribution.

The minimum wage and the people it was designed to help have been the victims of disregard for dire American poverty in the shadow of exorbitant wealth. There are 37 million Americans living below the poverty line, almost 13 percent of our population.[4] Since the 1970s, this reflects an increase of more than 50 percent in terms of the number of people living in poverty and a 10.5 percent increase in the proportion of the population below the poverty line.

This case study examines one of the oldest tools designed to prevent poverty in America, the minimum wage. The study chronicles how strategies used by business and their lobbyists have continually delayed minimum wage updates and blunted the force of minimum wage applications.

THE FAIR LABOR STANDARDS ACT OF 1938

The story of the minimum wage is a story of government helping the little guy. To understand the logic, you have to go back to the 1930s and the Great Depression. That's when employers operated factories with child labor, paid workers less than a dollar a day, and required employees to work endless shifts.

In the spirit of Franklin Delano Roosevelt's New Deal, Congress reasoned that employers have a responsibility to pay wages that allow workers a decent standard of living, to establish a normal workweek that is not oppressive, and to protect children from abusive practices. These principles were embodied in the 1938 law called the Fair Labor Standards Act. Initially, it set a minimum wage of $0.25 per hour, defined a maximum forty-four-hour workweek, and banned oppressive child labor practices.[5]

In the 1940s the leaders of the Wage and Hour Division, the agency established to enforce the new law, changed how workers in America were treated. They shut down sweatshops and saved low-wage workers and children from employer greed and recklessness.

Today, the Fair Labor Standards Act requires covered employers (defined as being involved in interstate commerce) to pay covered employees (not professionals) at least the federal minimum wage and overtime pay (time and a half) for all hours in a workweek worked beyond forty. Workers must be paid for all the time they are on duty or at a prescribed place of work and for any time an employee is permitted to work. This includes work performed at home, travel time, waiting time, and training and probationary periods. For young people up to eighteen years of age, there are restrictions concerning the type of work that may be performed and the number of hours that may be worked on any school day and in any school week; there are related guidelines for young people when school is not in session.

Those who wrote the Fair Labor Standards Act intended that the minimum wage would "eliminate labor conditions detrimental to the maintenance of the minimum standard of living necessary for health, efficiency, and general well-being of workers ... without substantially curtailing employment or earning power."[6] "The minimum wage redistributes income with no immediate budgetary consequence, increases the incentive to work, is administratively simple, and creates a wage floor that removes competition for wages at the bottom of the wage distribution."[7]

To allow the minimum wage to keep pace with increases in the general costs of living, Congress could have specified an objective process by which the minimum would be updated on a regular basis. For example, it could have directed that the minimum wage be raised every three years on the basis of increases in the cost of living, labor productivity (output per worker), gains in average hourly earnings, or combinations of these indicators. In that way, there would have been assurance that the safety net constructed by this wage floor would continue to provide sufficient income over time.

Unfortunately, Congress did not specify an unbiased procedure for the maintenance of the minimum wage. Congress did require the Wage and Hour Division to prepare annual reports that would gauge the need for and suggest the magnitude of future increases; however, the Federal Reports Elimination and Sunset Act of 1995 struck that mandate beginning in 1999.

Given the absence of an updating procedure that is based on time and data requirements, increases in the minimum wage have been implemented through Congressional amendments to the Fair Labor Standards Act. Therefore, to increase the minimum wage, a majority of

Congress and an agreeing President, or a veto-proof majority of Congress, is necessary. This has left the minimum wage vulnerable to the influence of special interest lobbying and political vagaries.

EVALUATION OF THE MINIMUM WAGE

The minimum wage must, at the very least, keep pace with increases in the cost of living, inflation, to maintain its value. Looking at the past three decades, this has not been the case. If one adjusts the annual minimum wage on the basis of the Consumer Price Index, it becomes clear that despite the seven increases implemented over the past thirty years, the dollars provided have not adequately compensated for the increased prices of consumer goods. For example, if the 2007 minimum wage were adjusted to match the value of the minimum wage provided in 1978, it would total $8.45 per hour. Instead, the minimum wage at the beginning of 2007 was $5.15.

The latest amendment to the Fair Labor Standards Act (the first in ten years), signed on May 27, 2007, provided for increases to $5.85 on July 24, 2007, $6.55 one year later, and $7.25 a year after that, still well below the income provided in 1978. If experience over the last thirty years holds for the future, there will not be another amendment for eight years. Therefore, as time passes, those dependent on the minimum wage will fall deeper and deeper into poverty.

Another tool that may be used to gauge the movement of the minimum wage is the average hourly earnings of non-farm production workers. Regardless of inflation, has the minimum wage behaved in a manner similar to average wage rates? When one adjusts average hourly earnings for inflation, one finds that deterioration of the minimum wage has been much more devastating than the decline in average wages. For example, between 1978 and 2007, average hourly earnings fell from $18.75 to $17.29, declining by 7.8 percent; in the same period, the value of the minimum wage tumbled from $8.45 to $5.15 for the first half of 2007 and to $5.85 for the second half. These data reflect income losses of 39.0 and 31.0 percent, respectively.

A third measure of the minimum wage is the extent to which it allows individuals or families to maintain purchases that allow for a standard of living above the poverty line. Once again, time and lack of adequate action by Congress and the President have not been kind to minimum wage workers. In 1978, the minimum wage was 74.5 percent *above* the poverty line for an unrelated individual; today, it is just 5.7 percent above that line. In 1978, the minimum wage would support a family of three; today, the minimum wage will not support a family of two. Therefore, the minimum wage worker with one or more dependents is no longer able to rely on employer income to sustain the family above the poverty line.

A final consideration is the ability of employers to pay the minimum wage. For this comparison, we look to data on labor productivity and corporate profits. In terms of productivity, over the three decades covered, output per worker averaged annual *increases* of 1.97 percent. At the same time, the minimum wage paid in real dollars (dollars adjusted for inflation) averaged annual *declines* of 1.62 percent.

In other words, while workers have been producing more, they have been receiving less for their labor. Assuming that increases in productivity for minimum-wage workers are typical of the all-worker average, this allows one to conclude that increased output per worker could have compensated for greater increases in the minimum wage without negative impact on employer finances.

Corporate profits over this time period showed significant increases, due in part to rising labor productivity and decreasing real wages (both minimum and average). Profits increased for nineteen of the thirty years included in the analysis. After adjusting for increased prices (using the Implicit Price Deflator), corporate profits grew from $491.49 billion in 1978 to $1.37 trillion in 2006, a whopping 179.3 percent. Again, it seems reasonable to assume that employers have been in a position to pay increased real minimum (and likely average) wages.

MINIMUM WAGE WORKERS

The Bureau of Labor Statistics estimates that 1.7 million U.S. workers in 2006 were earning hourly wages at or below the minimum wage of $5.15.[8] Half of these workers were under 25 years of age, and almost two-thirds were women.[9] Nearly three of every four were employed in service occupations, predominantly in food preparation and service jobs. The industry with the highest proportion of minimum-wage workers was the leisure and hospitality industry.

The Bureau of Labor Statistics recognizes that these numbers underestimate the total because those who are covered but were not hourly workers have been excluded. However, a more important exclusion is due to the extent to which the minimum wage has not been sufficiently updated. For example, if the current minimum wage were $8.45 per hour, a level that corresponds with the income provided by the 1978 minimum wage, there would be close to ten times the number of workers at that level.[10]

Therefore, the situation produced by Congress and the President, degrading the value of the minimum wage, creates an opportunity for critics of the mandated wage floor to question its relevancy on the basis of the modest number of workers at or below that rate. However, as we have seen, if the minimum wage had been updated appropriately, close to 17 million workers (not 1.7 million) would be considered minimum-wage workers.[11]

A minimum wage of $8.45 would mean that the percentage of wage and salary workers paid hourly rates up to that level would be 22.1 percent of the total (not 2.2 percent). Also, this group of workers would be more equally distributed among the array of industries. For example, while there are still large numbers in the leisure and hospitality industry at $8.45, there are also many workers in the education and health services sector who receive that wage.

SPECIAL INTEREST AND LOBBYIST TACTICS

The U.S. Chamber of Commerce and the National Restaurant Association have been the most vocal opponents to increasing the minimum wage; these organizations represent a large percentage of the employers who hire workers at that rate. Their arguments against minimum wage increases don't deal with the requirements of the law or how the rate might be fairly updated. Instead, their focus is on questioning the relatively large increases proposed, necessitated by continuing inflation and the many years between minimum wage gains. Also, they use negative opinions provided by small business owners, charges that the workers being helped by the minimum wage often are not poor, economist views based on theory rather than empirical research, and preference for increases in the Earned Income Tax Credit, a federal wage subsidy for the working poor.[12]

Another focus has been on establishing tax advantages to compensate for minimum wage increases. For example, as a result of industry lobbying, the latest minimum wage amendment included a $4.8 billion tax relief package for small businesses. The restaurant industry was targeted to receive $1 billion of that total.

The Chamber of Commerce also supports an organization, the Employment Policies Institute, which conducts research concerning the impact of the minimum wage. One such study, which is still quoted freely by the Chamber of Commerce, claimed that the $0.50 increase in the minimum wage initiated in 1996 resulted in 645,000 lost jobs.[13] That conclusion appears to be based on a questionable contention that the increase in the minimum wage was responsible for a small decline in the percentage of the teenage population that was employed. However, with no minimum wage increase between 1998 and July of 2006, there have been unprecedented declines in the percentage of the teenage population employed. For example, the employment–population ratio for teens in 1997 was 43.4, a figure that fell to 36.9 in 2006 and has been at historic lows since 2003.[14] Given that information, it is obvious that one cannot legitimately assign responsibility for lower teen employment rates to minimum wage increases without specific information that supports such a conclusion.

The Chamber of Commerce issues letters to members of Congress providing such information in association with requests for votes against minimum wage updating. These transmittals often carry the foreboding statement that votes on or in relation to minimum wage increases will be considered to be "key votes in the Chamber's How They Voted scorecard." Because the Chamber is by far the biggest spender in America for lobbying services ($317,164,680 from 1998 to 2006), requests to oppose minimum wage increases are considered seriously.

At the same time, the National Restaurant Association garners support through its campaign contributions, $8.6 million since 1990, 84 percent to Republican candidates. The National Restaurant Association also chairs a Coalition for Job Opportunities, a group of thirty organizations that lobbies Congress in opposition to government-mandated increases in the entry-level wage.

SUMMARY AND CONCLUSION

Together, the organizations noted above, and their lobbyists, have succeeded in keeping the value of the minimum wage well below that provided in 1978. As we will see in some detail in Chapter 14, such efforts have meant increasing profits for industries that employ many minimum-wage workers and growing numbers of workers who earn below the poverty line. The intent of the minimum wage, to establish a decent standard of living for all workers, has been frustrated by the powers of special interests.

CHAPTER 11

STEM CELL CURES THWARTED

How Special Interests and Their Lobbyists Limit Stem Cell Research

INTRODUCTION

National U.S. health expenditures in 2006 were $2.1 trillion, more than three times the $696 billion spent in 1990 and more than eight times the $246 billion spent in 1980.[1] Steep increases in the costs of health care have been caused by expenditures for patients contending with cancer, heart disease, high-risk pregnancies, and HIV/AIDS. At the same time, increased life spans and the chronic illnesses that accompany old age, which involve the use of prescription drugs and long-term and nursing home care, have pushed medical costs to 16 percent of the nation's gross domestic product.

Given our profound spending on health care, one might expect that infirmity would be on the decline, with heart disease, cancer, and diabetes relegated to the history books along with polio, smallpox, and diphtheria. But the truth is that while researchers have made great strides in combating the symptoms of disease and extending the lives of those afflicted, for too many years the word "cure" has been absent from the medical vocabulary. This has left our population in a twilight of health care insufficiency, scrambling to pay for diagnostic services, drugs, and care that allow them to live with a disease but fail to address the underlying causes that constitute their illness.

The promise of stem cell research is the promise of a cure. Unlike the drugs and care options available today, cell-based therapies offer the possibility of a renewable source of replacement cells and tissues that could cure Parkinson's disease, Alzheimer's disease, spinal cord injury, vision and hearing loss, cancer, stroke, burns, heart disease, diabetes, osteoarthritis, and rheumatoid arthritis. In fact, it has been estimated that 100 million Americans could benefit from stem cell treatments.[2]

Rather than spearheading advances in this hopeful field, the federal government has limited research to a relatively few stem cell lines and has failed to provide adequate funding to push the threshold of stem cell discovery. Annual National Institutes of Health (NIH) funding for human embryonic stem cell research since 2003 has averaged $33 million, just 5.5 percent of total stem cell funding and only approximately one-tenth of 1 percent of the $28 billion total annual NIH investment in medical research.[3]

This case study explains the basics of stem cell science, explores how stem cells might be manipulated to cure many of our most feared diseases, and discusses the ethical objections and tactics used by special interest groups that have spurred the movement against embryonic stem cell research. While new discoveries offer the possibility of stem cell replacements for those created by human embryos, there is no denying that the lobby against embryonic stem cell research has already cost society years in the search for desperately needed cures.

THE WONDER OF EMBRYONIC STEM CELLS

Embryonic stem cells are the fundamental cells from which differentiated cells are manufactured to form the body's many organs: the heart, lungs, brain, and so on. Embryonic stem cells form at an early stage of development, before the embryo becomes attached to the uterus. If the embryo's inner cell mass (about thirty cells) is removed before implantation (four or five days after fertilization) and cultured under controlled conditions, the derived cells can continue to divide and replicate themselves indefinitely. After six months, millions of embryonic stem cells might be generated from the original thirty. If they remain undifferentiated (that is, if they don't make the transition into cell types required for specific organs) and appear genetically normal, they constitute an embryonic stem cell line. These cells are pluripotent in that they maintain their ability to generate the specialized cells required for each part of the body.

The embryos from which human stem cells are obtained are created and exist outside the body; that is, these embryos are produced by in vitro fertilization (IVF), a process by which fertilization of the egg takes place in a culture dish, which is usually part of an effort to address the infertility of client couples. IVF clinics often create multiple embryos for client couples; after successful impregnation, the remaining embryos are no longer needed to assist with infertility problems. It is estimated that there are close to 400,000 IVF-produced embryos in frozen storage in the United States. Although most of these will be used to treat infertility, more than 11,000 will likely be discarded. Such embryos could form the basis of stem cell lines to supply further research initiatives.[4]

HOW STEM CELL THERAPIES MIGHT WORK

Application of stem cell knowledge to cure disease may take four different forms. First, embryonic stem cells may provide an unlimited supply of tissue for transplantation therapies that counter the impact of degenerative diseases. For example, stem cells might be converted into insulin-producing pancreatic cells for diabetics, healthy heart cells for heart attack victims, or dopaminergic neurons for patients with Parkinson's disease. The replacement of defective cells could offer lifelong treatment for such disorders. However, to achieve these ends, additional research is required to ensure that stem cells proliferate extensively and generate sufficient quantities of tissue, differentiate into the desired cell type, survive in the recipient after transplant, integrate into the surrounding tissue after transplant, function properly for the duration of the recipient's life, and avoid harming the recipient in any way.

Second, organ-specific cells produced through stem cell differentiation might constitute an extremely valuable ground for testing the safety and efficacy of new drugs. For example, without human heart cell lines, a new drug for the heart may first have to be tested in animals. Because animal models do not always replicate human reactions, after animal applications, the drug would have to be tested in humans with unpredictable and sometimes negative results. The availability of stem cell–derived heart lines could indicate dangerous drugs before they enter clinical trials. Therefore, one can see how stem cell drug testing could speed the drug discovery process and promote safer and more effective treatments.

Third, study of embryonic stem cell lines may improve our understanding of infertility, pregnancy loss, and birth defects, leading to more effective preventative or remedial procedures. Such steps would build upon enhanced understanding of early events in human development, including cell division and tissue differentiation, through the study of in vitro stem cell models. Furthermore, because cancer is caused by abnormal cell division and differentiation, greater insight into the genetic and molecular controls of these processes may help us develop new, more powerful cancer therapies.

Fourth, stem cells may be used in a procedure known as therapeutic cloning or somatic cell nuclear transfer. Under this process, the DNA would be removed from an immature egg cell and replaced with the DNA from a cell removed from a patient. Then the resultant nuclear transfer products would be cultured in vitro to the embryo stage, at which point stem cell development occurs. Next, the embryo's stem cells would be extracted, ending the life of the embryo. The stem cells obtained by this process would be encouraged to grow into a piece of human tissue or a complete human organ for transplant to the patient who provided the replacement DNA.

Successful therapeutic cloning has the potential to save many lives and cure diseases that devastate millions of Americans. The procedure would provide perfectly matched replacement organs to sick and dying people with no danger of rejection. Those waiting for organ transplants would have shortened periods of time required for relief, human donors would not be required, and the organs provided would be new and fully functional. Scientific challenges to therapeutic cloning include instances of mutating stem cells that have led to rejection, the formation of tumors in animals, and identification of an abundant source of eggs.

ETHICAL ARGUMENTS

The basis for the opposition to embryonic stem cell research is derived from a firm belief that each human embryo represents the early stage of a life that has a right to develop into an individual. As described in Chapter 1, our Declaration of Independence states that "all men are created equal, that they are endowed by their Creator with certain unalienable rights, that among them are life, liberty, and the pursuit of happiness."

Therefore, regardless of the possible benefits of stem cell studies, those opposed to federal funding of stem cell research believe that ending the life of an embryo constitutes murder and can never be justified. Embryonic stem cell adversaries are particularly opposed to somatic cell nuclear transfer cloning. They contend that this technique amounts to instrumentalization of a human being and that it could lead to "human embryo farms."

According to the National Right to Life Committee, "those who favor federal funding of research that kills human embryos sometimes claim that these embryos will be discarded anyway, but this need not be so. Many human embryos have been adopted while they were still embryos, or simply donated by their biological parents to other infertile couples. Today, they are children indistinguishable from many others."[5]

In a message to President Bush, Pope John Paul II stated the Catholic Church's opposition to embryonic stem cell studies:

A free and virtuous society, which America aspires to be, must reject practices that devalue and violate human life at any stage, from conception to natural death. Experience is already showing how a tragic coarsening of consciences accompanies the assault on innocent human life in the world, leading to accommodation and acquiescence in the face of other related evils such as euthanasia, infanticide, and, most recently, proposals for the creations for research purposes of human embryos destined to destruction in the process.[6]

In addition to making ethical, legal, and religious arguments opposing embryonic stem cell research, pro-life proponents have supported stem cell activities that do not destroy human embryos.

Those on the other side of the embryonic stem cell debate question whether thirty nondescript embryo cells constitute a human life and contend that the potential benefits of embryonic stem cell research to afflicted children and adults far outweigh the loss of embryo life. Supporters of stem cell research also insist that although some surplus embryos will be used in future fertility efforts, many still will be discarded and could be put to good use in embryonic stem cell research. Proponents of embryonic stem cell research also question the potential uses of adult stem cells and bemoan the time and resources being wasted on fringe studies while the bright promise of embryonic stem cells remains untapped.

VERY RECENT DEVELOPMENTS

Several new stem cell techniques are under development to promote the full potential of stem cell research while avoiding the funding restrictions of recent years.

- One new technique turns ordinary human skin cells into induced pluripotent stem cells without the use of embryos or a woman's eggs. The new method uses genetically engineered viruses to transform adult cells into embryo-like ones. However, the viruses may contaminate the cells, limit their beneficial potential, and cause tumors. Scientists predict that the development of virus-free techniques is not far away. Because the cells produced by this method are genetically identical to those of the skin donor, organ development and transplant may be possible without the fear of rejection.

- An experimental technique retrieves one stem cell from an embryo, without destroying the embryo, and then coaxes the stem cell removed to reproduce into stem cell lines that never result in an embryo. NIH funding is being denied, however, on the basis that the only sure way to tell that the embryos have not been harmed is to implant the embryos and examine the resulting babies. Since the NIH also believes that such a step would be unethical, the scientists are left without a means to prove their contention that the embryos are not abnormal.[7]

- A technique has been developed to create a mature cloned human embryo from single skin cells taken from adults. The objective is to harvest stem cells from those embryos and grow them into replacement tissues. Rejection of these cells would not be a problem, since the patient's immune system would recognize them as being identical to their own cells.

- Retrieving embryonic-like stem cells from the amniotic fluid that surrounds fetuses in the womb.

- Research and treatments using adult stem cells. These are rare stem cells (often difficult to obtain) that can only be used to repair the types of organs or tissues from where they came. Adult stem cells have been used in bone marrow transplants and skin and hair transplants.

SPECIAL INTEREST TACTICS

There are more than 150 pro-life organizations that oppose embryonic stem cell research and applications. The National Right to Life Committee, the Family Research Council, and Human Life International are three of the more prominent groups whose members work to combat federal funding of research that involves the destruction of human embryos.

Despite the fact that a clear majority of Americans favor expanded funding of embryonic stem cell research, these special interest groups have effectively lobbied to defeat bills that would have increased the availability of stem cell lines and provided additional funding for embryonic stem cell research.[8]

Since 1990, pro-life groups have donated more than $5 million to candidates who hold a federal office, almost all of them Republicans. Pro-life advocates are very vocal in their advocacy and have been known to boycott the products of corporations that are involved in the marketing of goods thought to be inconsistent with pro-life tenets.

President Bush established a policy under which only stem cell lines created before August 9, 2001, may be studied using federal funding. The NIH lists only twenty-two lines available for distribution to researchers. Furthermore, their use is constrained by a lack of genetic diversity, abnormalities, and poor growth characteristics.

Congress has passed legislation that was intended to expand the availability of embryonic stem cell lines, provide additional funding, and ease research restrictions, but these bills have twice been vetoed by President Bush. Because the NIH is the primary source of funding for academic laboratories in the United States, without new legislation, the efforts to move ahead continue to bog down.[9]

SUMMARY AND CONCLUSION

If the promise of very recent developments such as induced pluripotent stem cells is not interrupted by unanticipated setbacks, their funding is expected to grow substantially. However, those long involved in the stem cell debate caution that much work remains to be done to prove the value of the new processes. "No one yet knows, for example, whether the new cells will be as effective as conventional embryonic stem cells may prove to be against certain diseases, or whether the new cells will even prove safe for use in people."[10] According to U.S. Representative Diana Degette (D–Colorado), "I don't think this changes the debate. We still need to encourage all types of research, and we need to put ethical oversight in place."[11]

CHAPTER 12

HEALTH CARE: PROFIT VERSUS PUBLIC WELL-BEING

How Special Interests and Their Lobbyists Preempt Action to Provide the American Public with Universal Health Care

INTRODUCTION

When it comes to the provision of health care, the United States is unlike any other industrialized nation. For the rest of the developed world, the philosophy that people have a right to quality, affordable health care was adopted long ago. Rather than having this responsibility fall mainly on the individual, most countries assign the sponsorship of medical services and related products to government.

The great majority of industrialized nations have affirmed that the health of their populations is in the overall best interest of the nation; therefore, the nation as a whole, through government action, assumes the responsibility for the health of its citizens. In the United States, however, lobbying on behalf of the insurance and pharmaceutical industries as well as small businesses has ensured that Americans and their employers are for the most part on their own to make decisions regarding the purchase of health care in the marketplace.

If the unique American system functioned well, perhaps there would be no need for change. But the hodgepodge of America's health care is characterized by very serious problems. Comparing the United States with other developed nations, Americans pay twice as much for health care that is not as good. At the same time, 47 million Americans have no health insurance, and millions more are saddled with minimal coverage.[1] The U.S. system suffers from administrative waste, inefficiency, and depleted resources; racial and ethnic minorities receive lower quality care, and access to health care is constantly threatened by rapidly increasing costs.

This case study provides a brief description of our current healthcare system, examines the problems that contribute to its low ratings, chronicles how special interests and their lobbyists defeated the efforts in 1993 and 1994 to establish universal health care, and summarizes new initiatives proposed to enhance America's healthcare system.

AMERICA'S HEALTHCARE SYSTEM

Health care in the United States is provided by a variety of institutions and individuals at a great expense: hospitals represent about 32 percent of total expenditures; physicians and clinics, 22 percent; prescription drugs, 11 percent; nursing home and home health care, 9 percent; and other medical services and products, 27 percent.[2] America's health care is a product of both private and public sources.

For individuals under sixty-five years of age, the private sector is the dominant provider. Private, employer-sponsored insurance covers 62 percent of the population, and private, non-group (individual) insurance covers 5 percent.[3] Of the remaining population under sixty-five years of age, 18 percent have no insurance and 15 percent are enrolled in public programs, such as Medicaid. For individuals sixty-five years of age and older, most are enrolled in Medicare.

PRIVATE HEALTHCARE INSURANCE

Most employer benefit programs include some form of health insurance. This privately financed insurance is the most common way in which Americans receive their healthcare coverage. Administration of these programs may be by for-profit companies (Aetna, for example), by non-profit organizations (such as Blue Cross–Blue Shield), or, in the case of the self-insurance plans of very large corporations, through third-party contracts.[4] These plans are financed by both employers, who pay most of the costs, and employees. In 2006, the average annual cost of premiums for private healthcare insurance plans was $4,242 for individual coverage and $11,480 for family coverage.[5] The benefits, co-pays, and deductibles of such employer-sponsored insurance vary widely.

For those who are self-employed, retired, or simply unable to obtain health insurance from their employer, private, non-group policies are an alternative source of coverage. However, unlike employer-based insurance, under individual programs the insurance company may deny coverage due to preexisting conditions. These plans are administered by private insurance companies, financed by the individual being insured, provide a wide array of benefits, and incur costs determined by benefit terms and the health of the insured.

GOVERNMENT-FUNDED COVERAGE

Medicare and Medicaid were established on July 30, 1965, through Title XIX of the Social Security Act. At the federal level, these programs are administered by the Centers for Medicare and Medicaid Services.

Medicaid is the primary source of medical services for low-income parents, children, seniors, and those with disabilities. Medicaid is not insurance, but rather is a needs-based program for those unable to afford insurance. Eligibility is based on income, assets (not home ownership), and other resources. Medicaid is a jointly funded federal and state initiative, with the federal government paying 57 percent of annual expenditures.[6]

The states administer Medicaid under federal guidelines, but they may set their own eligibility requirements and may combine operations with other assistance programs. In recent years, Medicaid funding has been an increased burden for many states. In an attempt to lower the rate of cost increases, most have created Medicaid managed care programs. Under these schemes, recipients are enrolled in a private health plan that receives a fixed monthly premium from the state. The health plan, in turn, is responsible for providing required care to Medicaid enrollees.

Medicaid provides services to about 40 million Americans, almost half of them children, at a cost of nearly $300 billion per year.[7] Medicaid provides funding for nearly 60 percent of all nursing home residents, 37 percent of the total number of childbirths in the U.S., and more than half of individuals living with AIDS.[8]

Two additional government-sponsored healthcare programs include the State Children's Health Insurance Program (S-CHIP) and health care provided through the Veterans Administration (VA). S-CHIP has been designed to cover children whose families earn too much money to qualify for Medicaid but have too little to afford private health insurance. The program is authorized under Title XXI of the Social Security Act, is jointly financed by the federal and state governments, and is administered by the states.

Recent studies of the uninsured indicate that the number of uninsured children in the United States continues to rise. Most of these children are in families unable to meet the income eligibility requirements of S-CHIP. In response to this problem, in 2007, the Congress passed two bills to expand S-CHIP from an average cost of $5 billion yearly to $12 billion over the following five years. Both bills were vetoed by President Bush, and at the end of 2007, he signed an extension of the program to cover current enrollment levels through March 2009.[9] Another attempt to expand coverage failed when a January 2008 House vote did not attract enough representatives to override another presidential veto.

VA health assistance is provided to veterans through federal VA hospitals and clinics. VA medical services are financed through federal taxes and furnished free or at very affordable rates.

Medicare services are available to U.S. citizens and permanent residents who are at least 65 years old, those of all ages who have end-stage renal disease, and some who are disabled. Medicare is a single-payer program, with the federal government funding and administering the provision of medical services and related goods. Medicare provides coverage for close to 43 million seniors, with federal expenditures of $397 billion per year.[10]

Medicare is composed of four parts. Hospital insurance (Part A) helps cover inpatient care in hospitals, skilled nursing facilities (not custodial or long-term care), hospice, and some in-home health care. Medical insurance (Part B) helps provide doctors' services, outpatient care, and medically necessary physical and occupational therapy. Part C of Medicare, included in the Balanced Budget Act of 1997, provides an option for Medicare beneficiaries to receive coverage through private health insurance plans, known as Medicare Advantage plans. Medicare Part D, effective on January 1, 2006, as prescribed by the Medicare Prescription Drug, Improvement, and Modernization Act, offers prescription drug plans to those eligible for Medicare.

Most people don't pay a premium for Part A because they or a spouse, while working, already paid forty or more quarters of payroll taxes in accordance with the Federal Insurance Contributions Act. On the other hand, Medicare Part B usually requires a modest monthly premium and payment of an annual deductible; in 2007 the monthly premium was $93.50 and the annual deductible was $131.[11]

PROBLEMS THAT PLAGUE AMERICA'S HEALTH CARE

In addition to the systemic problems defined below, America's healthcare programs must deal with a complex of broad issues that present unprecedented challenges. Soon the nation's healthcare facilities must begin to absorb the huge number of Baby Boomers who will be reaching the age of retirement. For example, the number of those covered by Medicare is projected to increase by more than 65 percent between 2006 and 2025.[12] At the same time, the nation's political, fiscal, and healthcare structure is confronted by the challenge of managing rapidly increasing costs while maintaining quality care.

Specific health care problems are as follows:

- As a percentage of gross domestic product and per capita, the United States spends about twice as much for health care than most industrialized nations (based on data for the Organization for Economic Cooperation and Development [OECD] member nations).[13] Total U.S. healthcare spending has been forecast to average annual increases of more than 7 percent.[14]

- Despite the relatively high costs paid by American workers and their employers, comparisons with other OECD nations reveal few real advantages in terms of positive impact. For example, U.S. life expectancy is below the OECD average, and infant mortality exceeds the typical OECD experience. The United States has 2.3 practicing physicians per 1,000 population, which is below the OECD average of 2.9 per 1,000 population; 7.9 nurses per 1,000, which is below the OECD average of 8.2 nurses; and 2.8 acute-care hospital beds, which is below the OECD total of 4.1.[15]

- Among the thirteen wealthiest nations in the world, weighing ratings for the sixteen basic public health statistics, the United States ranks twelfth or thirteenth in each. The World Health Organization ranks the United States thirty-seventh in health care, above Bolivia but below Slovenia.[16]

- More than 47 million Americans, including 8.7 million children, are without health insurance.[17]

- Millions more have insurance that fails to cover major illnesses. This is exemplified by the fact that almost half of all bankruptcies result from burdensome medical bills, despite the fact that most of those people who are forced to file have healthcare insurance.[18]

- During a typical year, one-third of uninsured Americans are unable to fill a prescription due to cost.[19]

- When compared to those with health insurance, the uninsured often do not report or seek help for medical problems, they postpone treatment due to financial concerns, they do not have a regular place to go when sick, and they are much less likely to receive preventive care.

- For those without insurance, the consequences often mean late diagnosis of colorectal cancer, melanoma, breast cancer, and prostate cancer; and poor care for chronic diseases such as diabetes and end-stage renal disease.

- The problems of the uninsured lead to an excess annual mortality rate of 25 percent.[20] This translates to 18,000 unnecessary deaths each year for those between the ages of 25 and 64.[21] It has been estimated that their diminished health and shortened work life cost the nation $65 to $130 billion each year. [22]

- The combination of very limited preventive care for the uninsured, reliance on expensive hospital emergency room treatment for many relatively minor illnesses, and the likelihood of catching serious medical conditions at their late stages result in huge system inefficiency and wasted resources. For example, it has been estimated that more than 10 percent of emergency room visits are for non-emergency situations, costing billions in unnecessary expenses.[23]

- Children with no access to insurance suffer delays in development because of poor health, restricting their future earning capacity.

- The lack of universal coverage and the poor health it engenders increases costs to Medicare, Social Security Disability Insurance, and the criminal justice system.

- Communities that have high proportions of their population without health insurance are characterized by lower healthcare delivery capabilities due to uncompensated services that provide incentive for service providers to move, impaired access to emergency rooms due to uncompensated services and inappropriate use, weakened economies due to unsatisfactory health care facilities, and higher than average vulnerability to communicable diseases due to fewer vaccinations and less effective control of communicable diseases.

- One-third of healthcare expenditures result from administrative waste derived from reliance on private insurers.[24]

- Hospital expenses for billing and administration are almost double those of systems in which the government is the single payer.

- Between the spring of 2005 and 2006, the cost of premiums for employer-sponsored health care rose by 7.7 percent, faster than the rate of inflation, 3.5 percent, and wage gains, 3.8 percent.[25]

- Americans with employer-based healthcare insurance paid 79 percent more in 2003 than they did in 1996, and employers paid 89 percent more.[26]

- With health insurance premiums continuing to increase, many employers are shifting rising costs to their workers by increasing employee shares of premium bills and by cutting wage increases.[27]

- The percentage of employers offering health insurance declined from 69 percent in 2000 to 61 percent in 2006. At the same time, new policies offered often have high deductibles and fail to cover many healthcare requirements.[28]

- The high cost of health insurance premiums puts U.S. businesses at a disadvantage when competing with companies in Europe and with other industrialized nations in which the government assumes most healthcare costs.

- Health care disparities as a result of race and ethnicity result in more than 80,000 deaths each year.[29] African-American men and women are 1.4 and 1.2 times, respectively, more likely to die of cancer than their white counterparts.[30] Only 38 percent of Latina women over forty years old have regular mammograms, while Latina and African American women who get breast cancer are usually diagnosed at a later stage.[31] African American women experience higher rates of premature births.[32] In addition, diabetes is 1.6 times more prevalent among African Americans and 1.5 times more widespread for Hispanic/Latin Americans than in their white counterparts.[33]

SPECIAL INTERESTS AND THEIR LOBBYISTS DEFEAT UNIVERSAL HEALTH CARE

Given the problems described here, which have been evident for many years, why haven't enlightened politicians pushed for major reform? Why not use the legislative and fiscal power of the federal government to reform health care, eliminate the problem of uninsured Americans, and bring added efficiencies to a system rife with waste and bureaucratic paperwork? In 1993 and 1994, the Clinton Administration attempted such an effort. The following account chronicles how the health insurance companies, small businesses, and their lobbyists, with the help of the Republican Party, defeated this initiative.[34]

September 1993

President Bill Clinton proposed universal health care to a joint session of Congress. His proposal and the follow-up testimony by the First

Lady before five Congressional Committees were greeted with public enthusiasm. However, House and Senate Republicans criticized the lack of details provided, and the Health Insurance Association of America (HIAA) and the National Federation of Independent Businesses claimed that the Clinton plan would cause a huge dislocation of workers and prevent Americans from keeping the health care they already had.

October 1993

A staged media event by the President fell flat because the new legislation was still unavailable. Bob Michel, the moderate House Minority Leader, delivered a scathing attack on the premise of the Clinton initiative; other Republicans fell in line against the yet to be introduced bill.

November 1993

The HIAA launched a series of TV messages in which a typical American couple, Harry and Louise, sitting at their kitchen table, doggedly reviewed the Clinton healthcare plan, represented by a huge stack of paper. The couple criticized the plan's lack of individual choice and endless bureaucratic complications, and concluded that under the proposal, "They choose, we lose." First Lady Hillary Clinton attacked the insurance industry, which she claimed was lying about the reform program to protect their profits. However, the effectiveness of the lobbying effort was reflected in an extra $30 million raised by the HIAA to further their opposition.

On the last day of the legislative session, the Health Security Act of 1993 was introduced. It promised comprehensive benefits that could never be taken away; controlling healthcare costs for consumers, businesses, and the nation; improving the quality of health care; increasing choices for consumers; reducing paperwork and simplifying the system; and making everyone responsible for health care.

Under the proposal, every American citizen and permanent resident would receive a Health Security Card. The card would guarantee health insurance regardless of the state of your health, employment, or geographic location. The law would allow participants to choose their doctor, make it illegal for insurance companies to deny coverage, emphasize preventive care, and include prescription drugs. The plan was to be financed by Medicare and Medicaid savings, savings from federal employee health insurance, reducing the benefits of tax-free compensation, and some additional taxes. For the most part, it was estimated that consumer costs would be about 20 percent of current average health plan premiums, and the unemployed and the poor would receive subsidized insurance.

December 1993

A noted conservative journalist circulated a paper suggesting that Republicans should kill, not amend, the Clinton plan. He reasoned that if the bill passed, it would solidify middle-class support of the Democratic Party. Continued HIAA lobbying and stories about the Clinton Whitewater and Troopergate scandals began to erode public support for the Clintons and their proposal.[35]

January 1994

The Republicans tied the Whitewater scandal to health care and with the aid of the conservative talk radio network intimated that the Clintons couldn't be trusted in either case. In his State of the Union address, the President threatened to veto any healthcare legislation that didn't guarantee all Americans healthcare coverage. Senator Bob Dole (R–Kansas), in the opposition party's response to the President's address, used a chart that displayed a bewildering array of new government agencies and programs to make the point that the Clinton proposal was really government-run health care. Whitewater stories continued to be spread. The *Wall Street Journal* and the *New Republic* carried editorial page articles by a staffer of the conservative Manhattan Institute, painting a devastating picture of the Clinton plan's impact. Although most experts claimed that the articles were filled with falsehoods and distortions, they had a significant negative effect.

February 1994

Grass-roots lobbying by the No Name Coalition and Congressional Republicans changed the position of the U.S. Chamber of Commerce from support to opposition to the Clinton legislation. The Business Roundtable endorsed an alternative healthcare bill as the best starting point. The National Association of Manufacturers declared its opposition to the Clinton plan. Paula Jones filed a lawsuit against the President for sexual harassment and civil rights violations.

March 1994

The House Ways and Means Health Subcommittee considered the Clinton bill, labeled Medicare Part C, under the sponsorship of

Congressman Pete Stark (D–California). The bill moved to the full Committee. The Republicans again focused on the link between Whitewater and health care. Chairman Dan Rostenkowski (D–Illinois) faced legal challenges from federal prosecutors regarding possible misuse of official accounts.

April 1994

Democrats needed one more vote on the House Ways and Means Committee to move the bill forward. When Kansas Representative Jim Slattery (D) appeared ready to provide that vote, the National Federation of Independent Businesses launched a grass-roots lobbying campaign to its 8,000 Kansas members. They requested that their members contact Representative Slattery, imploring him not to vote for any employer mandate for health insurance. Slattery soon announced that he would not support a bill that included any employer mandate. The House Finance Committee began holding a closed-door session on the Clinton bill. Rush Limbaugh told his listeners, "Whitewater is about health care."

May 1994

As Senator Dole moved to develop an alternative healthcare bill, prominent conservatives warned that they would not support future candidates who were willing to compromise on behalf of Big Government. Chairman Rostenkowski stepped down after he was indicted on seventeen counts of conspiring to defraud the government. Without his influence, chances of passing health care through the House were dealt a serious blow.

June 1994

On the Senate side, arch-conservatives attacked moderates and labeled Senator Dole's Chief of Staff "a liberal Democrat." Senator Ted Kennedy (D–Massachusetts) delivered a strong version of the Clinton bill from his Labor and Human Resources Committee. However, convinced that some Republican support would be required once a health reform bill moved to the floor of the Senate, Senator Patrick Moynihan (D–New York) introduced his own bill. Senators Moynihan and Bob Packwood (R–Oregon) met with the President and informed him that they didn't have the votes needed to pass a bill that included healthcare mandates, universal coverage, or regional health alliances (groups of businesses and consumers who, under the Clinton bill, were to negotiate for high-quality care at affordable prices).

The HIAA funded new "Harry and Louise" TV spots nationwide, which attacked the Clinton plan's backup controls for healthcare spending and standard premiums for all the insured. The Democratic National Committee, unable to match HIAA funding, responded with ads that appeared only in the District of Columbia, not in the grass-roots regions, where such ads were most effective. First Lady Hillary Clinton met with representatives of labor, senior citizens, consumers, and supportive healthcare providers and warned that unless they forgot their individual interests and pulled together, no bill would be enacted. Bills were introduced by Republicans in the House and Senate that included no employer or individual mandates, premium caps, or price controls. The Republican National Committee funded ads that supported the Republican initiatives.

July 1994

The President and Congressional Democratic leaders decided to support a new bill introduced by Democratic Senate Majority Leader, George Mitchell of Maine. The bill had no employer mandates but came close to providing universal coverage. The Moynihan bill was advanced, but it was immediately broken apart. The Senate Finance Committee voted out a bill that didn't approximate universal coverage.

A new Republican strategy intimated that if the Democrats continued to push for health care, the Republicans would defeat ratification of international agreements that were made in the Uruguay Round of the General Agreement on Tariff and Trade (GATT). This new treaty would create the World Trade Organization, replacing the GATT Treaty; reduce tariffs, export subsidies, import limits and quotas; enforce patents, trademarks, and copyrights internationally; extend international trade law to the service sector; encourage foreign investment; and establish a new dispute-settlement procedure.

The President addressed the summer session of the National Governor's Association and appeared to retreat on universal coverage, instead saying that he would be satisfied with a "phased-in deliberate effort" to increase coverage. He also said that he would be open to new proposals detailing other ways to pay for the additional coverage. To reinvigorate the push for health reform, the White House organized a bus trek across America to generate grass-roots support.

Conservative interest groups (the No Name Coalition and Citizens for a Sound Economy) met the caravan in Portland, Oregon, with a broken-down bus, wrapped in red tape and labeled "Clinton Health Care." At almost every point, well-prepared protesters spoiled the

Clinton attempt at impressing Congress with grass-roots support. At a rally in Seattle, a mob of angry men, worked into frenzy by conservative talk show broadcasts, protested that if left unchecked, the Clintons would destroy their way of life, ban guns, extend abortion rights, protect gays, and socialize medicine. Fearing violence, many stops on the caravan route were canceled.

In a *New York Times* interview, Newt Gingrich, House Minority Whip, claimed that he had united House Republicans against healthcare reform and would use that issue to win back Congressional control.

August 1994

The Democrats rallied behind a new crime bill that had been passed by both Houses and agreed to in conference. Once that bill got final approval, the plan was to pass the Mitchell healthcare bill in the Senate and a comparable House bill sponsored by Dick Gephardt (D–Missouri), House Majority Leader. Then Congress would adjourn for the summer, and its Members would prepare for the upcoming November Congressional elections. The Mitchell bill postponed required employer coverage until early in the next century and exempted all employers with twenty-five or fewer employees. The target was to increase coverage from 85 percent to 95 percent of all Americans by 2000. The American Association of Retired Persons endorsed the Mitchell–Gephardt bills.

The Republicans in the House, led by Newt Gingrich, delayed a final vote on the compromise crime bill, thereby blocking action on health care. A procedural vote to begin consideration of the crime bill failed as fifty-eight Democrats switched sides and voted with the Republicans. Procedural tactics similarly blocked action in the Senate.

A new round of "Harry and Louise" TV spots appeared across the nation while opposition to healthcare reform was expressed in mountains of faxes, letters, and numerous telephone calls sponsored by the small business lobby. Conflict between Democrats over the course of healthcare reform (Ted Kennedy and Bob Kerrey) led the Party faithful to fear chaos among their leaders. Also, there was a spreading belief that the Republicans were in position to retake control of Congress, despite the relatively large Democratic majorities in place. Democratic leaders of both Houses announced that they were letting their Members return home for the remainder of the summer, thereby giving up on health care. Many Democrats running for new terms attempted to distance themselves from the President and his healthcare reform.

September 1994

Top staff members of Senators Kennedy, Mitchell, and moderate Republican John Chafee of Rhode Island worked furiously to prepare a new healthcare compromise bill to be ready for the September 19 return of Congress. When Congress reconvened, Mitchell attempted to set aside four days for consideration of the healthcare compromise bill, but the Republicans threatened a filibuster, which the Democrats didn't have enough votes to break. After Newt Gingrich told the President that continued action on health care would result in defeat for ratification of the new GATT Treaty, Senator Mitchell withdrew any Democratic plans to press for health care reform on September 26.

NEW HEALTH CARE INITIATIVES IN THE LIGHT OF PREVIOUS FAILURES

In late 1994, a Gallup poll reported that 72 percent of all Americans believed that healthcare reform should be a high priority for the government. Despite broad public recognition of healthcare problems and the need for reform, the alliance and funding of special interests—insurance, small businesses, and Congressional Republicans—were able to kill an effort to advance healthcare assistance.

There is no question that the Clinton effort was characterized by tactical errors and had to deal with inherent problems. First, the President's selection of the First Lady to head the Task Force to Reform Health Care denied recognized expertise at the initiative's lead position and weakened the respect of Congressional players whose support would be vital. Second, efforts to build grass-roots political support were late and inadequate in comparison with the skillful initiatives of the opposition. Third, the many scandals that plagued the Clintons made it too easy for the opposition to divert attention from the relevant issues and tarnish reform proposals with the smoke from allegations of wrongdoing, regardless of the veracity of the allegations. Fourth, the design of the Clinton plan appeared unconventional, complex, and difficult to understand, and lacked convincing evidence that revenues could be raised to fully support its design. This led many from the middle class to fear that the Clinton initiative would leave them worse off, while it would assist the poor and those with no insurance.

Despite those problems, had the Republicans viewed the issue on its merits and been open to compromise rather than seeing health care as an opportunity to condemn Big Government and its Democratic sponsors, perhaps real progress might have been made. In the absence of the

negativity and misinformation of the insurance and small business lobbies, the opportunity to address the legitimate need for healthcare
reform might have preempted the political opportunism that defeated
this initiative.

With the continued growth of the numbers of uninsured, premium
costs, and system waste and duplication, public understanding of the need
for reform and expanded government participation represents the sentiments of the great majority of Americans.[36] Whether such opinion, in
combination with electoral events, will result in significant change will
depend upon the design of reform proposals offered, the skill of proponents to generate meaningful grass roots and Congressional support, the
impact of special interest and lobbyist strategies to derail reform, and the
ability of politicians of both parties to solve problems instead of scoring
political points to discredit members of the other party.

Thus far, the new healthcare reform proposals may be divided into
three categories. The most extensive reform program would establish
Medicare for all, a universal, single-payer, not-for-profit healthcare system, similar to those in place in Canada and some European nations.[37]
This proposal is based on the assumption that access to comprehensive
health care is a right and that the provision of high-quality, reasonably
priced medical services and products is the responsibility of the federal
government.[38] When this basis is established, logically, there is no role
to be played by the private healthcare insurance industry, because their
primary function is to assign risk to individuals/groups to be covered
and to charge fees on the basis of those risk factors. Under the single-
payer design, risk is irrelevant; comprehensive health care is provided to
all regardless of risk.

By excluding private insurance companies from the provision of
health care, it has been estimated that $200 to $300 billion in administrative costs incurred for marketing, profit, underwriting, and billing
might be eliminated.[39] At the same time, the single-payer system is estimated to have the potential of saving another $109 billion in the bulk
purchases of prescription drugs, perishable medical supplies, and durable medical equipment.

Given these savings, plus new taxes (mostly on the wealthy), proponents of this proposal claim that the average consumer would see a
reduction in current health care/insurance costs of 75 percent. The
comprehensive health care provided to all would include primary care
and prevention, inpatient care, outpatient care, emergency care, prescription drugs, durable medical equipment, long-term care, mental
health services, dental services, substance abuse treatment, chiropractic
services, vision care and correction, and hearing services.

The second category of healthcare reform proposals would provide universal coverage but would not advocate a single-payer system.[40] Under one such scenario, four basic components would be combined to provide quality coverage for all at reasonable costs.

1. Businesses would be required to either provide a comprehensive health plan to their employees or contribute to the cost of covering them through Health Care Markets (see No. 3, below).
2. The federal government would offer tax credits to subsidize insurance purchased through Health Care Markets; expand the coverage of Medicaid and the State Children's Health Insurance Program; require insurance companies to keep plans open to everyone, charge fair premiums regardless of preexisting conditions, and include preventive and chronic care in policy offerings; and provide support for public hospitals, clinics, and community health centers.
3. The U.S. government would assist states or groups of states in the creation of regional Heath Care Markets. These non-profit purchasing pools would offer a choice of competing insurance plans. At least one plan would be a public program based on Medicare. Families and businesses could choose to supplement their coverage with additional benefits. The markets would be available to everyone who does not receive comparable insurance from their jobs or a public program and to employers that choose to join rather than offer their own plans. Over time, the system could evolve toward a single-payer approach if individuals and businesses prefer the public plan.
4. When insurance premiums are affordable, everyone would be expected to obtain health coverage. Special exemptions would be available in cases of extreme financial hardship or religious beliefs.

Financing of this system would be made possible by increased competition, investment in preventive care, better treatment of chronic diseases, and improved productivity through information technology.

The third category of healthcare proposals is characterized by less central control.[41] One such proposal would have the federal government fund the states to set up their own universal healthcare systems. Another proposal would rely on income tax deductions and tax credits to increase the purchasing power of insurance consumers. An alternative idea is consumer-directed health plans. They include a health savings account (a tax-advantaged, portable, health spending account), high-deductible medical coverage that includes preventive care not charged against the deductible, and access to informational tools that help consumers make informed decisions. Under such schemes, there would be price and quality transparency for the services and medical products of providers.

Since 1998, the pharmaceutical/health products industry, insurance industry, and major business associations have spent $2.8 billion to lobby government.[42] As healthcare reform initiatives are put forward, there is no doubt that these special interests will seek to have significant impact on the outcome.

The most recent example of such influence is reflected in the new Medicare Part D drug program. The idea behind this initiative was to reduce the cost of prescription drugs being paid by senior citizens. However, because of the influence of the insurance/pharmaceutical lobby, rather than receiving drug coverage through the single-payer Medicare program, those who need prescription coverage must select from one of more than forty plans offered by private insurance companies. Participants must pay a $250 deductible, and then 25 percent of costs up to $2,250 in total drug expenditures for a year ($750 total). At that point, the "donut hole" becomes effective, requiring consumers to pay 100 percent of further drug expenses until another $2,850 has been expended. In other words, after a participant pays a total of $750, there is no coverage at all until out-of-pocket expenses reach $3,600 ($750 + $2850). Then the insurance covers 95 percent of further expenses. However, according to *Families USA*, by this point, seniors living at the poverty level would be spending 41 percent of their income on prescription drugs.[43]

Inexplicably, Medicare Part D directly prohibits the negotiation of group-purchasing agreements and volume discounts with the drug companies.[44] Such arrangements save the Veterans Administration and the Department of Defense more than 40 percent on drug costs by establishing wholesale prices in consideration of the huge numbers of pharmaceutical products purchased.[45] It is estimated that the absence of such arrangements is adding billions of dollars to drug company profits.

In addition to drug company benefits, many corporations have been able to take advantage of Plan D by shifting their prescription drug costs previously paid for retirees on to the taxpayers. The *Boston Globe* claimed that one defense contractor would save more than $170 million through such action.[46]

SUMMARY AND CONCLUSION

We have seen that the U.S. healthcare system is unique and problem-ridden. On the one hand, its emphasis on utilizing private insurance is not in conformance with the government-run programs of most developed nations. On the other hand, the system is rife with duplication and unnecessary costs and fails to rank among the most respected healthcare providers in the world. Furthermore, the system leaves too many citizens without adequate coverage and taxes the budgets of those who strain to afford sufficient services.

Lobbyist power continues to mark the unfeeling characteristics of healthcare in the U.S.: 47 million with no coverage; no Medicare negotiations to provide quantity drug discounts; and the drug program "donut hole" are just a few examples. Perhaps, the most visible symbol of special interest/lobbyist success in shaping the nation's healthcare system is defeat of the effort to establish universal health care in the 1990s. In the coming years, new universal healthcare proposals of hopeful political candidates and the absorption of millions of Baby Boomers into the Medicare system will challenge the nation as never before to straighten-out its healthcare dilemma.

CHAPTER 13

INNER-CITY CRIME UNABATED

How Special Interests and Their Lobbyists Preempt Steps to Prevent/Reduce Inner-City Crime

INTRODUCTION

Crime rates in the United States in general, and in U.S. inner cities in particular, are extremely high. There are those who will point to substantial violent crime rate reductions that occurred from 1992 to 2004. During that period, violent crime was cut from 757.7 per 100,000 Americans to 463.2.[1] However, a resurgence of violent crime in 2005 and 2006, and comparisons with criminal activity in other developed nations, places America in embarrassing territory.

According to the Police Executive Research Forum, the twenty-four-month trend for the period beginning January 1, 2005, reveals an increase in the rates of several categories of violent crime: homicides, 10.21 percent; robberies, 12.27 percent; aggravated assaults, 3.12 percent; and aggravated assaults with a firearm, 9.98 percent.[2]

When compared with the violent crime experience of other economically mature nations, the United States is in a class by itself. For example, the rate of homicides for England, France, Germany, and Italy averages less than 1.5 per 100,000 population, with France having the highest rate at 1.73. The comparable U.S. homicide rate is 5.56, almost four times the average rate of the selected European countries.[3]

The sad story of runaway U.S. violence is far from invisible. For the majority of Americans who live within earshot of big cities, nightly newscasters reading the police blotter detail the horror of murder, forcible rape, robbery, and aggravated assault that occur daily. How can a nation of wealth and education permit this victimization to continue?

Analysis of the problem leads to difficult conclusions. For example, enormous resources are being spent, but they deal more with the symptoms of our epidemic of violence rather than addressing fundamental causes. Once again, powerful special interests and their lobbyists have led the nation astray while serving their own ends.

This case study will outline the parameters of America's criminal activity, underlying conditions that lead to crime, the manner in which special interests and their lobbyists have influenced relevant U.S. policy, and recommended steps offered by experts to obtain more positive outcomes.

OVERVIEW OF AMERICA'S RAMPANT CRIME PROBLEM

In 2005, in cities across the country, 7,723,696 criminal offenses were charged.[4] The all-city tally represented 74.8 percent of the 10,367,072 crimes perpetrated nationwide.[5] Crime in the United States is highest in the inner cities, the central areas of major cities characterized by high poverty and low levels of education and training. Inner-city rates of violent crime may be two to almost ten times the rates in associated suburban areas.[6]

The rate of violent crime in cities with populations of at least 250,000 is 58.2 percent higher than the overall U.S. violent crime rate.[7] The murder rate for these cities is 83.0 percent higher; for forcible rape, 18.6 percent higher; for robbery, 101.5 percent higher; and for aggravated assault, 48.6 percent higher. The rates for weapons offenses and drug abuse in cities of this size exceed the national averages by 60.5 percent and 52.6 percent, respectively.[8]

Of the total arrests in these cities, 46 percent of the individuals arrested were under twenty-five years of age.[9] Violent crime constituted 342,217 charges, 112,585 charges were for weapons possession, and 1,025,810 charges were for drug abuse.[10] Defendants under twenty-five years of age were charged with more than half (52.6 percent) of the murders reported, 45.2 percent of the rapes, 62.1 percent of the robberies, 41.1 percent of the aggravated assaults, 60.6 percent of the weapons charges, and 46.3 percent of the drug violations.[11]

In terms of race, 55.9 percent of those arrested for violent crimes in these cities were white (including Hispanic) and 41.9 percent were African American.[12] Whites commit 44.2 percent of murders and African

Americans 53.9 percent; whites account for 60.1 percent of rapes while African Americans account for 37.8 percent; whites commit 41.1 percent of robberies and African Americans 57.3 percent; and whites account for 60.3 percent of aggravated assaults while African Americans account for 37.3 percent.[13] Whites commit the majority of weapons and drug offenses, 56.8 and 61.1 percent, respectively, while African Americans commit 41.7 and 37.6 percent of those violations, respectively.[14]

With regard to the tendency of men versus women to commit crimes, men dominated all the selected categories. For example, men committed 75.2 percent of crimes overall, 81.8 percent of violent crimes, 92.0 percent of weapons offenses, and 80.4 percent of drug violations.[15]

Summarizing these data, one might simply conclude that the highest incidence of violent crime is among relatively young men, urban residents, and especially minorities in the inner cities. If the crime rates of these individuals could be reduced to approximate U.S. averages excluding that group, overall crime rates may be brought down to more moderate levels, closer to levels experienced by the rest of the developed world.

CURRENT STRATEGIES

Given the statistical information, how has the U.S. attempted to quell the trend of violent crime? A rational starting point could be to determine why individuals turn to a life of criminal activity. Once those causes were identified, we might work to remove the origins of high crime. While incarceration, anti-drug, and anti-gang programs could be concurrent initiatives, failure to address the underlying causes of unusually high crime rates would leave little if any hope of ever reducing crime in the future, instead leaving us to live with very high numbers of offenders.

Federal anti-crime initiatives have been shaped by three policy positions: "tough on crime" prison sentences first prescribed in the mid-1980s, continuation of the 1970s "War on Drugs," and relatively easy access to firearms.

1. "Tough on crime" sentencing has taken the form of mandatory (determinate) sentencing, abolition of parole and adoption of truth-in-sentencing requirements, lower rates of parole, passage of "three-strike" laws, and establishment of sentencing guidelines.[16] Under this regime, sentencing limits are usually determined at the time the sentence is issued rather than having a parole board set actual time served on the basis of progress made toward rehabilitation. Therefore, deterrence and punishment are being emphasized over rehabilitation. These policies, a reaction to the sharp increases

in the rate of violent crime recorded in the 1960s and 1970s, have led to an inevitable explosion in the number of people behind bars.

For example, stiffer mandatory sentences have driven the incarcerated population to more than 2.3 million people, or 737 per 100,000 residents. Comparable statistics for England (150), France (85), Germany (93), and Italy (67) highlight the aberration of the U.S. justice system.[17] America incarcerates more people than any other nation; with only 5 percent of the world's population, we have a quarter of the planet's prisoners.

Between 1982 and 2003, correctional spending in the United States grew by more than 570 percent, reaching $61 billion in 2003, greatly enriching the nation's prison-industrial complex.[18] This powerful special interest group is composed of corporations that build, supply, and operate prisons; prison guard unions; and legislators elected from depressed rural districts where prisons mean jobs and federal money.

Between 1970 and 2005, there has been a 700 percent increase in the U.S. prison population.[19] Another 13 percent rise is projected for state and federal prisons by 2011, at a cost of $27.5 billion. Since 1980, the total correctional population (including those on probation and parole) increased from 1.8 million to 7.0 million.[20] Therefore, one in every forty-three Americans is under some type of correctional supervision.

Each year, more than 600,000 people enter state and federal prisons and more than 10,000,000 are sent to local jails.[21] Almost two-thirds of those who are admitted to prison are individuals who failed to complete probation or parole.[22] In 2006, African Americans composed 12 percent of the U.S. population but accounted for more than 40 percent of those in adult correctional facilities.[23] Hispanics accounted for 15 percent of the general population but 19 percent of the prison population.[24] Annual costs to sustain each prisoner behind bars range from $13,009 in Louisiana to $44,860 in Rhode Island.[25]

While stiff sentences and incarceration surely act as deterrents to crime, recidivism rates have barely changed, and more than half of released prisoners are back behind bars within three years. With violent crime now on the rise again, locking up offenders does not seem to provide a long-term solution.

2. President Richard Nixon declared the War on Drugs in 1971 after Congress passed the Controlled Substances Act of 1970, which provided for prohibition of the manufacture, importation, possession, and distribution of selected drugs considered harmful. This

initiative followed the tumultuous years of the 1960s, which were characterized by increased drug use, including cannabis (marijuana and hashish) and LSD; assassinations (President John F. Kennedy, Dr. Martin Luther King, Jr., and Senator Robert F. Kennedy); racial riots; and massive anti–Vietnam War demonstrations. The Office of National Drug Control Policy, now a Cabinet-level agency, was established in 1988 to coordinate the anti-drug activities of the federal government. The Director of that agency has been labeled the nation's Drug Czar.

Federal expenditures to implement the nation's drug initiatives were close to $13.0 billion in 2007.[26] Of that total, 64 percent has been allocated to disrupt the illicit drug trade (domestic enforcement, destruction of foreign supplies, and anti-smuggling activities); 24 percent has been devoted to drug intervention and treatment programs (screening, therapy, and support); and 13 percent has been spent for prevention (education and outreach programs).[27] Indirect costs of the drug war include more than $30 billion expended to incarcerate drug offenders (including police protection, legal adjudication, and correctional charges) and the social and economic costs to families who lose members to prison.[28]

An ethical price being paid for the War on Drugs concerns the large numbers of African Americans and Latinos, relative to their composition of the population, who are incarcerated due to drug and related violations. For example, Congress dramatically increased prison time for offenses involving crack cocaine relative to usual sentences for use of cocaine in powdered form. Until recently, crack sentences were one hundred times more severe than those for powder. At the same time, 82 percent of crack cocaine convictions involve African American defendants, whereas African Americans constitute just 27 percent of convictions that involve powdered cocaine.

Given the nation's historical burden of slavery, convict leasing, and Jim Crow laws, it is not much of a reach for those who have experienced prejudice to interpret drug possession sentences as a new expression of America's disdain for the non-white population.[29] The motive for slavery and convict leasing was to obtain free labor; there are those who charge that the motives behind the rash of drug charges are to provide a sense of security to white Americans and to benefit the prison-industrial complex that is funded to keep those sentenced behind bars.

In addition to prisons benefiting from the huge annual number of drug abuse arrests, other groups that reap profits from the War on Drugs include manufacturers of planes and helicopters used for international spraying (destruction) of poppy and coca crops, some drug treatment programs that are contracted by criminal justice elements, and police and prosecuting agencies dependent on the proceeds from asset forfeitures.[30]

The primary result of the War on Drugs has been the incarceration of millions who are addicted to a drug and have been arrested on charges of drug possession, or who have committed a crime to obtain money with which drugs can be purchased. As noted above, in 2005 there were more than 1 million arrests on drug-abuse charges. At the same time, it is estimated that more than 20 percent of property crimes were drug related.[31] These offenses are usually committed by addicts who are dependent on heroin, cocaine, crack, and other high-dependency drugs.

Experts who are not tainted by the need for political slogans and those who are able to think realistically when it comes to drugs and addiction have reached conclusions that undermine the justification for a war on drugs. For example, Ethan Nadelmann, founder and executive director of the Drug Policy Alliance, claims,

> Prohibition has failed—again. Instead of treating the demand for illegal drugs as a market, and addicts as patients, policymakers the world over have boosted the profits of drug lords and fostered narcostates that would frighten Al Capone. Finally, a smarter drug control regime that values reality over rhetoric is rising to replace the 'war' on drugs.[32]

According to Nadelmann, current policies, which have been ineffective, have created "collateral casualties" that would never be accepted if drug addiction were treated as a health issue rather than a law enforcement matter. United States and global production and consumption of the coca bush, the cannabis plant, and opium poppy products have changed little over the past decade, despite the 1 million drug arrests each year and half a million Americans incarcerated for drug offenses. Drug addiction rates in the United States are the same as or higher than those in Europe, even though the United States practices a more punitive approach to the addiction problem.

Nadelmann advocates a "harm reduction" strategy to replace the false promise of "zero tolerance." While abstinence from dangerous drugs would still be the objective for most, for those who fall into the trap of addiction, procedures would be put in place to reduce the transmission of infectious disease through syringe-exchange programs, to reduce overdose fatalities by making antidotes readily available, and to allow people addicted to heroin and other illegal opiates to obtain methadone from doctors and even pharmaceutical heroin from clinics. Such strategies, already accepted by several European countries, appear to decrease drug-related harms, such as HIV/AIDS, without increasing drug use.

In terms of supply reduction, Nadelmann states that as long as profits from illegal drugs provide huge rewards to distributors, efforts at eradication simply shift production from one region to another. At the same time, aerial spraying destroys legal crops nearby, hurts impoverished farmers, and constitutes an environmental hazard without reducing overall supply.

Nadelmann raises the possibility of legalizing cannabis, the use of which accounts for 40 percent of U.S. drug arrests. He claims that "hundreds of millions have used it, the vast majority without suffering any harm or going on to use 'harder' drugs."[33] He contends that 40 percent of Americans believe that the drug should be legalized, taxed, controlled, and regulated like alcohol.

3. Easy access to firearms, while not treated as a conscious policy position, must be considered as the third leg of America's stance toward crime. While other developed nations have made possession of firearms a highly restricted privilege, in America almost anyone can find a way to purchase a gun, whether it's a handgun, a hunting rifle, or even an assault weapon. As a result, 68 percent of all homicides in America involve a gun.[34] While the 1993 Brady Act requires criminal background checks and waiting periods for gun purchases, and recently passed federal legislation provides $1.3 billion to help prevent the severely mentally ill from buying guns, only 20 percent of criminals get their guns from licensed dealers.[35] A flourishing black market is all too willing to provide unrestricted access to firearms.

Although some states and cities have passed laws intended to restrict firearm possession and use, without tough national regulation criminals may obtain weapons purchased in other areas without much effort. In addition, when restrictions limit purchasing guns from licensed dealers, gun shows often have methods to circumvent those restraints.

Fully automatic firearms, which can cost thousands of dollars, are legal in most states, but are restricted by federal law. For example, to be purchased legally, they must have been manufactured and registered before May 19, 1986; the local sheriff or chief of police must approve the purchase; fingerprints and a photograph must be submitted to the U.S. Bureau of Alcohol, Tobacco, and Firearms; and a criminal background check must be conducted.

On the other hand, semi-automatic firearms may usually be purchased over the counter if the buyer meets basic legal requirements, completes the necessary paperwork, and passes a criminal background check. Gun-control policies of many developed nations ban fully automatic weapons altogether as well as less deadly instruments.

In nearly forty states, law-abiding citizens, after completing a course of training, may carry handguns for self-protection. At the extremes, Alaska and Vermont have no restraints on lawful citizens carrying concealed weapons, whereas Illinois, Wisconsin, and the District of Columbia tightly restrict how citizens may carry personal firearms.

The special interest groups and their lobbyists, representing gun manufacturers, retailers, sportsmen, shows, and collectors, especially the National Rifle Association, cite the Second Amendment to the Constitution as evidence that free access to guns is guaranteed to American citizens:

> A well-regulated Militia being necessary to the security of a free State, the right of the people to keep and bear Arms shall not be infringed.

With no standing army at the time, the Second Amendment was originally intended to facilitate the quick formation of a fighting force if invasion or insurrection was threatened; if the general populace was already armed, an effective militia might be formed and put in the field to defend the nation.[36] Given its origin and purpose, one has to wonder what the Second Amendment has to do with allowing a desperate heroin addict, gang member, or mentally deranged youth, any of whom may choose to kill indiscriminately, to have easy access to weapons.

Experts working to reduce gun violence prescribe a number of steps that may be taken to combat illegal guns and gun violence.[37] Initiatives recommended include the following:

- Developing systems to trace the sales histories of guns used in the commitment of a crime.
- Running undercover sting operations on gun dealers suspected of illegal sales (1 percent of licensed firearms dealers sell more than half of the guns recovered in crimes).[38]
- Increasing the oversight and inspection of gun dealers.
- Revoking the license of problem gun dealers.

- Filing lawsuits against problem gun dealers.
- Requiring background checks for all gun sales, especially sales at gun shows (many shows advertise that they require no background checks).
- Requiring gun owners to lock up their guns (thereby reducing gun theft by criminals and also cutting down on teen suicides).
- Modifying state gun laws that prevent cities, most affected by gun violence, from enacting their own gun control legislation.
- Deploying special police units to detect and deter illegal gun carrying at times and places where shootings are common.
- Educating policy-makers and the public on steps to prevent gun violence, including model legislation.
- Requiring that guns are "personalized," only operable by designated users (this can be achieved through fingerprint/lock technology).
- Requiring microstamping of all guns, making ballistics matching far more accurate and efficient (achieved by using lasers to insert microscopic codes on multiple surfaces of the firing chamber of a gun).

SUMMARY AND CONCLUSIONS

In their fascinating book, *Freakonomics*, Steven Levitt and Stephen Dubner used statistical analysis to trace the 1990s crime reduction mainly to reduced numbers of young minority men in inner-city locations. "It shouldn't be surprising to learn that elderly people are not very criminally intent; the average sixty-five-year-old is about one fiftieth as likely to be arrested as the average teenager."[39]

Levitt and Dubner contend that this population phenomenon—many fewer minority teens—was caused by *Roe v. Wade* and the ensuing increase in abortions available to low-income inner-city women. They also credit tough sentencing, reduced profits in crack markets (lowering the incentive for dealers to murder their competition), and increased police presence as significant factors in the 1990s crime reduction.

The authors also identify the fundamental conditions that seem to result in high rates of inner-city crime: families characterized by low levels of education, single-parent households, poverty, teenage mothers, and children unwanted by their parents. Because we know where these conditions persist, and we know the enormous economic and social cost they extract from our society, one has to wonder why we persist on mainly funding efforts that deal with the results of crime rather than its causes.

Special interest groups and their lobbyists, who represent gun access, spraying foreign narcotics fields, and "tough on crime" prison solutions, seem to offer easy answers to complex problems, but their solutions come at a cost that perpetuates rather than eliminates the dilemmas the nation is experiencing. Of course, they curry the favor of Washington legislators with significant campaign contributions. For example, since 1990, gun rights groups have contributed almost $19 million to candidates campaigning for federal office.[40] This is just a small proportion of funds devoted to lobbying and campaigns by construction, aerospace, electronics, and union organizations that benefit from the boom in prison building, the private operation of prisons, and billions spent on elements of the War on Drugs.

If one examines the distribution of city criminal charges by age, it becomes easy to see what is happening. Those under eighteen years of age account for 10.0 percent of the murders committed, 15.8 percent of rapes, 26.0 percent of robberies, 16.8 percent of aggravated assaults, 24.3 percent of weapons charges, and 11.1 percent of drug violations.[41] However, if we look at the same data for those under twenty-five years of age, we see a very different picture: 52.6 percent of murders, 45.2 percent of rapes, 62.1 percent of robberies, 41.1 percent of aggravated assaults, 60.6 percent of weapons charges, and 46.3 percent of drug violations.[42] Young people, unprepared to enter the worlds of higher education or work, graduate or flunk out of high school. With no productive alternatives in sight, soon they turn to drugs and crime.

The above analysis seems to suggest that perhaps less attention might be paid to the more traditional reactive policies, and substantial resources should be freed to deal specifically with root causes. Why not prepare inner city youth to live lives of high promise? Instead of building more prisons, construct a network of up-to-date inner-city high schools, staffed with better teachers and excellent counselors, who might be available to both students and their family members.

These schools might provide free meals, health care, quiet study environments for extended hours, and college scholarships to community colleges and state universities for those who graduate. They could become centers of educational, vocational, job search, cultural, and athletic training to transform families from those who bear the burden of high-crime characteristics to those who have a better than even chance to fully succeed in American life. Given the incredibly high cost of current strategies, such initiatives would appear justified on economic as well as moral grounds. Furthermore, if successful, they would provide a long-term solution to many of the problems that mark America as a violent, crime-ridden society.

PART 4

IMPACT OF SPECIAL INTERESTS

The Winners and Losers of Special Interest Lobbying

In Part 3 we saw how special interests, their lobbyists, and the use of campaign financing have influenced five issues vital to the nation's well-being: global warming, minimum wage, stem cell research, universal health care, and inner-city crime. In those cases that were most suscep-tible to public observation, we saw clearly how special interests directed millions of dollars and huge numbers of hours to launch crusades that determined U.S. policy.

In the next three chapters we will quantify the results achieved by special interests in terms of winners and losers. Because there are many variables that affect industries and special interest groups, it's difficult to assign specific dollar gains derived from lobbyist initiatives. However, one can, in a general way, visualize how policy might have unfolded in the absence of special interest efforts and then trace the gains of indus-tries and organizations that have created their own environments. Part 4 also documents the extent to which special interest successes have denied the American public the policies it seeks and damaged the politi-cal leadership needed to guide the nation through difficult times.

CHAPTER 14

BENEFICIARIES OF MONEYED INTERESTS

Gains Reaped and Losses Incurred due to Special Interest and Lobbyist Achievements[1]

INTRODUCTION

How successful have special interests and their lobbyists been in promoting their own well-being? When it comes to major questions of U.S. policy, lobbyists often represent the status quo. Their clients have been clever enough, hard-working enough, or just lucky enough to take advantage of a given market or situation. With new information and fresh initiatives threatening a prosperous or comfortable existence, it is the lobbyist's job to head off the forces of change.

Throughout Part 3, we observed how lobbyists achieved their client's goals with regard to global warming, minimum wage, stem cell research, universal health care, and inner-city crime. Lobbyists utilized their effective arsenals of techniques to raise doubts, question motives, taint opponents and their ideas with the hint of scandal, deny and counter claims, mock proponent contentions, plant the seeds of fear, publicize justifications based on personal values, reduce complex issues to simple slogans, emphasize the importance of opinion rather than fact, creatively manipulate data to support arguments, invoke the loss of individual and corporate freedom in the face of Big Government, infiltrate the bases of political power, block legislation, propose alternatives to the preferred courses of action, and threaten withdrawal of campaign contributions.

In Chapter 14, where possible, we turn to the measurable gains of special interests that have, at least for now, won their battles. To what extent have they been able to translate victories into financial gains or other achievements, and how have their conquests affected others? For the leading industry or industries within the special interest areas described in Part 3, this chapter provides a business profile or description, vital statistics and trends, speculation as to how events might have unfolded if lobbyist efforts had been absent or ineffective, and identification of winners and losers in the current circumstances.

GLOBAL WARMING

Profile of the Oil and Gas Extraction Industry

The oil and gas extraction industry has been most closely tied to the campaign to deny global warming and blunt efforts to counteract its effects. Oil and natural gas provide about three-fifths of the nation's energy needs. Its products heat our homes, power our factories, and fuel our trucks, sport utility vehicles, and automobiles.

The principle role of this industry is to locate, develop, and extract oil and gas from the earth and sea. Seismic prospecting—a technique based on measuring the time required for sound waves to travel through underground formations and return to the surface—has greatly enhanced the accuracy of oil and gas exploration. Using computers and advanced software to analyze the data, scientists locate and identify structural oil and gas reservoirs and pinpoint the best locations to drill.

After scientific studies indicate that oil is likely present, the oil company selects a well site and installs a derrick to house the drilling equipment. Comparable techniques are used in offshore drilling, except the drilling rig is part of a steel platform that either sits on the ocean floor or floats on the surface, anchored to the bottom.

When the drilling enters the oil or gas reservoir, the drill pipe and bit are removed from the well, and a metal pipe (casing) is lowered into the hole. The casing is cemented in place, with its upper end connected to a system of pipes and valves called a wellhead, through which natural pressure forces the oil or gas into separation and storage tanks. Crude oil is transported to refineries by pipeline, ship, barge, truck, or rail. Natural gas is generally transported to processing plants by pipeline.

Vital Statistics and Trends

The oil and gas extraction industry in the United States employs about 316,000 workers.[2] Of those workers, about 40 percent are employed directly by oil and gas extraction companies, with most of the industry's employees working as contractors who perform support activities.[3] Although the industry operates in forty-two states, close to 75 percent of all workers are in California, Louisiana, Oklahoma, and Texas.[4] Most of the industry's employment is found in firms that employ twenty or more workers; however, just over 50 percent of industry establishments employ fewer than five workers.[5]

ExxonMobil Corporation, Royal Dutch Shell, and BP are the three largest industry producers. Shrinking oil and gas reserves, pressure from environmentalists, and consumer complaints regarding high oil prices have led the industry to invest in new energy technologies, including wind, solar, and nuclear energy. However, despite such challenges, the industry has tallied record profits in recent years. For example, from 1998 to 2006, after tax, annual profits have skyrocketed fourteenfold from $3 billion to $42 billion.[6] From 2001 to 2006, annual value added (the value of output produced less the cost of intermediate goods) has more than doubled from $118.7 billion to $256 billion.[7]

Sans Special Interests and Lobbyists

Let's assume that when the specter of global warming first appeared on the horizon, the U.S. response was spared the campaign launched by the Global Climate Coalition; let's further assume that the Senate's Byrd–Hagel Resolution failed to capture many votes as Senate Members decided to wait and see before they preempted action that might have been in the best interest of the nation and the world. Also, let's assume that once the great majority of Americans became convinced that global warming was real and needed to be addressed, the United States signed and ratified the Kyoto Protocol, becoming a full partner in the efforts to restrict carbon emissions. Finally, let's assume that the President recognized protecting the environment from global warming as a noble cause and rallied the nation to make every reasonable effort to reduce carbon emissions and develop and adopt alternative forms of energy.

Winners and Losers

How might the above assumptions have affected the oil and gas extraction industry? With the nation reducing its consumption of fossil fuels and seeking alternative sources of energy, it is safe to assume that demand for oil and gas would be reduced from the levels actually experienced. With a cap-and-trade system in place, industrial oil and gas customers would have a strong incentive to limit their consumption and design consumer goods that avoid excessive carbon emissions. In such an environment, energy companies would have heightened incentive to invest in new technology and forms of energy that would be free of characteristics that damage the environment.

Given such developments and the fact that the United States is the world's largest consumer of fossil fuels, the control that oil and gas firms would have over the price of their products would be diminished. Therefore, lower prices and reduced sales would likely result, having a negative impact on profits.

Such firms, undoubtedly, would continue to record healthy levels of return. However, one would expect that the ravenous levels of profit actually made—a 1,300 percent increase from 1998 to 2006—would be somewhat lower. And so it seems reasonable to conclude that the lobbying performed on behalf of the oil and gas extraction industry to block the recognition of global warming as a legitimate concern and then to restrict action to curb carbon emissions paid huge dividends. In a narrow and short-term sense, the industry's firms were the big winners.

In addition to the resources wasted on the high price of oil, there appear to be two types of loss that have resulted. First, current and future inhabitants of our world, including all Americans, will suffer the environmental consequences of our inaction with regard to global warming. The U.S. accounts for 24 percent of the world's carbon emissions, the largest national share. By refusing to take real action to curb carbon emissions, we have unnecessarily damaged the earth's environment.

With the issuance of the Third Intergovernmental Panel on Climate Change Assessment Report in 2001, all thoughtful parties knew that the problem of global warming was real and that avenues were open to repair the damage. This is when one would have expected that the political leadership of the nation would have initiated real action. Scientific evidence indicates that the carbon emissions sent into the air today will remain a problem for hundreds of years. Therefore, the time we have wasted will exact a serious price on generations to come.

Second, as a nation, Americans have lost an opportunity to pull together and tackle a challenge well worth its sacrifices. With the right leadership, global warming could have been the glue that united the nation for the benefit of our children and grandchildren. There is no more satisfying characteristic to nationalism than unity in the name of a noble cause. Through our politician's allegiance to the influence of special interest, we have forsaken that invitation to honor. Furthermore, according to the testimony of respected diplomats, by taking no serious steps to rein in global emissions, by rejecting the Kyoto Protocol, and by continuing to pretend that we desire remedial steps, America has been humiliated.

MINIMUM WAGE

Profile of the Food Service and Drinking Places Industry

The food service and drinking places industry has been most closely tied to the campaign to question the propriety of a minimum wage and to deny minimum wage updates. This industry is composed of close to half a million establishments, ranging from fast food to elegant, full-service restaurants.

The principle role of this industry is to prepare meals, snacks, and beverages to customer order for immediate on-premises and off-premises consumption. About 45 percent of the industry's establishments are limited-service eating places, including franchised fast food restaurants, cafeterias, and snack bars.[8] Close to 39 percent are full-service restaurants, usually providing table service and menus characterized by appetizers, entrees, salads, desserts, and beverages.[9] The remaining locations are drinking places (10.6 percent) and special food services (5.5 percent), including food service contractors, caterers, and mobile food services.[10]

With the aging U.S. population and dual-earner families with schedules that may preclude at-home preparation of meals, growth of the full-service sector, especially midscale or family-type restaurants, has been strong. In fact, many national chains have entered this market, which is expected to grow significantly. However, attracting qualified workers and experiencing very high labor turnover rates remain problems; another difficulty lies in the increasing costs for basic ingredients such as beef, corn, rice, and soybeans.

Point-of-service systems are being increasingly used to raise restaurant efficiency. Restaurant staff key in customer orders at the table using a handheld device or from a computer terminal in the dining room. These systems send orders to the kitchen, compute and print checks, function as cash registers, connect to credit card authorizers, and track sales. Other automated systems are being used to control inventory and minimize food costs and spoilage. High-speed cookers also are being used to increase levels of productivity.

Vital Statistics and Trends

The food services and drinking places industry employs more than nine million workers.[11] The industry ranks among the largest employers in the United States. More than 70 percent of the establishments in the industry employ fewer than twenty workers.[12] The fast food segment of the industry's labor force is characterized by many teenagers, often gaining their first experience in the labor market. Overall, industry employment is projected to grow by 16 percent between 2004 and 2014.[13] Many of the industry's workers earn the federal minimum wage, or less than the minimum wage if tips are included as a substantial part of earnings.

McDonald's Corporation, Sodexho Alliance, and Yum! Brands, Inc., are the three largest industry producers. Taking advantage of increased demand for restaurant services and the low-wage structure of the industry, after-tax annual profits have reflected significant gains. For example, profits in 2006 ($19.6 billion) were more than three times the level recorded in 1998 ($6.3 billion).[14] From 2001 to 2006, annual value added increased by almost one-third, reaching $349.9 billion.[15]

Sans Special Interests and Lobbyists

Let's assume that in 1978 the U.S. Congress, concerned with maintaining the value of the minimum wage, instituted objective rules for minimum wage updating. It was determined that every few years, the wage floor would be raised based upon increases in the cost of living.

Winners and Losers

From 1978 through 2007, on average, the actual minimum wage fell 24 percent below the value of the wage floor provided in 1978. Therefore, had Congress instituted inflation-based revisions, those companies who employed minimum wage workers would have experienced significantly increased costs for labor. This not only would be derived from those paid at the minimum wage but also workers up the wage structure whose remuneration must reflect differentials of skill and experience. With the food service and drinking places industry employing the largest number of workers paid the minimum wage, it is easy to see how their investments in successful lobbying against minimum wage increases have paid huge dividends.

The losers in this situation are as obvious as the winners: the millions of workers who have been and continue to be underpaid for their labor.[16] As noted earlier, two-thirds of minimum-wage workers are women, and half are under twenty-five years of age. By denying these entry-level workers an equitable income, we contribute to the growing number of people living in poverty and help raise the level of public support required by the needy.

HEALTH CARE

Profiles of the Health Insurance and Pharmaceutical Industries

The health insurance and pharmaceutical industries have been most closely tied to efforts to maintain or increase the privatization of America's healthcare system and protect the high prices of prescription drugs.

The insurance industry provides customers with protection from financial losses that result from a variety of risks. For example, health insurance policies cover the cost of medical expenses that result from accidents and illnesses. The industry is composed of insurance carriers and agencies. In general, carriers are large companies that offer insurance and assume the risk covered by the policy. Agencies and brokerages sell insurance policies for the carriers. While some agencies only sell policies for an affiliated carrier, others are independent and offer policies from a variety of carriers.

Insurance carriers set premiums based on the amount to be awarded and the likelihood that benefits will have to be paid. The insurance companies invest the premiums paid by customers in portfolios of financial assets and income-producing real estate as a means of paying future claims. Insurance applications are evaluated to determine the risk involved, the premium required, and whether the application should be accepted. Health insurance policies are usually issued to employers as group plans for the benefit of their workers.

Carriers have boosted productivity through expanded use of the Internet and new computer software. For example, some carriers have web sites that enable customers to access online account and billing information, and underwriting software automatically analyzes and rates insurance applications. Most insurance carriers employ 250 or more workers and are located near large urban areas.[17]

The pharmaceutical and medical manufacturing industry produces thousands of medications and equipment for diagnostic, preventive, and therapeutic uses. However, drug production usually represents one of the later stages of a long chain of research, development, and testing required before a new medicine may be presented to the U.S. Food and Drug Administration for approval. Once cleared for sale, the product must be manufactured, packaged, marketed, and distributed. Hundreds of millions of dollars and many years may be expended before it is known that a medicine may become available for sale. Efforts to improve productivity include automated production techniques.

Medications have been produced to treat infectious diseases such as pneumonia, tuberculosis, malaria, influenza, and sexually transmitted diseases. Compounds have been developed to help prevent and treat cardiovascular disease, asthma, diabetes, hepatitis, cystic fibrosis, and cancer. Antibiotics and vaccines have effectively eliminated the occurrence of diphtheria, syphilis, and whooping cough. New biotechnology-derived drugs, soon to be released, hold real promise to fight cancer, infectious diseases, autoimmune diseases, neurological disorders, and HIV/AIDS and related conditions.

Vital Statistics and Trends

Direct health and medical insurance carriers employ about 429,300 workers, most in establishments of 250 or more.[18] Since 1998, the number of workers in this industry has increased by close to 50 percent.[19] Medical service and health insurance is the fastest growing component of the insurance industry. While the increasing cost of premiums have made such coverage unaffordable for many, population growth among older Americans and expanded government participation are expected to stimulate further expansion in the sale of health and long-term care insurance. Large firms include United Health Group, Inc., WellPoint, Inc., and Aetna, Inc.

As a measure of the industry's growth and prosperity, the value of direct premiums issued between 2002 and 2006 increased by more than 40 percent to exceed $200 billion.[20] In 2006, these funds were supplemented by another $100 billion, reflecting the industry's increased participation in government programs.[21] The private health insurer's role in Medicare (Advantage and prescription drugs), Medicaid (managed care), and the Federal Employees Health Benefits Program generated an increase in government program premiums of 46 percent over the three-year period from 2004 to 2006.[22]

"Diversification into public programs permits private industry to continue growing despite the erosion of employment-based coverage and, of equal importance, limits its exposure to pressure from any one purchaser."[23] The profitability of these companies has been weighed by a health insurance stock price index that rose by more than 500 percent between 1996 and 2006.[24]

The manufacture of pharmaceuticals and medicines involves employment of about 292,400 workers.[25] Since 1998, the number of workers in this industry increased by almost 25 percent. The majority of the industry's jobs are in establishments of more than 500 workers.[26] Most jobs are located in California, Illinois, Texas, Indiana, New Jersey, New York, North Carolina, and Pennsylvania.

The pharmaceutical and medicine manufacturing industry is one of the fastest growing in the nation. It is predicted that demand for over-the-counter and prescription drugs will remain strong for use in hospitals, laboratories, and homes. Especially brisk demand is expected for medicines to treat cancer, Alzheimer's disease, heart disease, as well as for new "lifestyle" drugs that treat symptoms of chronic non–life-threatening conditions that result from aging or genetic predisposition. The increasing population, the larger proportion of the nation's older population, and growth of public and private health insurance programs support the expanding need for established and new medications.

Competition from generic drug makers, expiration of brand-name drug patents, and growing concern over the cost of products offered, costly litigation, and heightened regulatory scrutiny all represent continuing challenges to the industry's prosperity.

From 2000 to 2004, total assets of the pharmaceutical and medicine manufacturing industry grew by 80 percent from $402 billion to $725 billion.[27]

For that same period (the latest available from the Internal Revenue Service), the industry's net worth was up by 68 percent to $237 billion, and net income increased to $42 billion, a gain of 23 percent.[28]

Sans Special Interests and Lobbyists

For the health insurance industry, lobbying for the privatization of health insurance in the United States and the participation of private companies in publicly funded programs is a matter of survival. As was noted earlier, the manner in which health care is provided in the United States is the exception. For the rest of the developed world, the provision of medical care is not a matter of insurance coverage but of government responsibility.

Ironically, if one delves into the writings of the political philosopher from whom our Founding Fathers arguably drew the most, John Locke, we see that even in 1690 he reasoned that "the function of a legitimate civil government is to preserve the rights of its citizens to life, liberty, *health* and property"[29] (emphasis added).

When one considers recent calls for universal health care, demands for more competition among insurers, and proposals for more government responsibility with single-payer administration, such stands could represent serious threats to private health insurance vendors. When the industry rails against the specter of Big Government, it may not be Big Government that it is considering but the Big Profits that the absence of government responsibility and administration has permitted.

Without lobbying on behalf of the pharmaceutical and medicine industry, one would have difficulty believing that group purchasing agreements and volume discounts for bulk purchases would not be routine practices. As noted earlier, unlike Medicare, the Veterans Administration and the Department of Defense have reduced drug costs by 40 percent through such means. Furthermore, as also noted earlier, it has been estimated that if a single-payer system were adopted in the United States, $109 billion could be saved annually through the bulk purchase of prescription drugs, perishable medical supplies, and durable medical equipment.

Winners and Losers

Given this information, it is easy to see that both the medical insurance industry and the pharmaceutical and medicine industry have benefited greatly from their lobbying efforts. One could logically argue that the health insurance industry owes its very existence and continued profitability to lobbyist promotion of privatization and participation in public programs. At the same time, lobbyist efforts to maintain high prices for prescription drugs have significantly boosted profits for drug companies.

The losers are also easy to identify. They are the 47 million Americans with no healthcare coverage, the millions who cannot afford proper medical care and medications, and the millions more, including employers, who sacrifice to purchase overpriced health care.

INNER-CITY CRIME

Profiles of the Prison and Firearms Industries

Private sector elements of the American prison system have been instrumental in lobbying against reforms that might depopulate prisons through sentencing and rehabilitation initiatives. Lobbying on behalf of policies that expand the nation's prison systems has been assisted by the efforts of prison guard unions, companies that build prisons, companies and government entities that utilize prison labor, and surveillance technology vendors.

The objective of prisons and other correctional facilities is to protect society by confining offenders in controlled environments that are safe, humane, cost-effective, and secure. A secondary objective is to provide work and self-improvement opportunities to assist offenders in becoming law-abiding citizens.

Although prisons can be perilous places in which to work, prison populations tend to be more stable than jail populations. Within prisons, correctional officers generally know the security and custodial requirements of the prisoners with whom they are dealing. Prison facilities may include towers, gates, housing units, recreation areas, and mail rooms.

Correctional officers enforce rules and regulations to maintain order in these institutions. Efforts are routinely made to ensure proper behavior by monitoring and supervising work assignments, searching for weapons and drugs, settling disputes, and checking cells and other areas for fire hazards or tampering with locks and window bars. Officers report security breaches, disturbances, violations of rules, and suspicious occurrences. They work to prevent escapes, assaults, and contraband trafficking.

In jails and prisons with direct supervision of cellblocks, officers work unarmed; communication devices allow them to call for help when required. Such cellblocks are designed so that one or two corrections officers are able to manage fifty to one hundred inmates. In high-security prisons, which house the most dangerous inmates, facilities include centralized control centers with closed circuit television cameras and computer tracking systems that allow officers to monitor inmates in relative safety. In these environments, prisoners may see only officers for days or weeks at a time and may leave their cells only for showers, solitary exercise time, or visitors.

Small arms manufacturing covers the production of small firearms that are carried and fired by the individual. Included in this industry is the production of pistols, revolvers, rifles, and shotguns. Some firms in this industry also manufacture ammunition. The small arms manufacturing industry and the National Rifle Association have been instrumental in lobbying against gun control.

The production of small arms is part of fabricated metal product manufacturing. This work involves assemblers and fabricators putting together finished and semifinished parts, assembling gun components, and then joining them together. Materials are cut, aligned, and joined according to detailed specifications prior to welding. While steel is the most common material utilized, some high-performance plastics may also be used. Power-metallurgy techniques, such as injection molding, large presses and dies to stamp heavy sheet metal parts, and various machine tools facilitate the production process. The top firms in the industry include Remington Arms Company, Inc.; Sturm, Ruger & Co. Inc.; Smith & Wesson Corp.; The Marlin Firearms Company; and O.F. Mossberg & Sons, Inc.

Vital Statistics and Trends

Prisons and jails employ more than 418,000 correctional officers.[30] Since 1999, their employment has increased by close to 37,000 workers.[31]

Most correctional officers (61 percent) work for state government; 36 percent are employed by local governments; and about 4 percent work in federal correctional facilities.[32] The highest concentration of these workers is in Louisiana, Mississippi, Texas, New Mexico, and New York.

As of 2007, there were 114 federal prisons with a total population of 187,067 prisoners; 1,322 state prisons with 1.3 million inmates; 276 private prisons with over 100,000 inmates, and 3,751 local jails with over 600,000 prisoners at any given time.[33]

Over the past decade, the number of federal prisons increased by 30 percent, while the number of prisoners held in these facilities rose by 71 percent. In June 1997, there were no federal prisons that were privately managed. Ten years later, twelve prisons were under private supervision.[34]

Between 1997 and 2007, the number of state prisons increased by 62 percent, while the number of prisoners in those facilities rose by 33 percent. The number of privatized state facilities increased from 157 in 2002 to 264 in 2007, a gain of over 68 percent over five years. During the 1997–2007 period, the number of local jails and their occupancy both doubled.[35]

The current annual correctional system price tag of more than $60 billion will only increase as prisoner growth continues.[36]

Domestic small firearms manufacturers, many of which are foreign-owned, produce more than 3 million guns per year.[37] Of that total, 43 percent are rifles; shotguns and pistols each account for about 24 percent; and revolvers account for 9 percent.[38] Another 2 million firearms are imported into the United States each year.[39] Annual U.S. production reflects fairly steady reductions, while the import of foreign-made firearms is on the rise. For example, if one compares current year data with that of ten years ago, domestic firearms production is down by 27 percent, but imports are up by 69 percent.

The profitability of firearms manufacturing has been affected by rising materials and energy costs, increased foreign competition, and gains in employee fringe-benefit expenses. Increased costs of litigation, regulatory compliance, and public cries for stricter gun controls also threaten the industry. On the other hand, employment in recent years (about 11,000 workers) has increased somewhat, and the value added has gained significantly.[40]

Sans Special Interests and Lobbyists

Without the lobbying efforts of the prison-industrial complex, one could assume that tough sentencing reforms, greater efforts at prisoner rehabilitation, new approaches to drug addiction and rehabilitation, and even the provision of greatly improved education to inner-city residents would have a better chance of being established.

In the absence of gun lobby activity, there would be an improved prognosis for proposals to cut the rampant supply of firearms, better control of guns already in circulation, and implementation of suggested requirements to increase firearm safety and security features.

Winners and Losers

The increased funding required to maintain and support growth in our prison system will certainly advance the resources of those who benefit from our vast obsession with incarceration. Although it is difficult to express the financial gains in terms of profit and loss, prison lobbying continues to enrich those who build, supply, and operate America's prisons and jails.

For example, Corrections Corporation of America, the largest private prison company in the United States, had revenues of $1.33 billion in fiscal year 2006.[41] The GEO Group (formerly Wackenhut Corrections), the second largest private prison company, had sales of $1 billion over the past twelve months.[42] Both of these firms have been major funders of the American Legislative Exchange Council, a conservative public-policy organization that boasts the membership of more than 40 percent of state legislators.[43] This organization spent an average of $2.76 million on annual lobbying between 2004 and 2006.[44] In addition to the revenue gains of prison corporations and those who staff prisons, rural prison locations also reap significant benefits as their political representation and funding increase as prisoners are counted as a component of their population in U.S. Census counts.

According to the award-winning journalist Eric Schlosser,

> The prison-industrial complex is not only a set of interest groups and institutions. It is also a state of mind. The lure of big money is corrupting the nation's criminal-justice system, replacing notions of public service with a drive for higher profits. The eagerness of elected officials to pass tough-on-crime legislation—combined with their unwillingness to disclose the true costs of these laws—has encouraged all sorts of financial improprieties.[45]

The losers in this morass are the millions who will unnecessarily surrender their freedom by being placed behind bars and suffer interminable lives of crime and poverty. Because imprisonment has been demonstrated to be a revolving door to further criminal activity and incarceration, the nation as a whole loses as its resources continue to be invested in short-term measures that fail to address the fundamental issues responsible for many who turn to crime.

Also, by shifting the prison population from inner-city locations to rural areas, the political representation and funding represented by the prison population is shifted away from inner-city locations. Finally, the stature of our nation, having by far the largest number of prisoners, once again suffers in the eyes of the rest of the world.

In terms of the small firearms industry, it appears that the strong lobbying on behalf of firearm manufacturers and sportsmen has been required to head off even deeper reductions in domestic production. Without such lobbying, increased gun controls and suggested safety measures would surely increase production costs and gun prices, thereby reducing demand and cutting domestic production further.

When one considers the many years in which millions of guns have been produced and imported into America, it is easy to visualize the huge supply of weapons that may be abused. Without action to reduce the inventory of weapons and to increase regulations and safety measures, one would expect the nation's sad record of gun violence to continue.

CHAPTER 15

POLICY VERSUS NATIONAL INTEREST

Contrasting U.S. Policy and the Nation's Interest as Expressed in Public Opinion Surveys

INTRODUCTION

In Chapter 14, we saw how lobbyists representing special interests have promoted and protected their clients' bottom lines. This has been achieved through policies that have been established regarding global warming, minimum wage, universal health care, and inner-city crime. For some of these industries, such as oil and gas extraction, profits have grown incredibly.

On the basis that U.S. policy should promote the greater good of the nation, for each of the policy areas explored in the case studies in Part 3, it appears as though America has gone off track. But what of the will of the people? If American citizens overwhelmingly agree with the courses dictated by our political players, perhaps we should go no further. After all, to be truly representative, our democracy should reflect the sentiments of the population.

To test the popularity of the policies in question, we turn to the results of surveys conducted by respected national polling organizations. By studying their findings, we should be able to validate or dismiss the positions obtained by lobbyists for their special interest clients.

GLOBAL WARMING

During the period April 20–24, 2007, a nationwide CBS–*New York Times* poll was taken of a random sample of 1,052 adults. The results of these telephone interviews may contain a sampling error of plus or minus 3 percentage points. The objective was to weigh Americans' views on global warming and the environment. Here are selected survey findings:

- A very large majority—85 percent—believed that global warming is now having an impact (49 percent) or will have an impact (36 percent).

- A majority—52 percent—considered global warming as a serious problem that should be one of the highest priorities for government action.

- A very large majority—78 percent—is convinced that steps need to be taken right away to counter the impact of global warming.

- Only 33 percent approved of President Bush's handling of the environment; only 27 percent approved of his handling of the energy situation.

- A majority—57 percent—believed that the environment that greets the next generation will be less favorable than today's environment.

- A large majority—82 percent—believed that the federal government can take action to curb global warming.

- A large majority—79 percent—believed that average citizens can take steps to reduce global warming.

- A majority—62 percent—preferred the government to focus on developing new (clean) sources of energy versus protecting the environment.

- A significant majority—68 percent—believed that government should encourage the conservation of petroleum, coal, and natural gas versus increasing the production of those energy sources.

- A very large majority—92 percent—favored requirements to have car manufacturers make their products more energy-efficient.

- While just 38 percent favored increased taxes on gasoline, 64 percent said that they would favor such tax increases if the extra revenues were used for research into renewable sources of energy like solar or wind.

- A large majority of respondents—87 percent—viewed solar and wind energy favorably.

- Less than half of the respondents viewed energy from coal—43 percent—or from nuclear plants—36 percent—with favor.

- A large majority—85 percent—would *not* be less likely to vote for a candidate who expects citizens to sacrifice to help improve the environment; 48 percent said it would make no difference; 33 percent said they'd be more likely to vote for such a candidate.

- A majority—63 percent—agreed that protecting the environment is so important that requirements and standards can not be too high, and continuing environmental improvements must be made regardless of costs.

On the basis of these findings, one may conclude that the American public, in general, understands the seriousness of the threat of global warming and is ready to make sacrifices to reduce its impact. Clearly, such comprehension and willingness to take remedial and preventive action is contrary to long-standing U.S. policy. Furthermore, this is confirmed by the low grades given the Bush Administration concerning its handling of the environment and energy matters.

MINIMUM WAGE

During the period of March 8–12, 2006, telephone interviews of 1,405 adults, eighteen years of age or older, were conducted by the Princeton Survey Research Associates International on behalf of the Pew Research Center for the People and the Press. For results based on the total sample, one can say with 95 percent confidence that the sampling error is plus or minus 3 percentage points. The purpose of the survey was to gauge the American public's support for a substantial increase to the minimum wage. It is assumed that favoring a large increase in the minimum wage is a proxy for supporting a minimum wage that keeps pace with increases in the cost of living. Here are selected survey findings and relevant related information:

- An overwhelming margin—83 percent—favored raising the federal minimum wage from $5.15 to $7.15.

- Almost half of those surveyed—49 percent—strongly favored the $2.00 increase.

- Over the ten-year period from 1997 to 2006 in which no federal minimum wage increase was implemented, twenty states passed legislation raising their minimum wages above the federal rate.

- For those states in which their minimum wage did not exceed the federal rate, 82 percent favored the $2.00 increase.
- For those states in which the state minimum equaled or exceeded $7.15, 88 percent supported the $2.00 increase.
- Support for the increase was expressed by Democrats (91 percent), Independents (87 percent), and Republicans (72 percent).
- For people with annual household incomes below $20,000, 91 percent favored the increase; with annual incomes of $20,000 to $50,000, 85 percent supported the increase; with annual incomes from $50,000 to $75,000, 86 percent expressed support; and $75,000 and over, 76 percent also were in agreement.
- There was little difference in the degree of support on the basis of age, geography, or racial or ethnic lines.
- The strength of support for updating the minimum wage expressed in the 2006 survey is very similar to favorable expressions provided for surveys conducted for the periods of January 5 to 9, 2005, and February 9 to 12, 1995, carried out by the Princeton Survey Research Associates International for the Pew Research Center.

One can only conclude that there continues to be very strong support for updating the minimum wage to reflect increases in living costs. This favorable opinion has been expressed across all meaningful demographics despite established U.S. policy.

STEM CELL RESEARCH

The Gallup Poll conducted several surveys concerning embryonic stem cell research between the years 2001 to 2007. For the most part, these telephone surveys queried from 1,000 to 1,500 adults. It is estimated that findings may reflect a sampling error of plus or minus 3 percent. The purpose of the surveys was to assess the attitude of the American public with regard to this promising but controversial field of study. Here are the principle findings:

- A clear majority—61 percent—believed that medical research using stem cells obtained from human embryos is morally acceptable; only 30 percent believed it is morally wrong.
- Asked whether an embryo should be considered as all other human lives or as a potential life that cannot develop on its own, 60 percent agreed with the latter statement; 36 percent felt that it should be treated in the manner as all other life.

- A smaller majority—56 percent—believed that the federal government should fund research that would use newly created stem cells obtained from human embryos; 40 percent disagreed.

- A majority—60 percent—believed that current federal funding restrictions should be eased (38 percent) or eliminated (22 percent); only 20 percent agreed with the current restrictions and 16 percent opposed any federal funding.

- When asked if they would agree with a presidential veto of any expansion of federal stem cell funding, 64 percent said the President should *not* veto the legislation and 31 percent agreed with the veto threat.[1]

- Respondents were more inclined to approve of federal funding of the use of surplus embryos that have been created in fertility clinics than the use of embryos created specifically for stem cell research; a majority—55 percent—favored the former with 40 percent opposing, while almost half—49 percent—opposed the latter, with 46 percent approving.

- A large majority—66 percent—did *not* approve of federal funding for the production of stem cells from embryos that have been created by cloning cells from a living human being.

- Another large majority—68 percent—approved of federal sponsorship of research that uses stem cells that are obtained from adults, resulting in no injury to the individual from whom the cells have been obtained.

- A very large majority—82 percent—believed that it is very important for medical researchers to find cures for diseases such as Alzheimer's, diabetes, heart disease, and spinal cord injury.

- Only 30 percent felt it very important to prevent human embryos from being used in medical research.

- While most—67 percent—said they would in theory support the use of embryonic stem cells to help cure themselves or a family member, only 33 percent personally knew someone who might benefit from such treatments.

- The higher the level of education, the more supportive respondents were of embryonic stem cell research: postgraduate degrees—72 percent; less advanced college background—60 percent; and no more than a high school degree—45 percent.

- In terms of political affiliation, support is highest among Democrats (67 percent) and liberals (73) percent, then Independents (60 percent) and moderates (64 percent), and then Republicans (42 percent) and conservatives (42 percent). Majority opposition is expressed by Republicans (54 percent) and conservatives (54 percent).

Overall, it may be concluded that a majority of Americans believe that embryonic stem cell research is moral and approve of federal funding to advance the field. For the most part, the opinions expressed oppose the special interest positions that have been adopted as U.S. policy.

UNIVERSAL HEALTH CARE

A CBS–*New York Times* Poll was conducted during the period of February 23 to 27, 2007. A nationwide random sample of 1,281 adults was surveyed, yielding an estimated sampling error of plus or minus 3 percent. The purpose of the survey was to determine what Americans think about the U.S. healthcare system. Here are the major selected findings:

- Of those surveyed, 90 percent believed that the U.S. healthcare system needs either fundamental change (54 percent) or needs to be completely rebuilt (36 percent).
- When asked whether the federal government should be responsible for guaranteeing that all Americans have health insurance, 64 percent answered "yes" and 27 percent responded "no."
- When asked if it was fair or unfair to require all Americans to participate in a national healthcare plan funded by taxpayers, 48 percent felt it was unfair, and 43 percent felt it was fair.
- When asked whether government would do a better or a worse job than private companies in providing coverage, 44 percent felt that government would do a worse job; 30 percent, a better job; and 23 percent didn't know.
- On the other hand, 47 percent believed that government would do a better job lowering costs than private companies; 37 percent, a worse job; and 14 percent didn't know.
- At the same time, 47 percent believed that we would be better off with a government-run system that provided universal coverage; 38 percent preferred the current private system with many uninsured.
- When asked whether employers should be required to either provide health insurance to their employees or pay into a general fund for the uninsured, 46 percent weren't sure, 36 percent thought it to be a good idea, and 17 percent considered it a bad idea.
- A large majority—70 percent—characterized the problem of uninsured Americans as "very serious."

- When those surveyed were asked to choose between providing health care for all and keeping the costs of health care down, 65 percent selected the first option.

- When those surveyed were asked to choose between providing health care for all and maintaining the tax cuts enacted in recent years, a clear majority—76 percent—chose the first option.

- When those surveyed were asked if they would be willing to pay higher taxes so that all Americans could have health insurance that they couldn't lose, 60 percent answered "yes" and 34 percent "no."

- A very large majority—82 percent—said they would be willing to pay $500 a year in increased taxes to finance universal health care.

- When asked whether they would worry that providing health care for all might impact the quality of their own health care, 55 percent said they would *not* worry, but 40 percent said that they would.

- A very large majority—94 percent—felt that having many American children without health insurance was a serious problem; the problem was characterized as "very serious" by 78 percent.

- A very large majority—84 percent—favored expanding government programs to provide health insurance to all children without such coverage.

- When asked if an employer of a household member had cut back on healthcare benefits or increased employee costs in recent years, 49 percent had experienced this, while 46 percent had not.

- A very large majority—77 percent—believed that Americans should be able to purchase less expensive prescription drugs from Canada.

- In terms of the quality of health care, 57 percent were not satisfied with the quality of health care in the country on the whole, but 77 percent were satisfied with the quality of health care that they were receiving personally.

- In terms of the cost of health care, 81 percent were not satisfied with the cost of health care in the country on the whole, and 52 percent were not satisfied with the cost of health care that they were paying personally.

- A large majority—89 percent—were either very (52 percent) or somewhat (37 percent) concerned about future costs of health care.

- Of those insured, 59 percent were not concerned that they may lose their insurance in the next five years; 38 percent were concerned.

- According to the survey results, 11 percent of Americans were without health insurance; of those survey respondents without insurance, the most common explanations included unable to afford (52 percent), don't have a job (14 percent), and work part-time (8 percent).

- Among those *without* healthcare insurance, 79 percent were concerned about the possibility of major healthcare bills in the next few years; 61 percent have gone without medical treatment in the past twelve months because of the cost involved.

- Among those with health insurance, 64 percent were concerned about not having the funds to pay current healthcare costs, and 81 percent were concerned with healthcare costs as they age.

- Only 24 percent approved of the way President Bush has handled health care; 60 percent disapproved.

- Regarding President Bush's handling of health care, only 17 percent were confident in his abilities, and 77 percent were uneasy.

- There was a strong belief that the Democrats (62 percent) would do a better job than the Republicans (19 percent) in improving the healthcare system.

- Among the three leading Democratic candidates at the time of the survey, confidence in Clinton was expressed by 36 percent, 25 percent expressed confidence in Obama, and 22 percent expressed confidence in Edwards.

- Respondents believed that the healthcare issues most deserving of presidential candidate discussion are coverage for the uninsured (34 percent), reducing healthcare costs (28 percent), improving healthcare quality (18 percent), and improving the Medicare drug benefit (18 percent).

In summary, it is clear that Americans as a whole believe that major changes are required in our healthcare system to cover the uninsured and lower healthcare costs. On the other hand, while there seemed to be a preference for universal, government-run health care, there is apprehension about how well that would work.

INNER-CITY CRIME

The selected survey findings presented here are from three polls that sought to measure public opinion regarding crime in general, prison sentencing, and gun laws. Questions regarding drug violations and sentencing are included in some of these surveys. Two of the surveys (on crime and on gun laws) were conducted by the Gallup Poll in 2006 and 2007.

The survey specifically concerning sentencing was conducted for the American Civil Liberties Union in 2001 by Belden, Russonello, and Stewart. The surveys queried 1,000 to 2,000 randomly selected respondents and may exhibit a sampling error of plus or minus 2 to 3 percent for questions asked of the entire universe. Here are the key findings:

- A large majority—68 percent—believed that there is more crime in the nation today than there was a year ago.
- A small majority—51 percent—believed that there was more crime in their area than there was a year ago.
- A very large majority—97 percent—believed that crime in the United States was a serious problem (moderately serious, 41 percent; very serious, 39 percent; and extremely serious, 17 percent).
- In terms of the area where the respondent lived, a majority—53 percent—felt that crime was not a serious problem (not too serious, 35 percent; and not at all, 18 percent).
- A large majority—65 percent—believed that more money and effort should go into addressing the social and economic problems that lead to crime instead of putting more money and effort into improving law enforcement with more prisons, police, and judges.
- With regard to *buying* illegal drugs, 40 percent believed that the punishment should be prison some of the time, but 16 percent felt that prison should never be the penalty.
- With regard to *using* illegal drugs, 43 percent believed that the punishment should be prison some of the time, but 15 percent felt that prison should never be the penalty.
- With regard to *possessing* small amounts of illegal drugs for personal use, 42 percent believed that the punishment should be prison some of the time, but 25 percent felt that prison should never be the penalty.
- On the other hand, a large majority—81 percent—felt that the *selling* of illegal drugs should always result in prison (63 percent) or should result in prison most of the time (18 percent).
- When asked what the main purpose was of sending a person to prison, respondents said to rehabilitate the offender (40 percent), to punish offenders (21 percent), to protect society (21 percent), and to deter others (12 percent).
- When asked how effective prisons are in the rehabilitation of inmates, the most frequent responses selected were poor (40 percent), fair (25 percent), and very poor (18 percent).

- A very large majority—88 percent—agreed that prisons should be required to teach inmates skills so they are less likely to commit crimes once they are released.
- When asked if they favored replacing prison sentences with mandatory drug treatment and probation for people convicted of non-violent illegal drug use, a large majority—74 percent—either strongly favored (42 percent) or somewhat favored (32 percent) such a proposal.
- A majority—55 percent—believed that African Americans are treated unfairly by the criminal justice system.
- When presented with the choice of doing away with parole for people who commit non-violent crimes and spending more tax money to keep them in prison longer versus allowing parole and spending more tax money on training and education programs to help make them productive citizens, a very large majority—87 percent—favored the latter.
- A solid majority—61 percent—opposed strongly (35 percent) or somewhat (26 percent) the idea of mandatory prison sentences for certain types of non-violent crime.
- A solid majority—61 percent—believed that mandatory minimum sentences are not fair because the circumstances of each crime are different.
- A large majority—70 percent—agreed that laws should be changed so that fewer non-violent crimes are punishable by prison terms (37 percent strongly agreed, and 33 percent agreed somewhat).
- The largest proportion of respondents—49 percent—felt that gun laws should be made stricter, and 35 percent believed that such laws should remain the same. On the other hand, 14 percent believed that these laws should be made less strict.
- A majority of respondents—56 percent—felt that the laws governing the *sale of firearms* should be made stricter; on the other hand, 33 percent felt they should be kept as they are now, and 9 percent felt they should be less strict.
- A substantial majority—66 percent—believed that there should *not* be a law to ban the possession of handguns except by the police and other authorized persons; on the other hand, 32 percent favored such a law.
- A small majority—53 percent—said they would like to see current gun laws enforced more strictly; 43 percent favored new laws as well.

- Of those surveyed, 54 percent said they do *not* have a gun in their house, and of that group, 43 percent believed that having a gun in the house makes it less safe; on the other hand, 43 percent said that they *did* have a gun in their house, and of that group, 47 percent believed that this makes a house safer.
- Of those who own guns, the most common reasons stated were for protection against crime, target shooting, and hunting.
- The largest percent of those questioned—44 percent—believed that only safety officials should be permitted to carry a concealed firearm in a public place, 27 percent felt that any private citizen should have this right, and 26 percent agreed to this only for those who have a clear need.

In summary, these survey results indicate that Americans believe that crime is a serious problem in the United States; that criminal sentences are too strict for those guilty of non-violent crimes, including drug use and addiction; that prisons must do a better job of educating, training, and rehabilitating inmates; that, where possible, mandatory sentences should give way to parole, education, and training; and that gun laws governing the sale of firearms need to be made stricter. Once again, these conclusions contradict the policies built by special interest money and their lobbyists.

SUMMARY AND CONCLUSIONS

If one returns to Part 2 and reviews the interview transcript of our European diplomat in Chapter 8, there are two sentences that stand out: "We believe that American society is very raw. In Europe, we have a welfare state that takes care of our citizens."

Although welfare states are not compatible with American tradition, after reviewing the information provided thus far it is difficult to dispute the characterization of American society as raw. When an outsider views America, he encounters our official disregard for global warming, our failure to maintain an adequate wage floor, our reluctance to fully fund embryonic stem cell research, 47 million people with no health insurance, the dehumanizing environment of the inner city, 2.3 million people in prison, lax gun laws, and long prison sentences for drug addiction. How could any other conclusion be reached?

However, the survey findings reported in this chapter contradict that opinion. It is not the society that is raw, but the special interests that have been able to establish policies with which the American public clearly disagrees. The drive of special interests and the public's inability to blunt their influence has turned us into a nation that is betraying the Founders' dream of serving the will of the people.

In Chapters 17 and 18, we will explore remedial action to counteract special interest power, to restore our democracy, and reverse those abhorrent policies that betray our true tradition as a caring and for-ward-looking people. Before we take that journey, we will seek to understand how and why the nation's political leaders have allowed our decline, using the U.S. tragedy in Iraq as a telling example. These are the topics of Chapter 16.

CHAPTER 16

DETERIORATING POLITICAL LEADERSHIP AND THE TRAGEDY OF IRAQ

How Policy Formulation Has Been Undermined by Special Interest Considerations

INTRODUCTION

At its core, the tragedy of Iraq has been a matter of leadership long eroded by the force of special interest priorities. According to the available record, this foreign policy misadventure was not a miscalculation reached after rigorous analysis in the name of the nation's defense. Instead, it appears to have been a slick maneuver to retaliate for the mortifying attack on September 11, 2001, and to take out a dictator who showed no respect for the United States and its leaders.

This chapter exposes the lack of effective political leadership that spurred our involvement in Iraq, the march of special interests in America that damaged the war effort, and the high price exacted by these unfortunate developments. Then we turn to the principles of effective political leadership that are required to avoid future Iraqs and keep our nation on the right path.

INVADE IRAQ: POLITICAL LEADERSHIP OR LOBBYIST PITCH?

The justification for American aggression in Iraq was sold to Congress and the public just as a skilled and seasoned lobbyist would peddle proposed legislation to win favor for an inequitable tax break or to obtain funding for a bridge to nowhere. Neoconservatives in the Pentagon assembled bits and pieces of information and pasted them together to form a justification that would appeal to the masses. We were a people still in shock over our unfamiliar sense of vulnerability. We required a renewed feeling of national pride and safety.

Therefore, we would invade Iraq to remove the threat of nuclear weapons and other weapons of mass destruction. We would break that country's potentially lethal connection with al Qaeda. With no mention of the long history of ethnic strife in Iraq, we were told that an American liberation force of 100,000 that would stay "as long as necessary but leave as soon as possible" would be welcomed and could secure the country.[1] We would establish a true democracy in a Middle East Arab state, a nation that would naturally become our ally. We would remove a despotic dictator who had used weapons of mass destruction on his own people. These were the one-liners used to justify our aggression.

While the final justification was undeniably true, each of the other points used as grounds for war was questionable even before the invasion of March 2003 and the discovery that there were in fact no weapons of mass destruction in Iraq. For example, regarding the number of troops needed for the proposed invasion, the Army Chief of Staff, a former commander of the peacekeeping mission in Bosnia, publicly warned that several hundred thousand troops would be required to secure postwar Iraq.[2] His words were dismissed, and he was eventually encouraged to retire.

Joseph C. Wilson, a former U.S. Ambassador to the African nations of Gabon, Sao Tome, and Principe and Deputy Chief of Mission in Iraq under President George H.W. Bush, traveled to Niger in late February 2002 at the CIA's request. He reported that rumored Iraqi purchases of enriched uranium yellowcake were "highly doubtful."[3] Despite this report, the very rumor he debunked appeared in the President's January 2003 State of the Union Address. When Wilson stated his frustration with the President's Address in a July 6, 2003, op-ed piece in the *New York Times*, the Ambassador's wife, a covert CIA agent for many years, was outed through press leaks from within the Administration.[4]

Although a National Intelligence Estimate report on Iraq, representing the consensus of the U.S. intelligence community, reportedly cautioned that the claim of a long-standing relationship between al Qaeda and the Iraqi government was in doubt, those warnings failed to make it into Administration speeches.[5] At the same time, although most Senators said that they were briefed on the National Intelligence Estimate report before the invasion, it is likely that fewer than ten Senators outside the Intelligence Committee read the full ninety-two-page intel-ligence account.[6]

Pentagon budget specialists estimated the first-year costs of the war at $60 billion to $95 billion. In response, Deputy Defense Secretary Paul Wolfowitz said the numbers were too high, although he was unable to provide his own opinion of the likely costs because of "all the variables involved."[7]

Just as Congress has bought into lobbyist arguments against the exis-tence of global warming, against the need to continually adjust the minimum wage, against expanded embryonic stem cell research, against universal health care, and against realistic criminal sentences, gun con-trol, and drug addiction treatment, Congress accepted the Administra-tion's propaganda against Iraq. It voted to allow the President to "use the armed forces of the United States as he determines necessary and appropriate in order to defend the national security of the United States against the continuing threat posed by Iraq." The vote in the House was on October 10, 2002, with 296 for and 133 opposed; the vote in the Senate was on October 11, 2002, with 77 for and 23 opposed.[8]

POST-INVASION POLICIES

The serious errors of judgment and strategy exhibited immediately after the invasion of Iraq reflected the same lack of appreciation for objectivity, expert analysis, and experience evident in the events leading up to the War.

Initially, Jay Garner, a retired general with thirty years experience in the U.S. Army and six years in private-sector technology firms, was appointed Director of the U.S. Office of Reconstruction and Humani-tarian Aid in Iraq. Garner had directed the Reagan Administration Star Wars program, worked on the Patriot missile-defense system, and was head of Sy Technology, a firm that supplied much of the technical sup-port for missile defense systems used in the military.[9]

Garner had been admired for the job he did while in charge of humanitarian relief in the Kurdish area in the northern region of Iraq after the first Gulf War.[10] He arrived in Baghdad on April 21, 2003, just twelve days after coalition forces secured the capital.[11] His plan was to quickly push the Iraqis towards an interim government, elections, and a constitution.[12] However, he was replaced by L. Paul Bremer, who was named Director less than a month later.

L. Paul Bremer was appointed Director of Reconstruction and Humanitarian Assistance for postwar Iraq on May 6, 2003.[13] Bremer was a retired career diplomat who had worked for Henry Kissinger and

Alexander Haig during his Foreign Service career, and upon retirement he became managing director of Kissinger's consulting firm, Kissinger Associates, Inc.

Directly before his appointment, Bremer was chairman and chief executive officer of Marsh Crisis Consulting, a risk and insurance services firm that is a subsidiary of Marsh & McLennan Companies, Inc.; he was a trustee on the Economic Club of New York and a board member of Air Products and Chemicals, Inc., Akzo Nobel NV, the Harvard Business School Club of New York, and The Netherlands–American Foundation. He also served on the International Advisory Boards of Komatsu Corporation and Chugai Pharmaceuticals.[14]

Bremer admittedly had little knowledge of Iraq and his coalition staff has been criticized as inexperienced.[15] At the same time, according to Bremer, the planning upon which his mission was to be conducted was based on the "wrong assumptions."[16] With fewer than 200,000 troops on the ground (in spite of a Rand Corporation report that estimated troop requirements at 450,000 to 500,000), the Coalition Provisional Authority proceeded to turn a victorious military invasion into a disastrous occupation.[17]

- There was a failure to prevent or halt widespread looting that occurred for an extended period after the invasion; experts on Iraq's history, culture, and people "generally expected the ongoing violence and tenacious guerrilla warfare that the occupation is encountering."[18]
- By disbanding the Iraqi Army in May 2003, 400,000 former Iraqi soldiers were put out of work.[19]
- In June 2003, expulsion of 30,000 to 50,000 Baath party members from their government posts and banning them from the new government, public schools, and colleges left them disenfranchised;[20] all Baath party supporters were dismissed without distinguishing between active, criminal, and merely formal or reluctant Baathists.[21]
- Inadequate control of $8.8 billion in reconstruction resources originating from the United Nation's oil-for-food program wasted funds that could have contributed to reconstruction efforts.[22]

These misjudgments opened the door to Iraq for al Qaeda, fanned the flames of insurgency, and weakened efforts to revive the Iraqi economy. In addition to the inept leadership that contributed to the decision to invade and the inability to form rational policies directly after the invasion, one cannot ignore the economic visions of bounty that likely filled the dreams of Administration leaders used to favoring special interest needs. After all, Iraq is estimated to have about 10 percent of the world's supply of proved petroleum reserves.[23]

The Iraqi infrastructure, including its oil extraction industry and refineries, was decimated by the American attack, the eight-year war with Iran, the Persian Gulf War, an oil embargo, and other international sanctions. Had peace been restored, the award of innumerable private sector contracts to rebuild the nation's economic base could have greatly enriched numerous U.S. and other global corporations with little risk.[24]

"I would expect that even countries like France will have a strong interest in assisting Iraq in reconstruction," commented Deputy Defense Secretary Wolfowitz in February of 2003.[25] However, later that year, Wolfowitz issued a memorandum opening competition for $18.6 billion in reconstruction contracts, limiting bidders to those firms from nations that were Coalition partners and other countries that contributed to the war effort.[26]

Even with the insurgency and violence that have plagued post-invasion Iraq, the U.S. government has managed to award more than $30 billion in private-sector contracts.[27] Amounts awarded annually for private security and law enforcement contractors alone have increased to almost $4 billion.[28] Most contracts are extremely large, cover many unrelated tasks, and typically have been awarded to very substantial, politically active firms.

In fact, so many contracts have been awarded in Iraq that control of contract funds and contractor oversight has been jeopardized. This was reflected in the forced resignation of the State Department's security chief when an internal report concluded that his office failed to adequately supervise private contractors protecting U.S. diplomats in Iraq.[29]

THE PRICE PAID FOR DEFECTIVE LEADERSHIP

As of September 30, 2007, the Congressional Budget Office estimated the cost of the Iraq War to be $483.2 billion.[30] Thus, total dollar costs (Department of Defense expenditures plus contracts) have exceeded $513 billion and have therefore averaged $114 billion per year since the March 2003 invasion. That is 1.7 times the entire 2007 budget planned for the U.S. Department of Education; more than five times the Department of Energy's total budget; more than four times the budget for the National Institute of Health; and more than 2.5 times the budget of the Department of Homeland Security.[31] According to Nobel Prize-winning economist Joseph Stiglitz and Goldman-Sachs Vice-Chairman Robert Hormats, the overall costs of the war are likely to reach 2 trillion dollars, more than enough to put Medicare and Social Security on a sound footing.[32]

Of course, the tragically excessive price of the Iraq War must be expressed in more than dollars. As of March 2008, 3,981 American troops had lost their lives and 29,395 had been wounded, many suffering the loss of limbs and debilitating head injuries.[33] Official estimates of Iraqi security force and civilian casualties from the war exceed 38,000; and another 1,001 contractors and 307 non-U.S. coalition troops have also been killed. A recent study of the World Health Organization estimates that 151,000 Iraqis lost their lives from violence from March 2003 through June 2006.[34]

In addition to those losses, many families' lives have been seriously disrupted, including more than 1.5 million Iraqi refugees who have fled to Jordan, Syria, and elsewhere. Also, there has been ethnic and religious hostility aggravated by the conflict and irreparable damage to Iraqi cities, homes, businesses, and religious buildings.[35]

PRINCIPLES OF EFFECTIVE POLITICAL LEADERSHIP

The disastrous consequences of the Iraqi invasion and occupation exemplify how wrong-headed political leadership can affect the welfare of a nation, its people, and the people of other nations. Similarly, we have seen the damage done as special interests dominate other key U.S. policy issues.

In the concluding chapters we will discuss specific deficiencies in the execution of our democracy and how systematic changes might be initiated to rectify these shortcomings. However, without effective political leadership, the transformation suggested will not take hold.

Therefore, the following leadership principles—characteristics and skills—are advanced as suggested voter criteria for use in evaluating those vying for elective office. The principles have been derived from a search and review of prominent works on political leadership as well as from the author's own leadership perspectives. While most of the volumes reviewed approach leadership as instruction for those who aspire to leadership positions, this presentation focuses on how citizens might weigh the leadership ability and qualifications of candidates for elective office.

Political Leadership Principle No. 1

Exhibits honesty, virtue, and integrity in the manner in which the leader conducts personal and professional matters. Those who cannot follow accepted rules of behavior are not likely to be able to effectively lead the nation to develop enlightened policies. The day is gone when politicians can cover up indiscretions and lead invisible personal lives. Today, few indiscretions escape the press and the public. Scandals distract those involved from issues that may otherwise require a leader's full attention. Furthermore, leaders must be able to honestly assess people, problems, and issues, and present their ideas without hidden agendas that could erode public confidence.

Political Leadership Principle No. 2

True to American values of fair play, the rule of law, and the Constitution, possesses wisdom to discern and virtue to pursue the common good of society. Focus should be on promoting the greater good, not serving special interests to the detriment of the nation. From time to time, America faces enemies who exhibit an absence of moral discretion. During such times, the test of effective leadership is to trust in our laws and traditional beliefs and to maintain principled conduct. Ethical behavior encompasses compassion and sensitivity to citizen needs, regardless of the political strength of those requiring attention. America's ethical character is our strongest resource and most potent international asset.

Political Leadership Principle No. 3

Enthusiastic learner, capable of understanding complex issues and situations. Whether the problem is scientific, such as global warming, international, such as evolving Russian politics, or falls in another category of issues relevant to the nation's well-being, the leader must be able to absorb the subject matter, ask the right questions, and understand enough to make proper decisions. The leader should involve those with unquestioned expertise, encourage debate, listen to all sides, be open to suggestions, and base decisions on the nation's interest in light of the relevant facts and the judgment of those with suitable knowledge and experience.

Political Leadership Principle No. 4

Able to visualize innovative and realistic solutions to national and international problems, to identify noble deeds worth pursuing, and to define courses of action for overall betterment; demonstrates an impressive record of accomplishment on which future action may draw. The leader should have a clear sense of the people's needs and how they may be met. Noble objectives, beyond the imagination of most, might serve to inspire a sense of patriotism and national pride and to transform followers to a higher level of citizenship. All reasonable alternatives and likely consequences must be weighed before decisions are made, proposals advanced, and action taken.

Political Leadership Principle No. 5

Polished at conveying the sense of complex problems and issues in a clear and concise manner; able to inspire sacrifice and support for proposed courses of action. A leader should possess a personal magnetism that naturally attracts supporters. In an age of numerous and readily available forms of electronic media, the leader should take full advantage of opportunities to communicate problems, issues, and proposed solutions and keep citizens aware of status and progress made. Effective leadership also requires free and open communication with those working to support individual initiatives.

Political Leadership Principle No. 6

Adheres to a formal planning process that encompasses researching and forecasting contingencies, setting goals, establishing timelines, avoiding errors, and maximizing positive impact. Such a process facilitates the development of a step-by-step strategy for any endeavor. It draws a roadmap of activity to be followed and facilitates the identification of benchmarks that may be measured in order to evaluate progress.

Political Leadership Principle No. 7

Assemble the best and the brightest in teams to assess national needs, set courses for the future, and guide plan implementation. Must be able to effectively utilize all available and suitable resources. Although running "against Washington" has been an effective ploy for some politicians to get elected, it is illogical to be against the very resources you hope to inherit and must work with if elected. Enlisting the political parties, Congress, and the federal workforce as teams to be involved in carrying out objectives is a more rational course.

Political Leadership Principle No. 8

Recognizes that most problems will be difficult to solve and will require significant investments in both time and resources. In the short run, it's easy to accept the status quo and difficult to overcome the inertia that meets most plans for change. In the face of opposition, an effective leader must find ways to continue striving to reach goals that have been set, avoid deadlocks, and reconcile differences. Skill in negotiating compromises that don't sacrifice primary goals facilitates progress.

Political Leadership Principle No. 9

Determines levels of progress for initiatives through a formal evaluation process. A leader must recognize that success may only be confirmed through objective and transparent evaluations that base conclusions on data collection and analysis. A leader should utilize evaluation findings to inform teams of levels of accomplishment and to make midcourse corrections in strategy. A leader must keep the public informed of problems encountered and headway made, as well as celebrate major successes with responsible teams and beneficiaries.

Political Leadership Principle No. 10

Recognizes that as long as tasks require human input, mistakes will be made; doesn't hide errors but uses them to increase knowledge and adjust courses of action. A leader takes responsibility for missteps made, makes adjustments, avoids similar miscues in the future, and moves on. A leader avoids the blame game, only replacing subordinates when absolutely necessary.

SUMMARY AND CONCLUSIONS

We live in a dangerous world in which missteps can result in untold death and destruction. At the same time, well-reasoned, intelligently executed policies can greatly enrich and extend life. Trusting our leadership to thirty-second sound bites has not served us well. Perhaps it is time for Americans to demand better, to expand the universe of qualified candidates, to carefully scrutinize those who seek elective office, to assess candidate platforms relative to the nation's needs, and to guard against the influence of special interests.

PART 5

A PLAN TO REVIVE AMERICA'S FAILED DEMOCRACY

Through their knowledge of political philosophy and understanding of human nature, our Founding Fathers cleared a path for our democracy by declaring the equality of men and their unalienable rights to life, liberty, and the pursuit of happiness. They embodied the bravery, daring, and sacrifice necessary to win independence from the world's most powerful monarchy. To preserve their vision they constructed a constitution that applied their concepts of freedom to a vast land and its millions of inhabitants.

While the principles that guided the Founding Fathers endure, the environment within which their thought must be applied changes over time. After all, the Founders lived in a period of family farms, limited communications, and very modest requirements for campaign funds. While they were aware of the dangers represented by factions or special interests, they could not have conceived of the speed with which vast resources are marshaled to shape American policies to the detriment of the greater good.

By studying modern techniques of special interest lobbying, exploring the perspectives of today's political players, and documenting case studies that bear the corrosive mark of special interest dominance, we have seen how the power of factions has distorted our democratic process. Furthermore, we have confirmed that key policies won by special interests disregard the will of the American people. We have gauged the bottom-line benefits that special interest activists have accrued and reckoned the losses suffered by the nation and its people. Finally, we have seen how special interest dealings have weakened political leadership, wasted significant national resources, taken thousands of lives unnecessarily, and damaged our standing in the world.

Finding fault with the conduct of the nation without learning from our analysis is of little value. Therefore, this chapter identifies the root causes that have moved the country away from its democratic course. The final chapter presents the means to return America to its democracy.

CHAPTER 17

WHY AMERICA'S DEMOCRACY IS FAILING

How Special Interests, Their Lobbyists, and Campaign Financing Have Subverted Our Democracy

INTRODUCTION

As with most significant problems, the failure of our democracy is not caused by one single phenomenon. Instead, its origin is the product of an array of related developments that together empower special interests and weaken the will of the people. This chapter will describe each root cause of the American democracy's decline in the name of special interests and their lobbyists.

THE NATURE OF OUR ELECTED REPRESENTATIVES

Our democracy depends on the selection of the right kind of elected representatives. They are to be individuals of virtue and wisdom who will pursue the common good of society and seek to identify and perform noble deeds. While certain protections against inadequate representatives are in place, such as frequent elections, the proper functioning of our democracy assumes that the great majority of elected officials will be just and virtuous and will put the welfare of the people above the needs of narrow special interests.

We are all human beings and therefore are flawed. We are all capable of making mistakes. However, if one were to examine the individuals who rise to the office of President of the United States, one would hope that for the most part they should reflect the values prescribed by the Founding Fathers.

If we look to those who have held that office since 1970, we find a very different picture. For example, there is a president who was forced to resign over a cover-up of foolish political dirty tricks; one who was impeached over charges of perjury and obstruction of justice over extramarital activities; and a president who was elected twice despite having few achievements before his presidency, being the instigator of a costly and unnecessary war while in office, and consistently supporting special interests over the well-being of the people. Furthermore, a survey of presidential credits from 1970 to 2007 yields few substantive accomplishments or noble deeds that might have raised the level of our nation.

The poor quality of presidential candidates appears to be derived from two related forces. First, those who seek the office tend to be politicians who have accepted this era of special interest accommodation to obtain required campaign financing. Rather than basing positions on principle, proposing ultimate solutions, and compromising down the road if required, candidates discount positions and proposals up front, fearing that they might upset potential campaign contributors. The very candidates who might provide a more principled alternative turn away from a game that requires concessions before the competition begins.

Second, despite the length of recent presidential campaigns, the plethora of news coverage, and on-air debates, candidates are rarely scrutinized in a meaningful way. Before one buys an automobile, you can pick up *Consumer Reports* and review objective ratings both overall and for a number of meaningful criteria. When it comes to presidential candidates, too often we only see what managers and public relations experts want us to see. What has this individual accomplished in the past? What kind of judgment has the individual displayed? Is this an honest person? Is this candidate beholden to special interests? Certainly, you will not get an honest assessment from either political party or from television messages ("You really can sell ice to Eskimos"; see Chapter 4).

The Founding Fathers believed that the first responsibility of an enlightened citizenry is to be virtuous enough and wise enough to select the right kind of representatives. Today, the technology of television combined with the skill of political promoters have created an asymmetry of information that can confound well-intentioned voters. Whether it's the image building of smooth promotional pieces or the tear-down attack of a Swift Boat message, without an objective provider of relevant information, the voter is left in the dark.

AN ENLIGHTENED CITIZENRY

The Founders believed that for the democracy to function properly, citizens must not only be knowledgeable concerning candidates for elected office but also be well-informed regarding their own interests and the interests of the nation. When important issues such as global warming and universal health care arise, the democracy counts on its citizens to know what's best for them and for the nation as a whole. Citizens are to exert their influence in the favored direction, whether opposing or supporting special interest positions.

However, what we have seen in our studies is that, at least in the short run, citizens are not able to gather objective data, analyze special interest propaganda, develop a position, and provide policy makers with their best judgment in time to influence key decisions. While recent polls confirm that the public opposes established global warming and healthcare policies, those realizations were formed too late to be effective. In fact, even if those positions had been determined earlier, mechanisms might not have been in place to allow for public influence to overcome special interest leverage.

In the absence of meaningful federal action, as is true in the case of global warming, many corporations and state and local governments have begun to launch their own initiatives. However, despite their valiant efforts, U.S. carbon emissions continue to climb and the negative impact of having no effective national program will be felt for hundreds of years.

COUNTERVAILING CONSTRAINTS
TO SPECIAL INTEREST INITIATIVES

The Founding Fathers believed that if a special interest represented a minority, the majority would hold it in check. On the other hand, if a special interest were in the majority, its bounds would be limited by the wisdom of elected representatives, their view of the nation's true interest, and their love of justice and patriotic belief in the tenets of our country.

If we go back to the case studies provided in Part 3, the Founders' faith in countervailing forces appears to have been misplaced, at least in today's political environment. The examples of global warming and universal health care are two cases in which short-term but intense lobbyist initiatives have carried the day. However, more routine shortcomings come to the fore when we review the other case studies.

First, one wonders about the extent to which the public is even aware of the aberrations created by special interest lobbying. Does the average citizen understand that we spend over $60 billion annually to keep 2.3 million Americans behind bars, more than five times the rate of most developed nations? Is it common knowledge that the U.S. minimum wage routinely falls 24 percent below levels that would reflect increases in the cost of living? How many Americans understand that therapeutic cloning does not refer to the creation of human beings à la Dolly the sheep but would be a means of producing fully functioning replacement organs with no fear of rejection? Unless there is a mechanism to inform the public in an objective way of such complex issues and to highlight policies that deviate from reason and the greater good, it is unrealistic to expect that public support will arise to oppose special interest forces.

Second, assuming that there is public knowledge and opposition to special interest policies, there are two natural barriers that must be overcome. Public sentiment must be able to overcome the lobbyist inducements provided to elected representatives. On the one hand, special interests provide dollars to representatives to purchase TV time and other means used to capture votes. Unless elected officials understand that the public opposition to special interest positions represents enough votes to at least counteract lobbyist cash, special interests are likely to prevail.

The second barrier is an apparent natural alliance between special interest and conservative/Republican thinking. ("The Republicans operate differently. They have a different vision of the proper role of special interests. They're not embarrassed by it. They think that yielding to the demands of wealthy special interests is a good thing.") Because the goal of the special interest often is to maintain the status quo, those who naturally question the need for change and government involvement share a common bond with many lobbyist causes: oppose gun control, new increases in the minimum wage, and government-run health care.

Conservatives question increased government participation on the basis that "there is a new idea of equality wholly divorced from the Declaration that operates in modern liberals. Hence, the idea that equality means equality of outcome; not accepting the inequality which necessarily results from your equality of rights" (see Chapter 5). However, one might respond that it isn't equality of outcome that many seek, but adequacy of outcome. In a nation of wealth and education, should society tolerate the inadequacy of outcome that leaves 47 million Americans without health insurance?

Furthermore, to provide equality of opportunity, there should not be an assumption that citizens necessarily be treated equally. For example, to provide two young people an equal chance of success, it may be that an inner-city teen, coming from a single-parent household, would require much greater educational and other instructive resources than a teen brought up in a wealthy, suburban, two-parent home. Providing them with equal resources would result in an unequal opportunity of success.

It is this different perspective of equality that often blocks the ethics of responsibility and stands in the way of legislative compromise. While one party seeks to promote equality of opportunity through variable levels of expenditures and strives for an adequacy of outcome, the other party simply believes that treating all equally is in keeping with the tenets of American democracy.

THE CORRUPTIVE INFLUENCE OF CAMPAIGN FINANCING

The growing influence of funds required to finance campaigns corrupts the functioning of America's democracy in several important ways. First, demands for money are so great that raising cash has become a perpetual task for the nation's elected representatives. Significant portions of most workdays are spent contacting lobbyists and special interests and asking for campaign contributions. Efforts to obtain donations are especially time-consuming for Committee Chairmen and ranking Members. Time spent corralling dollars diverts Member attention from the substantive tasks of preparing legislation to promote the greater good.

Second, accepting special interest and lobbyist money, at the very least, indicates that recipients may compromise their positions on behalf of contributors. Campaign money buys the access that gives lobbyists the inside track for votes that support special interest causes, including thousands of earmarks that litter legislative calendars. Whether such money is a sign of corruption or just the appearance of corruption, its discouraging impact on voter regard for the nation's democracy is undeniable and can be gauged by low voter turnout (averaging just over 52 percent of eligible voters since 1980).[1] Furthermore, considerations given to future special interest contributions may shape legislative proposals to avoid special interest disapproval.

Third, special interest money can be a potent force to finance candidates who are likely to support the policy objectives of factions. ("An industry that big [oil and gas] can certainly put all kinds of money in the right place at the right time to get friendly candidates elected who will act to build up their industry.") At the same time, supporting such candidates reduces the likelihood that independent candidates will venture into elective contests.

Fourth, campaign contributions generally represent the wealthy, as less than 1 percent of all Americans make contributions of $200 or more.[2] Lack of concern by legislators for the poor may well be derived from the affluent source of most campaign contributions.

Fifth, keeping track of campaign contributions has to some extent eclipsed candidate positions and records as an indication of a candidate's worth. TV coverage of dollars amassed is presented as a live reality show, moving the focus of the contest from merit to money. Certainly, amounts gained may well be an indication of the appeal of a candidate's ideas. However, they may also reflect the extent to which a candidate is willing to compromise his or her principles for the benefit of special interest dollars or the extent to which special interests gauge a candidate's chances of success, hoping to back a winner and collect favors when the contest is over.

MISTRUST OF GOVERNMENT AND EXPERTS

Disregard for government capabilities and the need for expert judgment have led the nation astray in recent years. Such attitudes have been promoted by the conservative/Republican/special interest alliance, bolstered by the fact that lobbyists often represent private contractors who may benefit from initiatives to move government functions to the private sector.

> The Bush administration has doubled the amount of government money going to all types of contractors to $400 billion, creating a new and thriving class of post-9/11 corporations carrying out delicate work for the government. But the number of government employees issuing, managing, and auditing contracts has barely grown.[3]

While questioning expert judgment and involving private contractors in government work can be useful, experience leads one to conclude that extreme caution should be exercised with regard to such practices. We have already seen how a disregard for expert opinion resulted in misjudgment and tragedy in Iraq. One doesn't have to look very far to see other serious breaches of discretion. For example, inappropriate leadership and resource cuts at the Federal Emergency Management Agency (FEMA) resulted in the disastrous relief efforts after Hurricane Katrina, while the Bush administration's push for privatization of the Walter Reed Army Medical Center appears to have been responsible for the deplorable care provided to wounded soldiers.[4]

SUMMARY AND CONCLUSIONS

This analysis has identified five root causes of the nation's failed democracy: the deficient nature of elected representatives, the absence of an enlightened citizenry, insufficient constraints on special interest initiatives, the corruptive influence of campaign financing, and a mistrust of government capabilities and expert judgment. In Chapter 18, the task will be to design remedies for each of these shortcomings, allowing for the restoration of America's democracy.

CHAPTER 18

THE WAY OUT

Policy Alternatives to Lower the Impact of Narrow Forces, Fulfill the Promise of Our Founding Fathers, and Revive the Nation

INTRODUCTION

Restoring America's democracy will require the U.S. citizenry to get behind new ideas and push. Changing the culture of special interest cash established over many years will not be an easy undertaking. Watching the nation go down roads opposed by the public while short-changing other avenues deemed to be of great potential has robbed many of the will to get involved. "For them, the mantra that one person can make a difference has given way to the belief that the powers that be won't be moved."

But this is America, where the vote still trumps the money. Knowing that this holds true and being empowered by the following ideas should provide a stimulus for revival of the "people politics" envisioned by the Founding Fathers.

The plan to restore America's democracy calls on several sectors of the nation to make important contributions to this cause: professional associations, public interest organizations, academics, subject matter experts, government agencies, Members of Congress, and everyday voters. In some cases, groups may need to assume non-traditional roles that invite political risk and controversy. With the future of America's democracy at stake, those who truly value the nation's heritage must find the courage.

> The harder the conflict, the more glorious the triumph. What we obtain too cheap, we esteem too lightly; it is dearness only that gives everything its value. I love the man that can smile in trouble, that can gather strength from distress and grow brave by reflection. 'Tis the business of little minds to shrink; but he whose heart is firm, and whose conscience approves his conduct, will pursue his principles unto death.
>
> —Thomas Paine

To counteract the five root causes of the nation's democratic impairment as described in Chapter 17, a four-part initiative is proposed. Each applies to one or more of the cited deficiencies.

A FOUR-PART PLAN FOR DEMOCRATIC RESTORATION

The Right Kind of Elected Representatives: Candidate Information Profiles

The first step in improving the nature of candidates for federal elective office and sharpening the choices made by voters is to enhance the available information concerning the personal characteristics, capabilities, and accomplishments of the candidates. With relevant and objective information routinely provided to voters, those who seek office will become aware that their true record will become public knowledge. For those wrestling with the decision of which candidate to support, such information would be an invaluable addition to the base of data on which they make their choice.

It is proposed that the development of Candidate Information Profiles be entrusted to organizations that are expert in political leadership and political science. For example, a collaborative effort could be initiated by the International Leadership Association, which is the global network for all those who practice, study, and teach leadership, and the American Political Science Association, which is the leading professional organization for the study of political science. Drawing upon their substantial memberships, these organizations might organize and convene non-partisan committees to discuss and determine the process to be followed. For example, a subcommittee may be charged with the responsibility to select those criteria on which candidates will be assessed, such as the leadership principles presented in Chapter 16. A second subcommittee may tackle the issue of data collection, possibly including personal candidate interviews and requests for relevant medical information. A third subcommittee may determine the best format through which profiles may be presented and effective channels through which they may be transmitted to the voters.

By furnishing voters with accurate, in-depth profiles of those running for office, the Founding Father's prescription for the right kind of elected representatives may be fulfilled. At the same time, the quest for virtue, wisdom, the pursuit of the common good of the society, and noble deeds may become more of an American reality.

Countering Special Interest Misinformation: Federation of Public Interest Organizations

A Federation of Public Interest Organizations (FPIO) should be formed to identify, explain, and help resolve priority issues vital to the public and the nation. Operation of the FPIO would be modeled after the Nobel Prize–winning Intergovernmental Panel on Climate Change. The FPIO would be directed by a board selected from non-partisan, public interest leadership. The FPIO would be composed of five cooperating working groups, each with its own mission:

1. Identify high-priority issues and assess the progress made by the federal government and others in resolving those issues.
2. Weigh the vulnerability of people affected by the above issues and describe the ensuing consequences.
3. Sponsor annual Conferences of the Parties to develop options for resolving identified issues.
4. Facilitate action to implement selected options.
5. Maintain a strong program of public relations, explaining the rationale for issue selection, describing the complexities of selected issues in an easy-to-understand manner, revealing related special interest motives and tactics, and providing a means of quantifying how public support will be translated into votes for the benefit of presidential and Congressional decision-making.

Each working group would regularly issue reports that summarize their proceedings, findings, and progress. Reports would be prepared by a national network of academics, authors, contributors, reviewers, and experts. Before reports are issued, each would be reviewed by panels of experts and relevant government officials regarding accuracy, completeness, and overall balance.

The FPIO would maintain a quick-study capability to assess rapidly emerging issues and policies so that the public can receive expert feedback, explanations, and advice before official policies are established.

Finance-Free Politics: Public Financing
of All Federal Elections

The door must be opened to finance-free politics. Only in this way can our elected representatives return their focus to legislation and the quest for the greater good. Freedom from the need to raise enormous amounts of money will reduce special interest and lobbyist corruption and the appearance of corruption, remove the excuse to compromise positions sooner than necessary, reduce the capability of special interests to buy elections for candidate favors, and diminish the influence of wealthy contributors.

Finance-free politics may be achieved by implementing these four initiatives:

1. The presidential campaign finance system in place has become obsolete because of failure to adjust the timing and amount of funds to be provided.[1] However, it might be revived and applied to all federal elections based upon key features of the Common Cause proposal for public funding of Congressional elections:

    a. Candidates raise a limited amount of seed money in small contributions to launch their campaigns.
    b. Candidates prove that they are serious and viable by meeting an established contributions threshold.
    c. Once qualified, candidates are provided with campaign grants on a timely basis and may no longer accept contributions or spend personal money on their campaigns.
    d. If privately funded candidates significantly outspend publicly funded candidates, the latter would receive additional funding to keep them competitive.
    e. Participating candidates must comply with guidelines concerning how the public's money is spent and account for all expenditures.
    f. Funding levels would be indexed to increases in the cost of campaign expenditures, keeping the system viable over time.
    g. Candidates would receive vouchers for television airtime.
    h. Participating candidates must appear in election-related debates.

2. Encourage voter support for publicly financed candidates. As has been covered earlier, public financing systems must remain voluntary as a result of a Supreme Court decision. Because contributing money to a campaign has been deemed comparable to exercising

free speech, the government may not restrict the ability of candidates to run privately financed campaigns. However, while the court may allow continued private financing of elections, it cannot dictate the reaction of the voters to candidates who run privately financed campaigns. We have seen over and over that private financing of campaigns has been one of the most corruptive influences in the conduct of our democracy. To discourage special interest and lobbyist contributions and the evils that they bring, voters might favor candidates who accept public financing and the rules that accompany applicable systems.

3. Pledge finance-free conduct. Candidates and elected officials should be invited (by the Federal Election Commission) to sign a pledge that they will follow finance-free rules of conduct during campaigns and when they are in office. Such rules would prohibit the acceptance of any gifts or favors and would bar candidates and elected officials from soliciting funds, jobs, or any other object of value. Voters should be made aware of those who have signed such a pledge and should recognize such dignity with increased support. The Federal Election Commission should be charged with the responsibility of investigating reported violations. Public notice should be given of those found to be in violation.

4. Shift political party financing away from large contributors. In accordance with the objective of reducing special interest and lobbyist influence, the political parties should reduce their reliance on such contributors. This may be achieved through the provision of federal grants to established political parties, party membership drives, and initiation of membership dues systems. The political parties might establish communications with their members not just during campaign seasons but also on a continuing basis, communicating party positions regarding significant issues. Parties might also pledge that contributions will not be used to further special interest objectives unless they promote the greater good of the nation.

Revive the Vitality of the Federal Government and the Place of Qualified Experts

The capabilities of the federal government and the role of qualified experts have been systematically attacked by blatant political cronyism, the practice of ideology over analysis, and a rush to replace Federal Service capabilities with private-sector contracts. Too often, unqualified political appointees have been named to pay political debts or support special interest objectives over the interests of the people. If the government is to serve the public, its leaders must be fully qualified and oriented to promote the public good.

The combination of reduced federal employment (by more than 17 percent since 1990) and increased federal contracting strains the ability of the Federal Service to monitor contracts awarded.[2] Public service is a high calling and should be recognized appropriately so that it may attract the best and the brightest individuals to meet the nation's needs. These goals may be achieved through the following steps:

1. Before the names of political appointees are submitted to the Senate for confirmation, they should be provided to an independent unit within the Government Accountability Office, which should be charged with the task of conducting thorough investigations of the suitability of such nominees. The results of these inquiries should be provided to the public and the Senate before each nominee is formally considered.

2. The citizenry depends upon a vibrant and competent civil service to carry out Congressional and executive mandates. Excessive privatization reduces the scope of government capabilities, requires increased monitoring, and infuses profit considerations that may interfere with smooth and efficient operations. Therefore, the criteria used to weigh the advisability of federal privatization initiatives should be studied with a view toward making such transformations less common.

3. As the FPIO identifies policy issues for resolution, federal staffing and other capabilities should be assessed to determine if they are adequate to assume likely responsibilities. If not, streamlined procedures should be established to acquire exemplary professional staff and related resources required. Of course, new initiatives would be evaluated by appropriate FPIO working groups.

4. The Government Accountability Office should be charged with oversight responsibility regarding executive policy proposals and orders that appear to disregard expert consultation. As soon as they are available, reports on such instances should be released to the public. Consultation with appropriate FPIO staff should be encouraged.

SUMMARY AND CONCLUSION

Accepting these recommendations and working to put them in place will require thinking outside the box. Predictably, skeptics will raise numerous questions: Where will required resources come from? Don't these proposals introduce duplication into our political processes? Wouldn't special interests and their lobbyists oppose these proposals at every turn? How will the necessary legislation be developed and passed? Wouldn't these proposals contribute to more Big Government?

If we are serious about taking our nation back from those who rule by cash over the public good, the answers to these and other challenges will be found. If the will of the people is to be served, the people must persist in setting things right. Having completed this text, there should be no doubt that the democracy given to Americans by the Founding Fathers has been betrayed by special interests and political players unable to resist their lure. Now is the time to take action and reclaim our liberty.

Fixing America's democracy is not a subject solely for academic consideration. Every day, thousands of lives are lost unnecessarily as a result of inadequate health care, poverty, incomplete stem cell research, inner-city violence, global warming, and our misadventure in Iraq. For too many, this *is* a matter of life or death.

The Founding Fathers experienced the persecution of a distant monarchy and suffered the harsh conditions of an unsettled land. In response, they found the courage and stamina to free the people and establish a nation under a just democracy. With that democracy under siege by special interest and lobbyist power, we who have benefited from the sacrifices of those who came before must act to reestablish an honorable system of government. If we are to live up to the promise of our Founders, we can do no less.

NOTES

CHAPTER 1

1. Wesley Frank Craven, *The Legend of the Founding Fathers* (Ithaca, NY: Cornell University Press, 1956), v.

2. Samuel I. Mintz, *The Hunting of* Leviathan (Cambridge: Cambridge University Press, 1962); David Gauthier, *The Logic of* Leviathan; *The Moral and Political Theory of Thomas Hobbes* (Oxford: Oxford University Press, 1969).

3. E. J. Lowe, *Locke* (New York: Routledge, 2005); *Stanford Encyclopedia of Philosophy*, Stanford University, s.v. "John Locke."

4. W. Stark, *Montesquieu: Pioneer of the Sociology of Knowledge* (Toronto: University of Toronto Press, 1961).

5. W. Stark, *Montesquieu.*

6. W. Stark, *Montesquieu.*

7. Alf J. Mapp, Jr., *The Virginia Experiment, The Old Dominion's Role in the Making of America 1607–1781* (Lanham, MD: Hamilton Press, 1985).

8. David Price, *Love and Hate in Jamestown: John Smith, Pocahontas, and the Start of a New Nation* (New York: Alfred A. Knopf, 2003); Alf J. Mapp, Jr., *The Virginia Experiment.*

9. Francis J. Bremer, *The Puritan Experiment: New England Society from Bradford to Edwards* (University Press of New England, 1995).

10. Robert A. Dahl, *Democracy in the United States: Promise and Performance* (Chicago: Rand McNally, College Publishing Company, 1967).

11. Edmund S. Morgan, *Inventing the People: The Rise of Popular Sovereignty in England and America* (New York, W. W. Norton & Company, 1989).

12. Donald T. Phillips, *The Founding Fathers on Leadership: Classic Teamwork in Changing Times* (New York: Warner Books, 1997).

13. Thomas Paine, Thoughts on the Present State of American Affairs, in *The Life and Works of Thomas Paine*, ed. William M. Van der Weyde (New Rochelle, NY: Thomas Paine National Historical Association, 1925), II: 122–150.

14. Declaration of Independence, 1776.

15. *America Dead and Wounded*: John Shy, A People Numerous and Armed, 249–250.

16. James A. Henrietta, Microsoft Encarta Online Encyclopedia, 2007, s.v. "American Revolution."

17. James A. Henrietta, "American Revolution."

18. Roger A. Bruns, *A More Perfect Union: The Creation of the United States Constitution* (Washington, DC: National Archives Trust Fund Board, 1986).

19. Robert A. Dahl, *Democracy in the United States: Promise and Performance*, 66.

20. *The Federalist Papers* (Washington, DC: Library of Congress, 1788).

21. James Madison, *Federalist* 10, 1787.

22. The ten amendments eventually approved by the Congress and ratified by the states began as seventeen proposed additions to the constitution. Twelve were forwarded for ratification and ten garnered approval from the required number of states.

CHAPTER 2

1. Phillip Payne, *What Was Teapot Dome?* (New York: St. Bonaventure University, 2002); Susan Schmidt and James V. Grimaldi, "Abramoff Pleads Guilty to 3 Counts," Washington.com, January 4, 2006; "William J. Jefferson," *Beyond DeLay*, http://www.beyonddelay.org/summaries/jefferson.php (accessed June 13, 2007).

2. The majority of bills introduced in the U.S. Congress appear to be initiated by lobbyists rather than Congressmen who have analyzed public needs and prepared legislation to address a recognized deficiency.

3. The Center for Responsive Politics, http://www.opensecrets.org (accessed January 19, 2007).

4. Joseph E. Cantor, "Campaign Finance: An Overview," *Congressional Research Service* report to Congress and various releases of the Federal Election Commission (July 31, 2006).

5. Joseph E. Cantor, "Campaign Finance: An Overview."

6. Http://www.opensecrets.org. Accessed February 6, 2008.

7. Http://www.opensecrets.org. Accessed February 6, 2008.

8. Reports of the Center for Responsive Politics, 2002 and 2004. Candidate positions, campaigning skills, and incumbency also play significant roles in determining success, but as long as candidates consider private campaign funds as a prerequisite to victory, policy positions are likely to be compromised to obtain additional dollars.

9. Federal Election Campaign Finance Guide, The Campaign Legal Center, "A Brief History of Money and Politics."

10. "A Brief History of Money and Politics."

11. "A Brief History of Money and Politics."

12. "A Brief History of Money and Politics."

13. "A Brief History of Money and Politics."

14. Anthony Corrado, "Money and Politics: A History of Federal Campaign Finance Law," *The New Campaign Finance Sourcebook* (Washington, DC: Brookings Institution), 17–18.

15. "A Brief History of Money and Politics."

16. "A Brief History of Money and Politics."

17. *Buckley v. Valeo*, 424 U.S. 1 (1976).

18. "A Brief History of Money and Politics."

19. "A Brief History of Money and Politics."

20. These regulations may be found in The Campaign Legal Center's *Campaign Finance Guide*.

CHAPTER 9

1. *An Inconvenient Truth*, directed by David Guggenheim (Hollywood, CA: Paramount Classics, Participant Productions, 2006).

2. Assessment Report, Intergovernmental Panel on Climate Change (IPCC), World Meteorological Organization and United Nations Environment Programme, 2007. In Global Warming, Union of Concerned Scientists, Citizens and Scientists for Environmental Solutions, http://www.ucsusa.org/global_warming/science/global-warming-faq.html. Accessed February 26, 2007.

3. Assessment Report, IPCC, 2007.

4. Assessment Report, IPCC, 2007.

5. First World Climate Conference Report, World Meteorological Organization, Geneva, Switzerland, February, 1979.

6. Assessment Report, IPCC, 2007.

7. Global Warming: The Greenhouse Effect, The Union of Concerned Scientists, Citizens and Scientists for Environmental Solutions, http://www.ucsusa.org/globalwarming/html. Accessed July 2007.

8. Assessment Report, IPCC, 1990.

9. United Nations Framework Convention on Climate Change, official web site, http://www.unfccc.int/essential_background/items/2877.php. Accessed March 21, 2007.

10. Scientists believe that global warming may increase crop production in the short run; however, in the long run, such gains will disappear and be dwarfed by the negative impact of the phenomenon.

11. John Vidal, "Revealed: How Oil Giant Influenced Bush," *Guardian Unlimited*, June 8, 2005.

12. Assessment Report, IPCC, 1995.

13. Kyoto Protocol, United Nations Framework Convention on Climate Change, official web site, http://www.unfccc.int/kyoto_protocol/items/2830.php. Accessed March 9, 2007.

14. Assessment Report, IPCC, 2001.

15. "Marrakech, Morocco COP-7 Meeting," United Nations Framework Convention on Climate Change, official web site, http://en.wikipedia.org/wiki/United_Nations_Framework_Convention_on_Climate_Change.html. Accessed March 9, 2007.

16. "Montreal, Canada COP-11 Meeting," United Nations Framework Convention on Climate Change, official web site, http://en.wikipedia.org/wiki/United_Nations_Framework_Convention_on_Climate_Change.html. Accessed March 9, 2007.

17. Congressional Record: July 25, 1997 (Senate) Page S8113-S8139 and *Byrd-Hagel Resolution*, S Res. 98, 105th Cong., 1st sess., July 25, 1997, *The National Center for Public Policy Research*.

18. "Kyoto Protocol: Politics Position of the United States," Answers.com Encyclopedia, http://www.answers.com/topic/kyoto-protocol.html. Accessed February 27, 2007.

19. "Business Action on Climate Change," Wikimedia Foundation, Inc., http://en.wikipedia.org/wiki/Business_action_on_climate_change.html. Accessed March 1, 2007.

20. "Global Climate Coalition," Source Watch, Center for Media and Democracy, http://www.sourcewatch.org/index.php?title=Global_Climate_Coalition.html. Accessed March 15, 2007.

21. "Global Climate Coalition," Source Watch, Center for Media and Democracy, http://www.sourcewatch.org/index.php?title=Global_Climate_Coalition.html. Accessed March 15, 2007.

22. Assessment Report, IPCC, 2007. A paper issued in the *Journal of Geophysical Research Letters* in March 2008 presents the findings of new models that require zero carbon emissions by mid-century to avoid serious consequences.

23. "Clean Air: Clear Skies Proposal Weakens the Clean Air Act," *Sierra Club*, http://www.sierraclub.org/cleanair/clear_skies.asp.html. Accessed March 13, 2007.

24. "Fact Sheet: President Bush Announces Clear Skies and Global Climate Change Initiatives," *White House*, February 14, 2002.

25. "Fact Sheet: President Bush Announces Clear Skies and Global Climate Change Initiatives," *White House*, February 14, 2002.

26. "Issue Guide: Clear Skies Act," *Citizen Joe*, http://citizenjoe.org/node/225.html. Accessed March 13, 2007.

27. "The Bush Administration's Anti-Environmental Actions, January 20, 2001 to August 31, 2004: Global Warming," *National Environmental Trust*, http://www.net.org/reports/rollbacks/warming.vtml. Accessed March 13, 2007.

28. "Analysis of President Bush's Climate Change Plan," http://www.pewclimate.org/policy,html (accessed February 28, 2007); "Carbon Intensity," Wikipedia Encyclopedia, http://en.wikipedia.org/wiki/Carbon_intensity.html. Accessed March 13, 2007.

29. Bernie Fischlowitz-Roberts,"Carbon Emissions Climbing," *Earth Policy Institute*, http://www.earth-policy.org/Indicators/indicator5.htm. Accessed March 13, 2007.

30. "The Bush Administration's Anti-Environmental Actions, January 20, 2001 to August 31, 2004: Global Warming," *National Environmental Trust*, http://www.net.org/reports/rollbacks/warming.vtml. Accessed March 13, 2007.

31. "A New Direction for Bush Administration Climate Policy," *American Enterprise Institute*, January 19, 2007.

32. Asia-Pacific Partnership on Clean Development and Climate, Executive Summary of Task Force Action Plans, http://www.asiapacificpartnership.org (accessed October 31, 2006).

33. "Addressing Global Climate Change," *Council on Environmental Quality*, The White House, http://www.Whitehouse.gov/ceq/global-change.html (accessed February 28, 2007).

34. William A. Pizer, RFF Fellow, and Raymond J. Kopp, RFF Senior Fellow, "Summary and Analysis of McCain-Lieberman Climate Stewardship Act of 2003," S.139, introduced January 9, 2003, *Resources for the Future*, January 28, 2003.

35. "Pelosi Reveals Who's Who on Global Warming Panel," *Washingtonpost.com*, March 12, 2007, http://www.washingtonpost.com/wp-dyn/content/article/2007/03/11/AR2007031101044_p...html. Accessed March 12, 2007.

36. Daniel C. Esty, "Going Green: Is That the Way to Keep Business in the Black?" The Press of Atlantic City, March 12, 2007, Commentary.

37. "CEOs Lobby Bush to Curb Warming," *MSNBC.com*, Washington, DC, January 19, 2007, http://pnpoc.msnbc.com/id/16708004/print/1/display mode/1098/html (accessed February 28, 2007).

38. "Large Investors Back CO_2 Emission Curbs, Pension Funds, Merrill Lynch Urge Bush, Congress to Act," *MSNBC.com*, Associated Press, March 20, 2007.

39. "Large Investors Back CO_2 Emission Curbs, Pension Funds, Merrill Lynch Urge Bush, Congress to Act," *MSNBC.com*, Associated Press, March 20, 2007.

40. Michael Barbaro, "Wal-Mart: A Giant Store Gone Green," *International Herald Tribune*, The Times Center, http://www.iht.com/articles/2007/01/02/business/bulbs.php.html. Accessed March 21, 2007.

41. "Politics of Global Warming: United States State and Local Governments," Wikimedia Foundation, Inc., http://en.wikipedia.org/wiki/Politics_of_global_warming.html. Accessed March 1, 2007.

42. "Politics of Global Warming: United States State and Local Governments," Wikimedia Foundation, Inc., http://en.wikipedia.org/wiki/Politics_of_global_warming.html. Accessed March 1, 2007.

43. Juliet Eilperin, "EPA Chief Denies California Limit on Auto Emissions," *Washington Post*, December 20, 2007, p. A01.

44. "New Jersey Expected to Set Precedent by Passing the Global Warming Response Act," *Global Warming Solutions News*, U.S. PIRG, June 21, 2007.

45. "Regional Greenhouse Gas Initiative, An Initiative of the Northeast & Mid-Atlantic States of the U.S.," http://www.riggi.org. Accessed March 21, 2007.

46. John Ward Anderson, "E.U. Raises Bar in Fight against Global Warming," *Washington Post Foreign Service*, March 10, 2007 and "A European Auto Emissions Climate Plan," http://www.washingtonpost.com, January 28, 2008.

CHAPTER 10

1. Louis Uchitelle, "Age of Riches," *The New York Times*, July 15, 2007.

2. Louis Uchitelle, "Age of Riches," 2007.

3. Louis Uchitelle, "Age of Riches," 2007.

4. Historical Poverty Tables, Housing and Household Economic Statistics Division, *U.S. Census Bureau*, 2005.

5. Fair Labor Standards Act, 1938.

6. Fair Labor Standards Act, 1938.

7. Richard B. Freeman, "Minimum Wages—Again!" *International Journal of Manpower*, Vol. 15, No. 2/3, 1994, pp. 8–15.

8. U.S. Department of Labor, Bureau of Labor Statistics. Those reported under the minimum could reflect rounding errors, exemptions from Fair Labor Standards Act requirements, or violations of the law.

9. U.S. Department of Labor, Bureau of Labor Statistics.

10. Note that if the minimum wage had been increased to $8.45, some of the workers included in this analysis might be making higher rates due to employer efforts to maintain wage differentials; at the same time, additional workers may have been attracted by the higher rate and may have filled minimum wage jobs that are currently vacant.

11. Based on unpublished Bureau of Labor Statistics, Current Population Survey data for 2006. Beginning at the $8.00 level, data are only provided for the range of $8.00 to $8.99; therefore, the worker population at that level was divided in half.

12. The Earned Income Tax Credit program began in 1975 and has been increased to raise benefits substantially. Low-income workers who qualify receive tax credits that increase as income increases, providing an incentive to work; while the program often operates as a wage subsidy, its cost ($34 billion in 2004) falls on taxpayers in general, unlike the minimum wage that is borne solely by employers.

13. Employment Policies Institute, *Job Loss in a Booming Economy*, 2nd ed. (Washington, DC: The Employment Policies Institute, 1998). Summaries of other minimum wage impact studies, most of which indicate a negligible effect of minimum wage gains on employment, may be found in U.S. Department of Labor, Employment Standards Administration, Wage and Hour Division, *Minimum Wage and Overtime Hours under the Fair Labor Standards Act*, June 1998, 82–89.

14. Bureau of Labor Statistics, Current Population Survey. 1997–2006.

CHAPTER 11

1. National Health Expenditures and Selected Economic Indicators, Levels and Annual Percent Change: Calendar Years 2001–2006, Centers for Medicare and Medicaid Services, Office of the Actuary, 2007.

2. "Tell Me about Stem Cells," Professor David Gifford, MIT Department of Electrical Engineering and Computer Science; Professor Richard Young, MIT Department of Biology and Whitehead Institute; and Dr. M. William Lensch, Affiliate Member, Harvard Stem Cell Institute and Department of Biological Chemistry and Molecular Pharmacology, Harvard Medical School.

3. NIH budget documents.

4. D. I. Hoffman and others, "Cryopreserved Embryos in the United States and Their Availability for Research," *Fertility and Sterility* 79 (2003): 1063–69.

5. National Right to Life Committee, Inc., April 2, 2007.

6. Pope John Paul II, message to President Bush, July 23, 2001.

7. Rick Weiss, "Law Cites Stem Cell Advance," *The Washington Post*, January 11, 2008, p. A04.

8. See Chapter 16 survey results.

9. Recognizing the potential of embryonic stem cell research, the states of California and New Jersey are organizing their own stem cell research institutes and are providing funding to move ahead; however, while such efforts are hopeful, they will not compensate for the lost promise of a vigorous NIH initiative.

10. Michael Abramowitz and Rick Weiss, "A Scientific Advance, a Political Question Mark," *The Washington Post*, November 21, 2007.

11. Abramowitz and Weiss, 2007.

CHAPTER 12

1. Current Population Survey, U.S. Bureau of the Census, U.S. Department of Commerce, 2004.

2. Health Care Trends, Introduction to the Health Care Industry, Plunkett Research, Ltd., http://www.plunkettresearch.com. Accessed September 19, 2007.

3. Kaiser Commission of Medicaid and the Uninsured and Urban Institute Analysis of the March 2004 Current Population Survey.

4. Under self-insurance schemes, the employer is large enough to pay healthcare costs directly.

5. Kaiser Family Foundation. "Employer Health Benefits 2005 Annual Survey," 2005.

6. Kaiser Family Foundation. "Medicaid: A Primer," 2005.

7. Centers for Medicare and Medicaid Services, U.S. Department of Health and Human Services.

8. Centers for Medicare and Medicaid Services.

9. "State Children's Health Insurance Program," Wikipedia, http://www.wikipedia.org. Accessed January 23, 2008.

10. Centers for Medicare and Medicaid Services.

11. Centers for Medicare and Medicaid Services.

12. Centers for Medicare and Medicaid Services.

13. "OECD Health Data 2005: How Does the United States Compare," 2005.

14. "OECD Health Data 2005."

15. "OECD Health Data 2005."

16. "Ranking of the World's Health Systems: WHO World Health Report," *World Health Organization*, http://www.who.int/whr/en/index.html. Accessed October 29, 2007.

17. Institute of Medicine. "Care without Coverage: Too Little, Too Late," Kaiser Family Foundation, 2002.

18. D. Himmelstein and others, Illness and Injury as Contributors to Bankruptcy, *Health Affairs* (Millwood), February 2, 2005.

19. "Care without Coverage: Too Little Too Late," Kaiser Family Foundation, 2002; Institute of Medicine, "Undercoverage: The Uninsured and Uncovered Medical Services," American Medical Student Association, September 2007.

20. Institute of Medicine, "Care without Coverage: Too Little Too Late," 2002.

21. Institute of Medicine, 2002.

22. Institute of Medicine, 2002.

23. "National Hospital Ambulatory Medical Survey: 2000," National Center for Health Statistics, April 2002.

24. Kao-Ping Chua, "Strategies to Increase Healthcare Access," American Medical Student Association, 2005.

25. "Employer Health Benefits 2006 Annual Survey, Summary of Findings," Kaiser Family Foundation, http://www.kff.org/insurance/7527/index.cfm. Accessed January 23, 2008.

26. "Employer-Sponsored Single, Employee-Plus-One, and Family Health Insurance Coverage: Selection and Cost, 2003," U.S. Agency for Health Care Research and Quality, July 2005.

27. Kaiser Family Foundation, "Employer Health Benefits 2006 Annual Survey," 2006.

28. Kaiser Family Foundation, "Employer Health Benefits 2006 Annual Survey," 2006.

29. D. Satcher and others, "Trends: What if We Were Equal? A Comparison of the Black–White Mortality Gap in 1960 and 2000," *Health Affairs*, March/April, 2005.

30. African American to White Cancer Mortality Rate Ratios, U.S. 1997–2001, National Center for Health Statistics, Centers for Disease Control and Prevention.

31. "Preventing Cancer in Hispanics," The National Hispanic Leadership Initiative on Cancer: En Accion, 1998 and American Cancer Society, 2003.

32. S.J. Ventura and others, "Final Data for 1999 National Vital Statistics Report," National Center for Health Statistics, 2001.

33. National Diabetes Fact Sheet, American Diabetes Association, 2005.

34. Information on the 1993–1994 defeat of the Clinton healthcare initiative has been taken from "A Detailed Timeline of the Healthcare Debate," *The System*, The Public Broadcasting System.

35. Whitewater refers to controversy over a real-estate deal between the Clintons and the McDougals in the Whitewater Development Corporation, a failed vacation home venture during the 1970s and 1980s. Troopergate refers to

allegations that President Clinton offered jobs to Arkansas State Troopers in return for their silence concerning his alleged extramarital affairs. Neither scandal produced verified charges against either of the Clintons.

36. Pew Foundation survey, 2006.

37. See H.R. 676, the United States Health Insurance Act, introduced by Representative John Conyers, Jr., and co-authored by Representative Dennis Kucinich, among others.

38. In a 2004 poll conducted by the Kaiser Family Foundation, 76 percent agreed strongly or somewhat that access to health care should be a right.

39. H.R. 676.

40. A detailed example of this approach has been advocated by John Edwards. His proposal may be found on the John Edwards 2008 web site. Most of the other Democratic candidates for President in 2008 have also described their recommendations on corresponding web sites.

41. Features of these plans have been proposed by Republican candidates (see, for example, the web site of Mike Huckabee for President) and in proposals from healthcare insurance companies, such as Aetna.

42. http://www.opensecrets.org. Accessed March 16, 2008.

43. Families USA, The Voice for Health Care Consumers.

44. The drug companies routinely contend that higher prices are required to support the substantial costs of their research activities.

45. "Medicare Drug Disaster," *Socialist Worker Online*, January 27, 2006, http://www.socialistworker.org. Accessed October 1, 2007.

46. "Medicare Drug Disaster," *Socialist Worker Online*, January 27, 2006, http://www.socialistworker.org. Accessed October 1, 2007.

CHAPTER 13

1. "Crime in the United States, 2005," U.S. Department of Justice, Federal Bureau of Investigations.

2. "Violent Crime in America: 24 Months of Alarming Trends," Police Executive Research Forum, Washington, D.C.

3. Gordon Barclay and Cynthia Tavares, "International Comparisons of Criminal Justice Statistics 2001," E.U. Home Office and the Council of Europe, October 24, 2003.

4. These and related data are from "Crime in the United States 2005."

5. These and related data are from "Crime in the United States 2005."

6. "U.S. Central City and Suburban Violent Crime Rates: 1999," Demographia, derived from U.S. Department of Justice Uniform Crime Report, all metropolitan areas over 1,000,000 with required data.

7. "U.S. Central City and Suburban Violent Crime Rates: 1999."

8. Computed from "Crime in the United States 2005."

9. Computed from "Crime in the United States 2005."

10. Violent crime includes murder and non-negligent manslaughter, forcible rape, robbery, and aggravated assault.

11. Computed from "Crime in the United States 2005."

12. Hispanic individuals are counted mostly as white. While these data fail to break out separate information for those of Hispanic origin, information from the Department of Justice indicates that Hispanic violent crime rates are also well above the average. The remaining race categories are American Indian or Alaskan Native and Asia Pacific Islander.

13. Computed from "Crime in the United States 2005."

14. Note that the Federal Bureau of Investigation data do not provide population data by race for reporting cities. Census data for cities reveal a great deal of variability. For example, the African American population is 64.3 percent of the City of Baltimore's population but only 11.2 percent of the population of Los Angeles.

15. Computed from "Crime in the United States 2005."

16. In 2005, the Supreme Court struck down the mandatory federal sentencing guidelines and made them advisory. However, sentences issued often reflect the guidelines established.

17. "Home World Prison Brief, International Centre for Prison Studies," King's College, London, University of London, 2004.

18. "Public Safety, Public Spending, Public Safety Performance Project Report," JFA Institute, The Pew Charitable Trusts, June 2007.

19. "Public Safety, Public Spending"; based on data from U.S. Department of Justice, Office of Justice Programs, June 2007.

20. U.S. Department of Justice, Office of Justice Programs, Prisoners in 2005.

21. U.S. Department of Justice.

22. U.S. Department of Justice.

23. U.S. Department of Justice.

24. U.S. Department of Justice.

25. "Public Safety, Public Spending," iv.

26. Annual Report, Office of National Drug Control Policy, Executive Office of the President, 2007.

27. Annual Report.

28. Annual Report.

29. Ruth Wilson Gilmore, "From Military Industrial Complex to Prison Industrial Complex," *Creative Commons*, Stanford, California, 2005.

30. Under asset forfeiture, goods such as cars used to transport illegal drugs are confiscated by the police and sold at auction, with the proceeds used for law-enforcement purposes.

31. Annual Report.

32. Ethan Nadelmann, "Think Again: Drugs," *Foreign Policy Magazine*, September/October 2007.

33. Ethan Nadelmann, "Think Again: Drugs."

34. Crime in the United States 2006, Expanded Homicide Data Table 6, Murder, Types of Weapons Used, U.S. Department of Justice, Federal Bureau of Investigations, Criminal Justice Information Services, http://www.fbi.gov/

ucr/cius2006/offenses/expanded_information/data/shrtable_06.html.   Accessed February 25, 2008.

35. Daniel W. Webster, Jon S. Vernick, and Stephen P. Teret, "How Cities Can Combat Illegal Guns and Gun Violence," Center for Gun Policy and Research, Johns Hopkins Bloomberg School of Public Health, Baltimore, MD, October 23, 2006.

36. This interpretation has been supported by nine of the eleven federal appeals courts. The U.S. Supreme Court recently agreed to hear a case regarding District of Columbia gun law restrictions and Second Amendment rights.

37. Daniel W. Webster, Jon S. Vernick, and Stephen P. Teret, "How Cities Can Combat Illegal Guns and Gun Violence."

38. Bureau of Alcohol, Tobacco and Firearms, "Commerce in Firearms in the United States," (Washington, DC: U.S. Department of the Treasury, 2000).

39. Steven D. Levitt and Stephen J. Dubner, *Freakonomics* (New York: William Morrow, HarperCollins Publishers, 2005).

40. Opensecrets.org, Center for Responsive Politics.

41. "Crime in the United States, 2005."

42. "Crime in the United States, 2005."

CHAPTER 14

1. The issue of embryonic stem cell research is excluded from Chapter 14 because this is an ethical matter rather than one of revenues or profits.

2. "Career Guide to Industries," U.S. Department of Labor, Bureau of Labor Statistics, 2006–2007.

3. "Career Guide to Industries."

4. "Career Guide to Industries."

5. "Career Guide to Industries."

6. U.S. Department of Commerce, Bureau of Economic Analysis, National Economic Accounts.

7. U.S. Department of Commerce.

8. "Career Guide to Industries."

9. "Career Guide to Industries."

10. "Career Guide to Industries."

11. "Career Guide to Industries."

12. "Career Guide to Industries."

13. "Career Guide to Industries."

14. U.S. Department of Commerce; data include the Accommodation component of the industry.

15. U.S. Department of Commerce.

16. The Bureau of Labor Statistics, as noted earlier, counts about 1.7 million workers at or below the minimum wage; however, this excludes those paid the minimum who are not hourly workers.

17. Bureau of Labor Statistics.

18. Bureau of Labor Statistics.

19. Bureau of Labor Statistics.

20. National Association of Insurance Commissioners (NAIC). These data do not include premiums for disability and long-term care insurance.

21. National Association of Insurance Commissioners.

22. National Association of Insurance Commissioners.

23. Jamie Robinson, "The Commercial Health Insurance Industry in an Era of Eroding Employer Coverage," *Health Affairs*, 25 (6), November/December, 2006.

24. Lehman Brothers Global Equity Analysis, in Jamie Robinson, "The Commercial Health Insurance Industry."

25. Bureau of Labor Statistics

26. Bureau of Labor Statistics.

27. The Bureau of Economic Analysis data combine pharmaceuticals with all other chemical manufacturing; therefore, these data were obtained from the Internal Revenue Service.

28. Internal Revenue Service.

29. John Locke, *Second Treatise of Government*, 1690.

30. Bureau of Labor Statistics.

31. Bureau of Labor Statistics.

32. Bureau of Labor Statistics.

33. Estimates based upon data from the "Census of State and Federal Correctional Facilities," The Office of Research and Education of the Federal Bureau of Prisons; and the American Correctional Association (note that prison totals include related facilities).

34. Same as note 33.

35. Same as note 33.

36. "Public Safety, Public Spending," Public Safety Performance Project Report, JFA Institute, The Pew Charitable Trusts, June 2007.

37. "Annual Firearms Manufacturing and Export Report," Bureau of Alcohol, Tobacco, and Firearms, 2004.

38. "Annual Firearms Manufacturing and Export Report."

39. "Annual Firearms Manufacturing and Export Report."

40. U.S. Department of Commerce; note that another 30,000 workers are employed in industries that primarily produce ammunition, bombs, and artillery.

41. Corrections Corporation of America, Annual Report 2006.

42. Annual Report.

43. Brigette Sarabi and Edwin Bender, "The Prison Payoff: The Role of Politics and Private Prisons in the Incarceration Boom," Western States Center and Western Prison Project, 2000.

44. Center for Responsive Politics, "Corrections Corporation of America—Client Summary," Opensecrets.org, September 19, 2007.

45. Eric Schlosser, "The Prison-Industrial Complex," *The Atlantic*, December 1998.

CHAPTER 15

1. Polls taken immediately after President Bush vetoed legislation to expand stem cell funding and delivered a speech on the subject reflected approval of presidential action by 50 to 60 percent of respondents. However, these surveys included fewer than 600 participants and were subject to additional error or bias. Given that these findings are consistently contradicted by surveys that have been conducted over several years, one must conclude that the opinions expressed likely were influenced by the President's speech and would not be maintained over a reasonable period of time.

CHAPTER 16

1. Eric Schmitt, "Pentagon Contradicts General on Iraq Occupation Force's Size," statement by Deputy Defense Secretary Wolfowitz, *The New York Times*, February 28, 2003.

2. Eric Schmitt, "Pentagon Contradicts General on Iraq Occupation Force's Size."

3. Joseph C. Wilson, "What I Didn't Find in Africa," *New York Times*, July 6, 2003.

4. Joseph C. Wilson, "What I Didn't Find in Africa."

5. Walter Pincus, "Report Casts Doubt on Iraq-Al Qaeda Connection," *The Washington Post*, June 22, 2003.

6. Manu Raju, Elana Schor, and llan Wuman, "Few Senators Read Iraq NIE Report," *The Hill*, June 19, 2007.

7. Eric Schmitt, "Pentagon Contradicts General on Iraq Occupation Force's Size."

8. Sourcewatch Encyclopedia, Congresspedia, "Congressional Actions on the Iraq War Prior to the 2003 U.S. Invasion," 107th Congress (2001–2002), http://www.sourcewatch.org/index.php?title=Congressional_actions_on_the_Iraq_war.html. Accessed October 22, 2007.

9. Gail Martin, *Iraq in Transition*, Online NewsHour, http://www.pbs.org/newshour/indepth_coverage/middle_east/Iraq/keyplayers/garner.html. Accessed October 24, 2007.

10. Frontline Interview with L. Paul Bremer, "The Lost Year in Iraq," PBS, posted October 17, 2006.

11. Gail Martin, *Iraq in Transition*.

12. Frontline Interview with L. Paul Bremer, "The Lost Year in Iraq."

13. Iraq, MSN Encarta Premium, http://www.encarta.msn.com/text_761567303_0/Iraq.html. Accessed on October 20, 2007.

14. *L. Paul Bremer*, Wikimedia Foundation, Inc., http://en.wikipedia.org/wiki/L._Paul_Bremmer.html. Accessed on October 23, 2007.

15. Frontline Interview with L. Paul Bremer, "The Lost Year in Iraq."

16. Frontline Interview with L. Paul Bremer, "The Lost Year in Iraq."

17. Frontline Interview with L. Paul Bremer, "The Lost Year in Iraq." Bremer himself, in an October 4, 2004, speech at a resort in White Sulfur Springs, West Virginia, implied that lawlessness in Iraq might have been under better control by having more troops on the ground earlier on.

18. Robert McC. Adams, "Contexts of Iraqi Looting," November 14, 2003, published in *Proceedings of the American Philosophical Society*, 149 (1): March 2005.

19. *L. Paul Bremer*, Wikimedia Foundation, Inc.

20. Frontline Interview with L. Paul Bremer, "The Lost Year in Iraq."

21. Frontline Interview with L. Paul Bremer, "The Lost Year in Iraq."

22. "Audit: U.S. Lost Track of $9 Billion in Iraq Funds," http://www. CNN.com, January 30, 2005.

23. Iraq, MSN Encarta Premium.

24. Joshua Holland, "Iraq's Reconstruction a Boondoggle by Design," *Alter-Net*, July 17, 2006.

25. Eric Schmitt, "Pentagon Contradicts General on Iraq Occupation Force's Size."

26. Joshua Holland, "Iraq's Reconstruction a Boondoggle by Design;" "Iraq Reconstruction Contracts for Firms from Supporting Nations," http://usainfo. state.gov.html. Accessed December 10, 2003.

27. Joshua Holland, "Iraq's Reconstruction A Boondoggle by Design."

28. John M. Broder and David Rohde, "Use of Contractors by State Department Has Soared," *The New York Times*, October 24, 2007.

29. Karen DeYoung, "State Department Ousts Its Chief of Security," *Washington Post*, October 25, 2007.

30. Ken Dilanian, "Iraq and Afghanistan Wars May Total $2.4 Trillion," *USA Today*, October 24, 2007.

31. U.S. Office of Management and Budget, 2007.

32. Bob Herbert, "The $2 Trillion Nightmare," *The New York Times*, March 4, 2008.

33. http://www.GlobalSecurity.org.

34. http://www.Icasualties.org. and "New Study Estimates 151,000 Violent Iraqi Deaths since 2003 Invasion," World Health Organization, January 9, 2008.

35. At the time of this writing, a change in leadership at the U.S. Department of Defense and on the ground in Iraq, a "surge" of 30,000 additional U.S. troops, and a change in attitude of some Iraqi factions appear to have raised hopes that the tide may be turning in favor of peace. With new threats of possible Turkish–Kurd conflict in the north and increased danger of Iranian confrontations, one can only pray that real progress is being made to reconcile Iraqi divisions and restore the nation. However, if that hoped-for eventuality is achieved, it should not be used to disguise the defective leadership of the past and the necessity to ensure that it does not continue to erode national policy in other vital areas.

CHAPTER 17

1. Infoplease web site, http://www.infoplease.com.html. Accessed November 12, 2007.

2. "Breaking Free with Fair Elections: A New Declaration of Independence for Congress," Common Cause, March 2007.

3. John M. Broder and David Rohde, "Use of Contractors by State Department Has Soared," *New York Times*, October 24, 2007.

4. "Exposed by Katrina, FEMA's Flaws Were Years in Making," *USA Today*, 2005; "Walter Reed Army Medical Center Scandal," *SourceWatch*, 2007.

CHAPTER 18

1. See, for example, *Breaking Free with Fair Elections: A New Declaration of Independence for Congress*, sponsored by Common Cause and other public interest organizations.

2. U.S. Department of Labor, Bureau of Labor Statistics, 2007.

BIBLIOGRAPHY

Adams, Henry. *Democracy: An American Novel*. Middlesex, UK: The Echo Library, 1925.

Ameil, Barbara. *John Locke and America*. Oxford: Clarendon Press, 1996.

Appleby, Joyce. *Liberalism and the Republican Imagination*. Cambridge, MA: Harvard University Press, 1992.

Ashcraft, Richard. *Revolutionary Politics and Locke's Two Treatises of Civil Government*. Princeton, NJ: Princeton University Press, 1986.

Bailey, Thomas A. *The American Spirit: United States History as Seen by Contemporaries*. Lexington, MA: D.C. Heath & Company, 1963.

Bailyn, Bernard. *The Ideological Origins of the American Revolution*. Cambridge, MA: Harvard University Press, 1967.

Bell, John Fred. *A History of Economic Thought*. New York: The Ronald Press Co., 1953.

Bellomo, Michael. *The Stem Cell Divide: The Facts, the Fiction and the Fear Driving the Greatest Scientific, Political, and Religious Debate of Our Time*. New York: AMACON, 2006.

Berlin, Isaiah. "Two Concepts of Liberty," in *Four Essays on Liberty*. Oxford: Oxford University Press, 1969.

Burns, James MacGregor. *Leadership*. New York: Harper & Row Publishers, 1978.

Burns, James MacGregor. *Running Alone: Presidential Leadership—JFK to Bush II: Why It Has Failed and How We Can Fix It*. New York: Basic Books, 2006.

Chambers, John Whiteclay II, ed. *The Oxford Companion to American Military History*. Oxford: Oxford University Press, 1999.

Craven, Wesley Frank. *The Legend of the Founding Fathers*. Ithaca, NY: Cornell University Press, 1956.

Dahl, Robert A. *Democracy in the United States: Promise and Performance*. Chicago: Rand McNally, College Publishing Company, 1976.

Dietze, Gottfried. *The Federalist: A Classic on Federalism and Free Government*. Baltimore: The Johns Hopkins Press, 1960.

Diggins, John Patrick. *The Lost Soul of American Politics: Virtue, Self-Interest, and the Foundations of Liberalism*. New York: Basic Books, Inc., 1984.

Elting, John R. *The Battle of Bunker's Hill*. Monmouth Beach, NJ: Phillip Freneau Press, 1975.

Erwin, R.E. *Virtues and Rights: The Moral Philosophy of Thomas Hobbes*. Boulder, CO: Westview Press, 1991.

Gardner, John W. *On Leadership*. New York: The Free Press, 1990.

Gauthier, David. *The Logic of 'Leviathan': The Moral and Political Theory of Thomas Hobbes*. Oxford: Oxford University Press, 1969.

Gilmore, Ruth W. *Golden Gulag: Prisons, Surplus, Crisis, and Opposition in Globalizing California*. Berkeley: University of California Press, 2007.

Grant, Ruth. *John Locke's Liberalism*. Chicago: University of Chicago Press, 1987.

Hulliung, Mark. *Montesquieu and the Old Regime*. Berkeley: University of California Press, 1976.

Jackson, Brooks. *Honest Graft: Big Money and the American Political Process*. New York: Alfred A. Knopf, 1988.

Jonas, Steven, Goldstein, R., and Goldstein, K., eds. *An Introduction to the U.S. Health Care System*. New York: Springer Publishing Co., 2007.

Judis, John B. *The Paradox of American Democracy: Elites, Special Interests, and the Betrayal of Public Trust*. New York: Routledge, 2000.

Kaiser, Robert G. "Citizen K Street": How Lobbying Became Washington's Biggest Business," *Washington Post*, March 26–May 8, 2007.

Kavka, Gregory S. *Hobbesian Moral and Political Theory*. Princeton, NJ: Princeton University Press, 1986.

Kennedy, John F. *Profiles in Courage*. New York: Harper & Brothers, 1961.

Laslett, Peter, ed. *John Locke, Two Treatises of Government*. Cambridge: Cambridge University Press, 1988.

Levitt, Steven D., and Dubner, Stephen J. *Freakonomics*. New York: HarperCollins Publishers, 2006.

Lienesch, Michael. *The Order of the Ages: Time, the Constitution, and the Making of Modern American Political Thought*. Princeton, NJ: Princeton University Press, 1988.

Lowe, E.J. *Locke*. New York: Routledge, 2005.

McCleskey, Clifton. *Political Power and American Democracy*. Pacific Grove, CA: Brooks/Cole Publishing Company, 1989.

McCullough, David. *John Adams*. New York: Simon & Schuster, 2001.

McDougall, Walter A. *Freedom Just Around the Corner: A New American History 1585–1828*. New York: HarperCollins Publishers, Inc., 2004.

Mapp, Jr., Alf J. *The Virginia Experiment: The Old Dominion's Role in the Making of America 1607–1781*. Lanham, MD: Hamilton Press, 1987.

Mintz, Samuel I. *The Hunting of Leviathan: Seventeenth-Century Reactions to the Materialism and Moral Philosophy of Thomas Hobbes*. Cambridge: Cambridge University Press, 1962.

Morgan, Edmund S. *Inventing the People: The Rise of Popular Sovereignty in England and America*. New York: W. W. Norton & Company, 1989.

Morris, Richard B. *Seven Who Shaped Our Destiny: The Founding Fathers as Revolutionaries*. New York: Harper & Row, 1973.

Nordlund, Willis J. *The Quest for a Living Wage: The History of the Federal Minimum Wage Program*. Contributions in Labor Studies. Westport, CT: Greenwood Press, 1997.

Pangle, Thomas. *Montesquieu's Philosophy of Liberalism: A Commentary on the Spirit of the Laws*. Chicago: University of Chicago Press, 1973.

Phillips, Donald T. *The Founding Fathers on Leadership: Classic Teamwork in Changing Times*. New York: Warner Books, Inc., 1997.

Philp, Mark, ed. *Rights of Man, Common Sense, and Other Political Writings*. Oxford: University Press, 1998.

Prewitt, Jeffrey L. *Dilemma of American Political Thought*. New York: Pearson Higher Education, 1995.

Rawls, John. *A Theory of Justice*. Cambridge, MA: Harvard University Press, 1971.

Rutland, Robert A. *The Birth of the Bill of Rights, 1776–1791*. Chapel Hill: University of North Carolina Press, 1955.

Sanders, Bill. *Youth Crime and Youth Culture in the Inner City*. New York: Routledge, 2005.

Shain, Barry A. *The Myth of American Individualism: The Protestant Origins of American Political Thought*. Princeton, NJ: Princeton University Press, 1994.

Shy, John. *A People Numerous and Armed: Reflections on the Military Struggle for American Independence*. New York: Oxford University Press, 1976.

Smith, Hedrick. *The Power Game: How Washington Works*. New York: Ballantine Books, 1988.

Stark, W. *Montesquieu: Pioneer of the Sociology of Knowledge*. Toronto: University of Toronto Press, 1961.

Stem Cells: Scientific Progress and Future Research Directions. Washington, DC: National Institutes of Health, 2001.

Time Magazine Editors. *Global Warming: The Causes, the Perils, and the Politics—and What It Means for You*. New York: Time, 2007.

Vaughan, Alden T., and Billias, George A., eds. *Perspectives on Early American History: Essays in Honor of Richard B. Morris*. New York: Harper & Row, 1973.

Waltman, Jerold. *The Politics of the Minimum Wage*. Chicago: University of Illinois Press, 2000.

Weart, Spencer R. *The Discovery of Global Warming*. Cambridge, MA: Harvard University Press, 2003.

Wheeler, Tom. *Leadership Lessons from the Civil War: Winning Strategies for Today's Managers*. New York: A Currency Book, Doubleday, 1999.

About the Author

ALAN L. MOSS is an economic consultant and author. He has served as an American Political Science Association Congressional Fellow in the U.S. Senate, Chief Economist of the U.S. Department of Labor's Wage and Hour Division, and Adjunct Instructor in Economics at the University of Virginia's Northern Virginia Center. He is the author of *Employment Opportunity: Outlook, Reason, and Reality.*